How to Read Middle English Poetry

How to Read Middle English Poetry

Daniel Sawyer

Great Clarendon Street, Oxford, OX2 6DP,
United Kingdom

Oxford University Press is a department of the University of Oxford.
It furthers the University's objective of excellence in research, scholarship,
and education by publishing worldwide. Oxford is a registered trade mark of
Oxford University Press in the UK and in certain other countries

© Daniel Sawyer 2024

The moral rights of the author have been asserted

All rights reserved. No part of this publication may be reproduced, stored in
a retrieval system, or transmitted, in any form or by any means, without the
prior permission in writing of Oxford University Press, or as expressly permitted
by law, by licence or under terms agreed with the appropriate reprographics
rights organization. Enquiries concerning reproduction outside the scope of the
above should be sent to the Rights Department, Oxford University Press, at the
address above

You must not circulate this work in any other form
and you must impose this same condition on any acquirer

Published in the United States of America by Oxford University Press
198 Madison Avenue, New York, NY 10016, United States of America

British Library Cataloguing in Publication Data

Data available

Library of Congress Control Number: 2023946100

ISBN 9780198895237

DOI: 10.1093/oso/9780198895237.001.0001

Pod

Links to third party websites are provided by Oxford in good faith and
for information only. Oxford disclaims any responsibility for the materials
contained in any third party website referenced in this work.

Acknowledgements

For suggestions on specific points I must thank Caroline Batten, Joanna Bellis, Julia Boffey, Penny Boxall, Lucy Brookes, Colleen Curran, Mary Flannery, Bernardo Hinojosa, Llewelyn Hopwood, Lorna Hutson, Ayoush Lazikani, Micah MacKay, Richard McCabe, Jenni Nuttall, Ad Putter, Lotte Reinbold, Tessa Roynon, Hannah Ryley, Elizabeth Solopova, Daniel Wakelin, Lawrence Warner, and Michael Whitworth. Cosima Gillhammer kindly offered guidance on my attempts to cover some linguistic matters. The late Anne Hudson and E. G. Stanley taught me valuable things and personified, in different ways, lively inheritances of teaching and scholarship. Rey Conquer has been a stalwart weekly writing partner. John Colley helped to check some chapters, and Charlotte Ross double-checked references. I am grateful to the two anonymous readers for Oxford University Press, who understood my aims and offered corrections and suggestions alongside enthusiasm. My editors at the Press have shepherded the undertaking along with professionalism and skill. Much labour goes into making a book, and I must thank all those, many unknown to me, who have turned typescript into codex.

I drafted while working at Merton College, Oxford and I revised while working at St Hilda's College, Oxford. The staff of these two colleges, particularly in catering, maintenance, and IT, made work possible. The fellows at both colleges provided vital environments, full of learning. The staff of the Bodleian Library and the English Faculty Library worked magic to ensure access to books despite a global health crisis. My colleagues in Oxford's Faculty of English have been wise and helpful.

This book emerges from sixteen years being taught about and teaching about Middle English. The being taught did not cleanly precede the teaching: I've learned much from my students, who always ask the best questions. I wrote this as a teaching book despite a national academic environment emphasizing research-driven publications. It is a book of practical solutions to problems in the reading of Middle English verse, as faced by people—most commonly, undergraduates—with sometimes-messy lives. I myself wrote it in the middle of a mess, during a pandemic, around the pressures of teaching, lockdown, and chronic illness. I hope it helps everyone who reads it, but most especially I hope it helps readers who have lives as complex as mine has been during its making.

Finally, I am very grateful to my parents.

Contents

List of Figures	viii
List of Abbreviations	ix
List of Conventions	x
Introduction	**1**
1. Why Old Poetry?	13
2. Wording	20
3. Phrasing	31
4. Metre (I): Alternating Metres	46
5. Metre (II): Alliterative Verse	70
6. Rhyme	89
7. Stanzas	102
8. Grander Designs	114
9. Manuscripts, Texts, Editions	131
10. Poetry of Many Tongues	149
11. Verse Takes Breath	164
Epilogue: Craft in an Unfixed Time	177
Appendix	183
Bibliography	189
Indexed Glossary of Technical Terms	201
General Index	209

List of Figures

1. Opening lines of *Troilus and Criseyde* in Oxford, Bodleian Library, MS Rawlinson poet. 163, folio 1 recto. Reproduced by kind permission of the Bodleian Libraries, University of Oxford, under Creative Commons licence CC-BY-NC 4.0 (<https://creativecommons.org/licenses/by-nc/4.0>). 132

2. Poetry presented as a charter held out by Jesus from the cross. © The British Library Board; London, British Library, MS Additional 37049, folio 23 recto. 137

List of Abbreviations

c.	*circa* ('about')
DIMEV	Linne R. Mooney and others, eds, *The 'DIMEV': An Open-Access, Digital Edition of the 'Index of Middle English Verse'*, <https://www.dimev.net>
DOST	*A Dictionary of the Older Scottish Tongue*, in *Dictionaries of the Scots Language / Dictionars o the Scots Leid*, <https://dsl.ac.uk>
EETS e.s.	Early English Text Society, Extra Series
EETS o.s.	Early English Text Society, Original Series
EETS s.s.	Early English Text Society, Supplementary Series
MED	Hans Kurath and others, eds, *Middle English Dictionary* <https://quod.lib.umich.edu/m/middle-english-dictionary/dictionary>
MS	manuscript
NIMEV	Julia Boffey and A. S. G. Edwards, eds, *A New Index of Middle English Verse* (London, 2005)
OED	*Oxford English Dictionary*, <https://www.oed.com>
TEAMS	Teaching Association for Medieval Studies
trans.	translated by

List of Conventions

Technical words printed in **bold type** are explained in the indexed glossary. A second index covers authors, works, and more general topics. The Appendix details basic points of the spelling, sound, and grammar of Middle English. Sections in the Appendix are numbered, and the main text occasionally refers to them by number.

Within in-line quotations, a stroke (/) indicates a line-break, and a pair of strokes (//) indicates a transition between stanzas. In quoted lines of alliterative verse, a vertical bar (|) indicates the metrical caesura. To describe rhyming patterns, I use italicized letters, with *a* representing the first rhyming sound, *b* the second, and so on; *x* represents a line with no end rhyme. When necessary, I indicate the number of metrical beats in lines using a subscript number: the rhyme-and-metre pattern of 'Amazing Grace' is $a_4b_3a_4b_3$, that of a normal Shakespearean sonnet, $ababcdcdefefgg_5$.

In some quotations, I silently alter editors' punctuation and capitalization. For the sake of readers new to earlier forms of English and Scots, I silently modernize letters specific to the period throughout: thorn (þ) and eth (ð) have become 'th', yogh (ȝ) has become 'gh' or 'y' depending on the sound it would have represented, and in some early texts ash (æ) has become 'ae' (see Appendix section 2). I supply present-day English glosses in italics parallel to quotations; semicolons (;) separate distinct glosses. I supply full translations of some more challenging quotations within parentheses, and unless I specify otherwise these translations are my own.

Items in the bibliography are sorted by author's name; multiple items by the same author appear in order of publication date. Editions are referenced in the main text and listed in the bibliography by author's name, or by editor's name when the work is anonymous or is part of a multi-author anthology. Provinces of Canada and states of the USA appear in publication details only when there is a real risk of confusion. Editions preceded at their first mention by an asterisk (*) are available in Medieval Institute Publications's TEAMS Middle English Text Series, and for free online at—at the time of writing—<http://d.lib.rochester.edu/teams/text-online>. Editions preceded at their first mention by a dagger (†) are out of copyright, and freely available online. Conscious of a readership of newcomers, I have prioritized editions that are easily found and that provide accessible texts with helpful glossing and notes. Readers should bear in mind that such editions intervene, rightly, in spelling, metre, and textual detail, in ways that make them unsuitable for primary research in metrics. When a work was composed in English but titled in Latin, I capitalize the title according to English conventions ('*Speculum Vitae*').

Quotations of Chaucer come from *The Norton Chaucer* (2019). Quotations from *Troilus and Criseyde* are referenced by book and line number ('IV.392'), those from the *Canterbury Tales* by section and line number ('II 201'). Quotations of William

Langland's *Piers Plowman* come from A. V. C. Schmidt's second edition of the B text (Langland 1995), which I reference by passus number and line number ('XI.27'). Quotations of John Gower's *Confessio Amantis* come from Russel A. Peck's edition, (*2000–2004), and, in its first and second volumes, Peck's partial second edition (*2006–2013). Quotations from *Pearl* come from Sarah Stanbury's edition (*2001) because it is available for free online; those from *Patience*, *Cleanness*, and *Sir Gawain and the Green Knight* come from the edition of the works of the *Pearl* Poet edited by Ad Putter and Myra Stokes (eds 2014). I quote Shakespeare from *The Arden Shakespeare, Third Series: Complete Works* (2021), and his plays are referenced by act number, scene number, and line numbers ('1.2, 50–61'). Modern English quotations of the Bible come from the New Revised Standard Version.

Medieval manuscripts are referenced by place, library, 'MS' (for 'manuscript'), and then a shelfmark, e.g. 'Oxford, Bodleian Library, MS Digby 99', 'Manchester, John Rylands Library, MS Eng. 1'. Specific leaves are referenced as 'folios', e.g. 'folio 28', and specific pages are referenced as sides of folios, e.g. 'folio 28 recto' for the first, right-hand side, then 'folio 28 verso' for the second, reverse side. Full digital facsimiles are available online for some of the manuscripts I reference, and when this is the case I give the current facsimile URL next to the manuscript's entry in my bibliography.

New students and other readers less used to historical dates should remember that 1150 is in the twelfth century, not the eleventh, 1450 in the fifteenth, and so on. For readers less used to talking about the relevant geography, Great Britain is the single island containing Scotland, Wales, and England; England, Scotland, and Wales form parts of Great Britain; the British Isles are the full archipelago of islands including Ireland, Great Britain, and several thousand smaller islands. The United Kingdom postdates Middle English and Older Scots by some centuries, and so falls outside this book's period.

Introduction

This book explains how to read Middle English poetry for pleasure and study. It maps out the topic and sets readers up to adventure further. Middle English is vital to literary criticism and cultural history, both as a lively body of work in its own right and as a unique vantage from which to view modern English, showing how some things taken for granted now are strange and accidental. The first chapter explores this vitality. Chapters 2 to 8 explain the craft and workings of Middle English verse and show how they might be discussed. The discussion begins at the small scale with poets' word choices, and gradually broadens its coverage through phrasing, metre, rhyme, and stanzas, finishing with the over-arching forms of whole poems. Chapters 9 to 11 map out three aspects of Middle English verse helpful to close reading: manuscripts and modern editing, the many other languages present in the British Isles, and the fact that audiences often didn't see poetry, but rather heard it aloud. The chapters do come in a logical order, but each can also stand on its own. The Appendix advises on Middle English spelling, pronunciation, and grammar, while the indexed Glossary provides a reference guide to technical terms. Readers will finish this book equipped to enjoy poems from the period, able to find accessible copies of such poems without expense or hassle, and prepared to discuss those poems in detail should they want to, or be asked to, at school or university.

That bald sketch for readers judging whether to buy the book—please do!—invites some questions. Why care about reading closely? Why think about craft? What is Middle English, anyway? And how does this book fit into the wider landscape of help for novice readers of Middle English? What follows will tackle each of these questions in turn. After that, the rest of the introduction explains the choice of examples studied in the book and advises on tools which assist the reading of poetry from this period.

Why close reading? Some student readers might answer, with feeling, that they have simply been told to read closely, and so their interest is purely utilitarian. Outside force is an understandable reason to do something, of course. The practice has better justifications, though, than arbitrary necessity handed down from on high. It is an underpinning insight of literary study that a work's form and content affect each other and can't wholly be divided. We can't safely try to understand a work's matter (content) without understanding its manner (form). Close reading offers tools for tracing the connections between manner and matter and for following the effects of form into arguments with wider implications. Close reading does not oppose the more theoretical or even philosophical parts of literary study: it can and should serve those parts too. Some fine theorists proceed by reading closely, and of course those critics who think they only attend to the text do, with that very thought, take a theoretical stance. Close reading also works with, rather than against, the wider study of texts using quantification and computer assistance: such work stands or falls on the quality of the questions humans ask their tools, and the best examples of it draw on precise instincts about form. And close reading has strong links to the rest of life. Humans persist in reading for pleasure, and good close reading enhances that process rather than killing it off. And, what's more, a newspaper article, a legal statement, or a personal message on a phone screen can all offer challenges similar to those involved in reading literature closely.

Various fine if sometimes slightly over-traditional books can guide readers through the appreciation of modern English texts (e.g. Vendler 2010; Mikics 2013). There are helpful general guides to the technical side of reading literature (Lennard 2005; Greenham 2019; Hodgson 2021). But these guides say little about the first three-fifths or so of the history of English verse, before modern English, and they get some of what little they do say wrong. Existing works covering Middle English for novice readers, by contrast, tend to offer only limited help with close reading and with grasping form. Some useful aids for beginners map cultural context (Turville-Petre 2007; Gray 2008, 1–153), outline the relevant conditions for writing in the period (Burrow 2008), explore 'reading strategies' (Johnson and Treharne eds 2005), or tour timelines, genres, and reception (Galloway 2006). Collections of essays offer chapters on specific approaches and authors (e.g. Strohm ed. 2007; Turner ed. 2013). Wise critics have written literary histories (Bennett 1990; Gray 2008) and spirited reassessments (Simpson 2002; Ashe 2017). But no past book explains the details of Middle English verse itself, its forms and systems, with a special focus on ways of reading and writing helpful to those meeting Middle English poetry for the first time.

In recent decades, form has regained prominence in literary study generally (e.g. Wolfson and Brown eds 2006; Attridge 2013), and in Middle English studies in particular (e.g. Lerer 2003; Prendergast and Rosenfeld eds 2018). At the same time, scholars have honed our knowledge of the making of verse in this period. For example, we can now say more about the uses of rhyme or the workings of alliterative verse than we once could. Advances of this sort are still, though, filtering their way towards introductory knowledge. This book tries to hurry them along and to fold them into a fuller gathering of useful facts, tips, and tricks. It doesn't exhaustively cover every possible verse form. Nor does it explain all the most basic principles underlying the making of verse: it's not a total reconstructed poetics. But it does lay out the landscape of Middle English verse-craft for beginners.

So much for this book's mission and context. As a teaching book rather than a research monograph, it doesn't doggedly pursue one argument. It does, though, have some recurring interests: craft, pleasure, and tangibility.

Craft is not art, a word which—especially in its more modern senses—tends to distance and exclude (Williams 1983, 'Art', 40–43). Craft is learned skill, partly conscious and partly habitual, in doing something. In this book, that something is writing verse. Like most concepts, craft can be misused to make unsupportable claims or to paper over other matters—historical or ethical ones, say—which should sometimes take priority. I nevertheless find craft a useful idea because it makes reading and writing approachable. One of the Middle English words for a writer was *maker*, which sounds more practical today than *poet*—though in fact the Greek word from which *poet* comes also meant someone who makes things. This book's cover image depicts people rebuilding the city of Troy: Troy has long gripped poets' imaginations, but I also chose this picture because it shows work and craft. I don't ask here whether the poets under discussion possessed genius or produced art. I do try to show how they worked through learned, traceable, practical choices. Learning about that craft makes their poetry more understandable and more fun today. The focus on craft doesn't mean that I think poetry lacks deeper and more mysterious facets. But if those exist, then the road to them runs through reading many poems, and walking that road becomes easier with a craft map to hand. This book also implicitly argues that literary criticism too is a craft: people aren't born with an aptitude for it, but rather learn to do it bit-by-bit. Every day that we spend at least a little time grappling with reading and writing, we improve our literary-critical craft.

Pleasure is not quite love. I do love literature—on a good day—but loving literature might itself be a fairly recent idea (Lynch 2015), and the concept of literature isn't universal. Still, we can safely say that people enjoyed Middle English verse. Our pleasure need not always echo their pleasure: sometimes the value of studying an early poem lies in grasping how and why audiences then enjoyed something that we would now reject. Yet pleasure was the counterpart and response offered by readers to the craft unleashed by poets. Close reading often benefits from asking, early in the process, just what it was in a poem or a passage that engrossed people.

Tangibility is linked to pleasure: though people often think of verse as particularly intangible, it is a most solid, concrete topic. All poetry known from this period is known because it survives in physical books, of course, and that's one kind of tangibility. More broadly, though, all reading, aloud or silent, requires physical action: even in silent reading some speech muscles usually move, a process called subvocalization. Verse also tends to deal in repeated physical patterns, like dance. Some Middle English poems are really dancing songs, making the link clearer still, but all verse presents things to feel and touch. It often helps to conceive of literary study as a set of very graspable problems. This book makes the poetry of one time friendlier and more approachable by talking through ways to grasp it.

Bounds and choices

Middle English is English after it was Old English but before it became modern English. These are modern categories, nailed down in the nineteenth century. Scholarship normally puts the beginning of Middle English somewhere at the start or middle of the twelfth century, around 1100 or 1150, and its end somewhere during or at the end of the fifteenth century, around 1450 or 1500. For this book's purposes, 1150 and 1500 are the rough cut-off dates. Researchers sometimes also subdivide Middle

English into early Middle English, up to about 1350, and late Middle English after about 1350. All of these are round numbers. Their roundness proclaims their arbitrary nature, as limits placed on what is really a continuous history: nothing so terribly significant happened in 1150 to separate Old from Middle English (Faulkner 2022), or in 1500 to part Middle and modern English (Simpson 2002; Weiskott 2021a). People certainly didn't wake up one day speaking differently.

These dates do, though, roughly coordinate with shifts in English's workings and status. Around the twelfth century, the disappearance of many of the grammatically meaningful word-endings of Old English sped up, while the long aftermath of the Norman Conquest of England in 1066 reduced English's social prestige, by making Norman French the language of the nobility, government, and the law. At the other end of the period, during the fifteenth century, the sounds of English began to alter in something linguists call the Great Vowel Shift. In the same decades, English saw increasing use among the powerful, returning slowly to greater social prestige. This social change began a process of standardization in writing, and the use of moveable-type printing for English from the 1470s on hastened that standardization. Provided that readers bear in mind that these divisions slice through continuities, they can be useful.

Alongside Middle English, this book's examples also include some Older Scots poems. Scots poetry of this period is by no means subordinate, and has different periods—Early Scots to about 1450, Early Middle Scots from about 1450 to about 1550—but it comes from the same linguistic ambit as English verse. No hard break in speech, writing, or verse-craft ran along the hazy, oft-crossed border dividing Scotland and England: in pronunciation and vocabulary the Middle Englishes of the North of England sat closer to Scots than to the Middle Englishes of London or Southampton. In some cases, scholars disagree over whether a poem is English or Scots, and it's not clear that this question would always have made sense to readers at the time. Scots and English verse shared much in their poetic vocabularies and underlying principles of metre, rhyme, and alliteration. Indeed, confusingly for future readers, Scots writers of this period routinely called their own language, which we now call Scots, *English* (Barbour 1997, IV.253), reserving *Scots* to describe Gaelic (Smith 2012, 8). In including Scots poets, this book doesn't assert that they must count as English writers: placing Scots writing is a political and cultural question for present-day Scotland, above the heads of southrons such as I. Older Scots verse is often excellent, though, and since it forms part of the same linguistic and craft tradition, a guide which left it out would ill serve readers.

The topic of language opens a broader problem. Someone might reasonably ask whether this book should take English verse as its topic at all. In some ways En*glish* was not the most important written language in En*gland* in these centuries, and neither was Scots in Scotland. In both countries, and throughout western Europe, Latin was the normal and model literary language, dominant in education and scholarship: learning to read often meant learning to read Latin, and the very idea of literacy came bound up with Latinity. French, meanwhile, was an alternate living language in Great Britain, and a much more prestigious and international one.

A book seeking purely to describe the past might, then, focus on writings in French and Latin. Chapter 10 does explore the literary effects of this multilingual situation and, as I note there, some works defy labelling as either 'English' or 'not English', troubling the category of English verse. As a whole, though, this book doesn't pursue French and Latin rather than English. A literary critic's final goal is not to describe the past, still less to recreate it. Twenty-first-century audiences rarely arrive armed with Latin and French, and teachers must meet students and the public where they are. Non-specialists would struggle with a book about the intricacies of Latin and early French verse. Plus, despite the huge influence of verse from other languages, the alliterative, rhyming, and metrical systems found in English and Scots poetry during these centuries stayed somewhat distinct from those of other tongues in the British Isles or nearby on the European mainland.

There is also a good present-day reason to attend to Middle English. The fractured state and humble status of Middle English in its own time make it vital to the study of English now. In the twenty-first century, when prestigious standard English far too often seems like a default, see-through medium, both first- and second-language English-speakers can learn much from looking at the language when it was neither prestigious nor standardized. Among all periods, including Old English, Middle English fills this important role best, thanks to the language's uniquely low levels of prestige and standardization during the Middle English centuries.

Verse form and language history thus drew the limits of this book's topic. The examples of poetry given here come from many genres, origins, modes, and forms written in the period. Accessibility has often driven choice: some poems appear because they are more easily available for readers. Indeed, for longer discussions I have sought out verse which readers might access quickly and without paying, rather than verse only found in expensive editions rare outside large university libraries. To break down the process of close reading into observable steps, I have also often rolled up my sleeves and made more basic, granular arguments than I would use in pure research: the chapters below model the process of reading closely, rather than every later stage of literary criticism.

Two other factors have shaped my choices of examples. First, where accessibility makes it possible, the quotations here draw on poems and poets less commonly taught. Geoffrey Chaucer appears often in this book, but—whenever I can—I place him in the context of other Middle English poetry. Chaucer is the one Middle English poet at all known to general readers, and often takes centre stage when Middle English is taught. He inhabited the ideas which surrounded him just as much as any of his contemporaries did, of course (Turner 2019); he displayed wit and craft because he lived in crafty, witty times. Posterity has treated him kindly: by luck, the type of English he wrote became dominant in government and education, while his major metrical innovation became a successful elite-culture metre, the line of Shakespeare and Milton (see Chapter 4). Both of these lucky breaks happened after his death and might have surprised him. Besides his good luck, Chaucer was also a great poet, and I shall have much to say about him. But I shall also seek wit in other poets before, during, and after the age of Chaucer. These other works offer context for Chaucer and have their own intrinsic interest too: readers aren't obliged to like just one poet, or to make him the core of their studies.

Second, more verse in later Middle English (from about 1350 on) appears here than verse in early Middle English (about 1150 to 1350). This disparity does not stem from a lack of early Middle English works in general: more survives than is sometimes imagined. English might have lost much of its social purchase after the Norman Conquest, but a range of works still emerged, including chronicles, sermons, and the fascinating *Ancrene Wisse*, an early thirteenth-century guide to life for monastic women. Most of these works are in prose, though. Surviving early Middle English poems are more limited in number. Partly this lack must stem from the loss of books during the centuries since; partly it must be because countless more poems simply never made it into writing in the first place. This book therefore has an unavoidable tilt towards later Middle English verse. It still, though, folds in earlier verse where it can, and should help anyone reading early Middle English too.

Modern and present-day poets also crop up in the following chapters, where they have written work that draws directly on Middle English or Older Scots, or where their verse does something helpfully similar. Those modern poets who appear make up a haphazard selection, not by any means a full survey of those who have reached back to earlier English verse for forms or inspiration. I include them because I like them, because they show earlier poetry's lasting influence, and because poetry and literary criticism have continuity. Nothing wholly splits early verse from verse today: although the details might differ, poetry from every time opens itself to an open-minded reader, and it matters that—for instance—Emily Dickinson wrote many poems in, or in tension with, a verse template that emerged in the twelfth and thirteenth centuries.

In talking of times, I shall use *modern* to describe the period from about 1500 on, and *present-day* for the first decades of the twenty-first century and the third millennium. I shan't use the word *medieval*, because I don't need it, and because its range and force could cause problems. Bede—who died in 735—and King Richard III—who died in 1485—are both medieval, yet more time divides them than divides Richard III from us. Their contexts differed greatly, and Richard III lived alongside many things we might consider 'early modern' (Strohm 2000, 88–96). What's more, to focus on a set of Middle Ages seems to me to risk wandering from what this book pursues: not a time, but a body of poetry. I'm content for others to speak of the medieval, and in some contexts the word might serve well, but I haven't found it necessary here.

Editions and reading

Where to find Middle English verse, especially beyond Chaucer's work? This book particularly leans on editions in the TEAMS Middle English Texts series, because they are available for free online (at the time of writing, at <https://d.lib.rochester.edu/teams/text-online>) and as relatively cheap paperbacks; because they are aimed at novice readers of Middle English, with suitable glossing; and because they tend to publish works on the borders of the taught canon, making them natural allies to this book's interest in poems that receive less attention. When an asterisk (*) precedes a mention of any poem, that poem can be found through TEAMS. At times, for some poems not edited in TEAMS, I rely on editions which have aged out of copyright, and so can be found at no cost online. Any poem whose title is preceded by a dagger (†) is in this category. Asterisks and daggers mark the same things in the bibliography. In other cases, the argument sticks to editions which help novices with glossing, are likely to be in libraries, and are not outrageously priced. Precisely because they are more accessible for inexpert readers, many of the editions I have used cannot support primary research in, for instance, metre: such editions serve well for reading and studying a poet, but to propose a new thesis about that poet's metre, one must go to scholarly editions and to manuscripts—and then think very hard about those.

My mention of manuscripts brings up another key topic. Until the later fifteenth century, hand copying was the only method known in the British Isles for reproducing large amounts of text. This fact shaped all literature from the time. Almost all of the poetry considered in this book persists today because people repeatedly copied it by hand in handwritten books: manuscripts (*manu-* means 'hand', *-script*, 'written'). Only a small minority of the manuscripts which existed during the period have endured to the present. Therefore, very few poems from the time survive in copies which their poets made, or even saw. No manuscripts of any of Chaucer's works exist in Chaucer's own handwriting, and every surviving copy of the *Canterbury Tales* was probably made after his death. This situation is standard for Middle English and Older Scots poets. A few exceptions exist: we have manuscripts of verse by the poets Orm, Thomas Hoccleve, George Ashby, and John Capgrave copied in their own hands, for example. Even these, though, are not working drafts created during composition, and almost no examples of drafts endure from these centuries (for a survey, see Beadle 1994). Only very rarely can we read a poem with any confidence that its appearance in surviving copies reflects the wishes of the poet.

In manuscripts, spelling varies. Often new readers of Middle English notice this variation first of all. Different editing practices are partly responsible for our impression of a sharp break between Middle English variation in spelling and early modern English conformity. The modern editors of Shakespeare, for instance, tend to present him in standardized and modernized spelling, but in the First Folio of his works (1623) Hamlet's 'slings and arrows of outrageous fortune' (F 3.1, 58) are the 'Slings and Arrowes of outragious Fortune' (1623); in the Second Quarto text of *Hamlet* (1604–5) they are the 'flings and arrowes', with a long s, ſ. It is also true, though, that through the twelfth to the fifteenth centuries spelling varied even more than it did in the sixteenth and seventeenth. Spelling varied for multiple reasons, reasons that reinforced each other. In part, variation happened because no particular variety of English was firmly established as a prestige or standard form. Texts and spellings were not, as they would become, subject to the choices of a print publishing industry based primarily in one city and fired by a practical desire to standardize. Both pronunciation and spelling therefore varied a great deal: there are more than 500 different recorded Middle English spellings for the word we now know as *through*, including *thurgh, thorutgh, þurðh*, and *turght*. Sometimes variation between Middle Englishes happened at the level of words rather than spelling, with words from one local variety of English supplanting those from another as works travelled between regions. Needing no general standard, individual scribes also varied within their own practice: the same scribe could use two distinct spellings of the same word just a few lines apart.

Although such quirks can now seem comic or difficult, or both, Middle English spelling made more sense than present-day English spelling does. People tended to spell more as they spoke, representing their speech more closely than we do in spelling today. (For more on Middle English spelling, see Appendix, sections 1–8.) However, because very few poems in this period survive in the handwriting of the poets themselves, the spellings found in writing from this time are almost always scribal rather than authorial. One word of caution for close reading, therefore: though spellings in this period have their own interest for language history, they cannot help critics close-read poems in the way that the spelling of more modern poets, from the hands of the poets themselves, sometimes can.

In almost all editions of Middle English works, modern editors add modern punctuation and capitalization for readers' convenience. Such editorial intervention misrepresents the text—but does so helpfully. In some ways, it produces a reading experience more, not less, like those of the original audiences: these poems looked and sounded normal and modern to them, and modernization helps make the poems look and sound normal to readers now. This idea matches a standard argument for the performance of Shakespeare in modern dress: that is how his plays were performed and received in his lifetime. Readers must, however, bear in mind this editorial addition of capitalization and punctuation when reading closely. A nineteenth- or twentieth-century poet's choice between semi-colon and em-dash might bear meaning. In an edition of a Middle English work, though, these features have been added by editors. They can't enter direct close reading of the verse. I say more about the changes wrought in the editing of Middle English verse, and about how editions themselves can help close reading, in Chapter 9.

The best way to build a facility with Middle English and Older Scots is to read a lot. Each line makes the next easier. The simplest advice I can offer on reading Middle English is therefore a repurposing of Helen Gardner's line on the hard parts of T. S. Eliot's poems: 'read on, preferably aloud' (1949, 54). Much more so than today, poetry at this time was written to be heard, and reading such poetry aloud clarifies confusing words and phrasings. Often what seems alien to sight sounds familiar when given breath. Granted, reading aloud with a stab at reconstructed pronunciation carries an unavoidable falseness: the right sounds sound strange today, though they were normal in their time. But it is still worth trying to get the sounds right. The sounds serve an understanding of the poetry, clarifying rhymes, puns, and rhythms, and they don't have to pursue an elusive, illusory authenticity. Our present-day reconstructions will never be perfect and will always vary from each other somewhat, just as different types of Older Scots and English varied. Readers shouldn't feel silly if they slip up: everyone with a right to complain about pronunciation died long ago. When and where it's possible, there are other, broader benefits to reading aloud, too, ones which matter well beyond early poetry, for most literature benefits from being heard (Akbari 2019). To help in reading the poetry, the Appendix to this book offers a basic guide to spellings, pronunciations, and grammar, written for those who are not historical linguists.

No book could cover close reading as a technique, in general, alongside Middle English and Older Scots verse, in particular. I shall limit myself to a few broader remarks. Close reading cannot only record a reader's emotional response: technical knowledge must support it, and this book supplies a lot of that knowledge. Equally, though, close reading shouldn't entail a dry naming of parts, murdering to dissect. The careful study of poetry is not a business of spotting and cataloguing. Rather, such study combines both the technical and the impressionistic, so that in the best literary criticism deep knowledge supports an appreciative ear for the text. In a way, close reading involves readers carefully observing themselves in the act of reading. Every critic has one unique and highly sensitive measuring instrument: their own mind. They read poetry with half an eye on their own reactions, using those reactions as a guide to which passages and lines seem most potentially fruitful. Then, perhaps after copying out a particularly interesting passage and sitting with it for a few minutes, the technical abilities come into play, and they can look again to see how and why the poetry piques their interest, not destroying their response, but rather coming to appreciate the craft behind it. Close reading combines craft knowledge and self knowledge.

Because close reading is knowledgeable work, literary critics don't rest once they have spotted poetry's features and effects. They ask what those features and effects do. A poem's craft details are best understood together, acting with or against each other, and in concert with what the poet says. This book's initial chapters discuss different aspects of verse separately because clarity calls for separation. They still, though, gesture towards what their example quotations might do in their larger poetic contexts and link each facet of verse-craft discussed to others. Literary form is often at its most exciting when individual aspects of writing work together or cut against each other. Readers are encouraged to think in this holistic manner as they read.

Tools and resources

I must also introduce three types of tool. The first of these is the dictionary, and in particular the invaluable *Middle English Dictionary* (*MED*), which lives online, free to everyone (<https://quod.lib.umich.edu/m/middle-english-dictionary/dictionary>). Good editions often have their own specialized glossaries at the back, or on-page glosses, and readers should turn to such aids first of all. But the *MED* offers support when local glossaries fail. Sometimes it offers cantankerous support, picky about the queries it is fed, but it remains very useful. Besides clearing up meanings, its quotations also show a word's likely contexts of use and probable connotations, topics which I cover in more detail in Chapter 2. More developed practical advice on the use of the *MED* appears in Simon Horobin's helpful *Chaucer's Language* (2013, 180–184), but here are two key tips: keep trying different spellings if the right entry doesn't turn up at a first enquiry, and make liberal use of the drop-down box which controls which elements of the dictionary are searched—the 'Modern English word equivalent' search, for example, lets users enter present-day words and find their Middle English counterparts. The *MED* often helps with Older Scots words too, but for further assistance readers can consult the *Dictionary of the Older Scottish Tongue* (*DOST*) as part of the *Dictionaries of the Scots Language* (<https://dsl.ac.uk>). Readers lucky enough to have electronic access to the *Oxford English Dictionary* (*OED*)—often available to university students—will find it very helpful for understanding the histories of words, which will receive more discussion in Chapter 2. Topical dictionaries (e.g. Corèdon and Williams 2004) can help with contextual vocabulary.

The second type of tool to exploit is translation. Few Middle English works have received multiple translations, and most have no full translation at all. This clustering of translations follows the unequal distribution of prestige and critical attention. Where a translation exists, readers should feel no shame in turning to it. But they must avoid the trap of treating a translation as the primary text: far better to read the Middle English, wrestle with the knotty bits, and only then bring in translation. The translator attends as a consultant whose opinion is never final.

Every translation creates a new text. Take, for example, the long poem telling of the fall of King Arthur that is now known as the *Alliterative Morte Arthure*. At the height of his power, Arthur relates the beginning of a nightmarish dream which he has just had:

> Me thought I was in a wood | willed mine one,
> That I ne wiste no way | whider that I sholde.
> (*Benson ed. 1994, 3230–3231)

Simon Armitage translates these lines as follows:

> I believed I was in a wood, wandering alone
> Wholly unaware of which way I should walk.
> (Armitage 2012, 3230–3231)

Various changes leap out here. 'Me thought' in Middle English has a less active quality than present-day 'I believed'—the original phrase uses 'me' and not 'I' for a reason—and its sense is closer to 'It seemed to me'. The Middle English 'willed' in the first line is not a present participle as 'wandering' is, and because 'willed' contains the element 'will', it points to something very much at issue at this point in the poem: Arthur's will—to power, to conquest—and its coming subordination to reversals of fortune. This thematic echo disappears in Armitage's 'wandering'. In his translation,

Armitage takes on the formidable task of echoing the original's regular alliteration. Translating 'whider that I sholde' while reaching for alliteration, he introduces the specificity of 'walk'. In the Middle English the 'sholde', with only at best a vague sense of implied 'go', specifies less and therefore opens up more questions: is this actually about the direction of Arthur's life and reign, not his footsteps? The wood where Arthur finds himself threatens dangers:

> There lions full lothly | licked their tuskes
> All for lapping of blood | of my lele knightes!
>
> (3234–3235)
>
> Lions lurked there, licking their lips,
> That would love to lap at the blood of my lords.
>
> (Armitage 2012, 3234–3235)

Armitage lets in lurking, a new idea, and loses the lions' loathliness. For alliteration's sake, the 'tuskes', teeth, have become 'lips'. To lick one's lips is no doubt a potentially threatening gesture, but it brings other associations—cookery, for instance—while the Middle English, by contrast, attends directly to the sharp points at issue: the teeth. Set alongside Armitage's change of 'lapping' into an infinitive in the more hypothetical 'would love to lap…', the threat in the Middle English feels sharper, more immediate.

These differences don't mean that Armitage somehow gets it wrong, or that his translation can't offer help. All translations always change things, and Armitage makes these choices because he must prioritize and select, taking some routes and spurning others. Translations open possibilities up, and comparison can clarify. In this case, for instance, the modern version casts light through contrast on the physicality of the threatening teeth in the original. Translations can assist in many ways, then, but the original must be kept firmly in mind.

The third type of tool which I must introduce is the verse index. Almost all known Middle English poems have been indexed, and assigned individual, identifying numbers. This invaluable work makes it possible to indicate reliably the host of more obscure verse pieces, which have no original or agreed titles. By the early twenty-first century, many hours of scholarly labour had produced two dominant tools, the *New Index of Middle English Verse* (*NIMEV*), which is a printed book (Boffey and Edwards 2005), and the *Digital Index of Middle English Verse* (*DIMEV*), which is an online database (<http://www.dimev.net>). The two provide a textbook contrast between electronic and print transmission. The *NIMEV*'s printed stability is a strength: my *NIMEV* will always be the same as any other *NIMEV*, and no copy will ever read 'page not found'. Print is also a weakness: the printed book is a large, unhandy object, and won't accommodate improvements in scholarship unless I add them to my copy, uniquely, by hand. The *DIMEV* accepts updates and is highly portable, but requires electricity, internet access, and stable hosting. Each tool is useful and each contains quirks. The very category of Middle English verse has complications and edge cases. Nevertheless, these tools offer vital aid in the consistent and universal identification of Middle English poems. I give *NIMEV* and *DIMEV* numbers for less well-known works.

Both indexes descend from the original *Index of Middle English Verse* and its *Supplement*, flawed-yet-mighty achievements of scholars who worked before word processing and digital information storage. Carleton Brown and Rossell Hope Robbins published the original *Index* during the Second World War, assigning it the 'purpose of proclaiming the freedom and recognition of learning among the United Nations' in hopeful anticipation of 'the final victory over international fascism' (1943, xiii). For the 1943 *Index*, the study of Middle English poetry couldn't just be an escape from the present. This idea runs between and behind the readings that make up this book. It's time to consider why we of the present should care about Middle English poetry.

1
Why Old Poetry?

Why read early poetry? Friends, students, and well-wishers who think I should have more ambition—all have asked me. The question's a fair one: most English-speakers live their lives without ever reading any, or perhaps without ever getting the chance to read any. Even at those universities which do offer that chance to students, and even within many introductions to the field, the question isn't always tackled. Silence on the topic has not, on the available evidence, successfully promoted it, and so I offer some possible answers here.

It's true that experience of Middle English will not serve a person as, say, understanding healthy living can. On its own, though, utility is not much of an objection, since we might object on the grounds of utility to all kinds of things, ancient and modern, which nevertheless enhance our lives. Even within the discipline of English studies, however, where one might expect to find people who think poetry important, plenty of departments forgo English before Shakespeare. So: why early poetry?

One reason is that the verse we think of as 'early' makes up the majority of the history of English and Scots literature. The earliest substantial English text of any kind to survive, a prose law code, might come from c.589–616 (Oliver ed. 2004). In terms of raw time, then, the mid-point of the history of English literature falls somewhere around the year 1300. The entirety of printed English falls within that history's second half, for English first appeared in print in the 1470s. To read only writings from (say) the nineteenth and twentieth centuries is therefore to experience about fifteen per cent of the full chronological range on offer. It seems wise to try more of that range: no one at a buffet wants to be restricted to just fifteen per cent of the food's variety. (To travel earlier than this book's coverage, see, for example, Marsden ed. 2015, Treharne ed. 2010, and Terasawa 2011.) That comparison might seem unfair because more writings survive from more recent times. Yet sufficient works survive from any century after the eighth to fill a university course. Despite great losses, enough Middle English and Older Scots writing survives that one lifetime's detailed study can't cover it all. Since these limits form the real constraints on reading, we need not regard the overwhelming mass of surviving early verse as different on a human scale from the overwhelming mass of contemporary verse.

Middle English verse deserves special attention, though, for a quality which does sharply distinguish it from present-day English writing: its lack of assumed dominance. Middle English writings had a more uncertain status than either Old or Modern English. English today is the world's most spoken language and serves as the most widespread—though far from only—shared language of trade and diplomacy. It has more second-language speakers than first-language speakers. The use of English itself

How to Read Middle English Poetry. Daniel Sawyer, Oxford University Press. © Daniel Sawyer (2024).
DOI: 10.1093/oso/ 9780198895237.003.0002

therefore sometimes goes unquestioned by twenty-first-century students and critics. But English's prevalence is not natural or ahistorical, or, for that matter, necessarily good. Reading early English reminds us of these facts and helps us begin thinking around and beyond them.

Middle English poetry offers one especially useful escape route from the default position of present-day English, because it was never normal or normative. Middle English poetry was an uncertain verse-craft, practised near the known world's edge by people speaking a little-known, little-learned tongue, turning out poetry shot through with its own oddity. England in these centuries exported wool, not words. Reading earlier English literature, we uncouple ourselves from the language's present dominance. While much else in this chapter applies also to the study of Old English poetry, these facts apply particularly to Middle English. Old English had a less troubled status, since, among linguistic groups in Western Europe, earlier English-speakers were precocious in shifting some ideas from Latin into their first language. Only the Norman Conquest in 1066 raised up another vernacular language, creating the conditions for Middle English's strangeness, its estrangement from writing and power.

In reading Middle English we encounter an English literature which is tentative about itself, and so divided among its different local varieties that writers report problems with mutual understanding: the fifteenth-century printer and translator William Caxton tells an anecdote about an Englishman travelling a short distance within England and being taken for a French-speaker when he tries to buy eggs (1490, A i verso). This uncertainty lends Middle English verse more fascination: it was less standardized, less centralized, more in play, and hungry for influence from other traditions. English poetry in these centuries fizzed with experimentation because what English poetry was, or should be, was unsettled. It was towards the end of the time assigned to Middle English, too, that English writing cautiously began to make claims for a concept of literature as something self-sustaining and valuable in itself rather than as—in the sense this book tends to use—'something written' (Cannon 2008, 150–186; Meyer-Lee 2010). Studying this period at once challenges assumptions about English literature and lays bare the roots of those assumptions.

While English itself felt less normal as a literary language at this time, verse itself felt more normal. Poetry commonly served a wider range of purposes than it does today. People wrote short, personal poems expressing strong emotion—that is, they wrote what someone on the street today might call a poem—but they also wrote poems to transmit medical guidance, to teach, to pray, to keep and inflect the historical record, and to tell long stories. Poets more rarely take on these tasks today, and almost never tackle some of them, such as medical advice. As a proportion of the writing population, perhaps more people composed poetry more often during these centuries, and they found proportionally larger audiences than modern poets, excepting modern songwriters. Poetry was also more commonly read aloud to groups as a social entertainment (Coleman 1996). This period of literature therefore lets readers study poets who didn't regard poetry as a minority interest. Such a context, in which English writing felt less natural but poetry felt more natural, exactly flips today's state of affairs.

Middle English and Older Scots therefore serve as a vital testbed for literary-critical assumptions: any general theory about literature must work for literature from this period too. If it does not, critics must either reject it, modify it, or reduce it to a thesis about a specific time. When I was a new undergraduate, my whole cohort of students attended a lecture hall discussion in which we tried to define poetry. This famously tough question gave us plenty of grief: not all poetry has regular rhyme or metre, for example, and saying that poetry is written by poets merely shunts the problem one stage back. At last, I suggested 'text in which the author, not the publisher, decides where the lines end on the page'; this idea was hardly original to me (Eagleton 2007, 25), and has persisted: it still appears in contemporary guides (Greenham 2019, 57; Hodgson 2021, 61). The definition received general approval, with the lecturer using it to wrap things up. I felt smug. Middle English taught me humility, though, for I later spent months studying earlier manuscripts in which scribes copied English poems in big paragraphs, with no line divisions, like prose. Scribes, not authors, had decided where these lines ended. The now-agreed convention that separate English verse lines come separated visually developed during the Middle English centuries: the greatest ever change in how pages present verse. I had taken this idea for granted when it really had a history of its own. Ideas which hold true for modern literature ought to be tested on writings from other times. The study of early literature keeps the rest of criticism honest.

For those with any interest in writing poems, meanwhile, verse before print is a significant source of influence. Middle English is one of the layers underpinning the work of modern poets: to name just a few, W. H. Auden, Patience Agbabi, Thom Gunn, Vahni Capildeo, Carter Revard, Lavinia Greenlaw, and Caroline Bergvall (Revard 2003; Capildeo 2013; Agbabi 2014; Greenlaw 2014; Bergvall 2019; Leahy 2019; Sawyer 2021b; for more examples, see Saunders 2010). Early modern writing, too, reverberates with the long echo of Middle English. Shakespeare adapted elements of *Troilus and Cressida* from Chaucer's greatest poem, *Troilus and Criseyde* and John Lydgate's *Troy Book*, while the plot of his play *As You Like It* descends from the Middle English *Tale of Gamelyn*. He borrowed from Chaucer's Knight's Tale in both *A Midsummer Night's Dream* and—writing with John Fletcher—*The Two Noble Kinsmen*. In *Pericles*, which Shakespeare also co-authored, much of the story comes transmitted through the poetry of Chaucer's acquaintance John Gower. The dramatized figure of Gower himself takes the stage to open each act, and Shakespeare himself might have played Gower in early performances. Gower's dialogue in Acts I–IV varies from the customary five-beat line of the Jacobean stage, so that Gower's own older four-beat couplets are recalled in the play's first words:

> To sing a song that old was sung
> From ashes ancient Gower is come,
> Assuming man's infirmities
> To glad your ear and please your eyes.
>
> (1 Chorus, 1–4)

To feel what the play is up to here—to feel it rather than merely knowing it—one must have met at least a little of Gower's work, as Shakespeare himself could have, in printed editions of the middle of the sixteenth century.

Note further that, although only two centuries separated John Gower from the writing of *Pericles*, the play makes either Gower or the ashes from which he comes 'ancient'. The perceived difference and distance of Gower lets the play flatter its audience for their modernity:

> If you, born in these latter times
> When wit's more ripe, accept my rhymes,
> And that to hear an old man sing
> May to your wishes pleasure bring,
> I life would wish, and that I might
> Waste it for you like taper-light.
>
> (1 Chorus, 11–16)

Gower lived, it is implied, in a time of 'unripe' wit, and in staking out this separation in *skill* the play conveys one of the things many people who haven't read any early English poetry believe: that it's less sophisticated.

This belief errs. Craft changes, but it doesn't progress, and it doesn't fit framing metaphors of evolution or technological advancement. Consider an analogy with architecture. The nondescript 1990s block within which I sit, writing this paragraph, sits itself atop a long history of technological improvements. Its construction benefitted from thousands of changes in planning, precision, materials, safety, and supply chains which were unavailable to those who built, for example, the rock-cut church of St George in Lalibela, or the Temple of Heaven in Beijing. In some respects *engineering* has improved. But those improvements don't make my building more worth seeing than those monuments: I get no tourists. Moreover, some of the sophisticated techniques used in the building of my block are simply irrelevant to other buildings: the artisans at Lalibela had less need for supply chains, for instance, for they carved their churches out of the ground itself.

So it is with verse. Verse has changed over time, true, but the wit of its readers and writers hasn't strengthened. Indeed, poets and their readers today lack some abilities they had six centuries ago, when fewer people could read, but those who did read read better. The first audiences for Middle English poetry lived in a time where writing was costly; they cultivated better memories than ours; many of them spoke more languages than most first-language speakers of English today do; and most of them encountered more poetry, more often, than most readers today.

No wonder, then, that Middle English poetry is finely worked: poets and readers had more time and space than most people today to play with words, think lines over, and chew through their influences. Those seeking psychological sophistication can turn to works such as Chaucer's *Troilus and Criseyde*, long celebrated for its sensitivity to its characters' inner lives (Spearing 1964, 96–117). Equally, some Middle English works, such as many of the surviving romances, invite us to rethink how text crafts character through action and description. The whole period predates the cluster of ideas about realism in narration, voice, and consistent characterization which shape the modern novel, for even novels today which react against realism are, in their very reaction, controlled by it. Surviving Middle English works should hold plenty of interest, too, for anyone who favours playful postmodern writing. Middle English examples of polyvocality, open-endedness, and circularity abound; the period also fostered non-realist traditions of drama (discussed in Chapter 11), and poets who willed themselves anonymous, or wrote works designed for other voices to inhabit. The postmodern is not identical with what came before modernity, but it does echo, for much postmodern writing attempts to undo things done in, or to, European writing after the fifteenth century. Early poets possessed a model of writing that stressed response and adaptation: what we might today call intertextuality was the default and serves as a core element in some Middle English poems. *Piers Plowman*, for instance, keeps up so dense a dialogue with other works and others' ideas that some critics treat the poem as a kind of reading diary. Thematically and conceptually, Middle English poetry at least equals any other period.

Verse-making itself, too, could achieve extraordinary levels of detail, sometimes to the point of what might seem like rococo excess, as in *Three Dead Kings*:

> An a byrchyn bonke | ther bous arne bryght,
> I saw a brymlyche bore | to a bay broght;
> Ronke rachis with rerde | thai ronnon aryght;
> Of al hore row and hore rest | lytil hom roght.
>
> (On a birch-tree'd bank, where boughs are bright, I saw a fierce boar brought to bay; strong hounds with a cry ran rapidly; they cared little for all repose and rest. *Three Dead Kings*, *Audelay 2009, art. 38, 1–4)

This extraordinary poem marshals four obligatory ornamental features:

1. Alliteration both within and across lines, grouping lines into pairs: in these lines, an *aabb* pattern, alliterating on **b** and **r**.
2. Rhyme at line ends, alternating here in an *abab* pattern, rhymed on *-yght* and *-oght*.
3. Something technically called 'pararhyme' or (more precisely) '**total consonance**', in which syllables match each other in both the consonant clusters preceding and following a vowel but differ in the vowel itself; here, this effect links the final words of the first two lines (*br-ght*) and of the third and fourth lines (*r-ght*) for a second *aabb* pattern.
4. Simple consonance, in which words match through single consonant clusters; here all four lines quoted end in *-ght*, for an *aaaa* pattern.

The next four lines of the poem (5–8) all share the same *-ght* consonance, making up an *aaaaaaaa* pattern; the pairing of lines into 'couplets' based on total consonance and alliteration also continues, extending the *aabb* pattern to *aabbccdd*; and so does the rhyme pattern, making the eight lines *abababab*. Those eight lines make up but the first part of a thirteen-line stanza—perhaps the most decorated and ambitious stanza-form ever used in English (Turville-Petre 1974, 6–7)—but explaining the first four lines has taken enough space. Not all readers want this level of ornamentation in poetry; I seek only to show that Middle English poets worked with extraordinary formal precision when they wished. These were not centuries of weakness or incompetence in verse.

What, though, of the ideas in these works which we might oppose and repudiate? For instance, one of the *Canterbury Tales*, the Prioress's Tale, is an antisemitic story, and some early poem dehumanize people, in ways that past scholarship did not always properly grasp (Rajabzadeh 2019). There is also much in the history of the twelfth to the fifteenth centuries themselves from which we might turn away. Actually, my working assumption is that any one of the poets I study would have seen me, personally, as dangerous and objectionable. Might this not be a reason to avoid them?

My provisional answer to this question begins with the thought that the poems are not the time that produced them. The practice of studying the poems doesn't commit us to agreement with them, or with their time. In reading, we build a critical relation with early poetry, rather than just nodding along. The poems are in some ways twenty-first-century works. We read them today, and our interest in them is anachronistic. Even a desire to touch something authentic of the past through them is itself anachronistic. I think, then, that we shouldn't treat Middle English poems as conduits to the time that produced them, positively or negatively. There is, as I noted at the end of my introduction, no real escape from the world in which we live; Middle English verse is as much a part of the twenty-first century as mRNA, meteorological chaos, and machine learning; let us therefore read the poetry as part of our present-day world. It contains some of the roots of present-day fissures and prejudices, it offers test cases in the reading of difficult, troubling works, and in its very difference from the present it creates chances to step outside, and reassess, our own assumptions. And it is often good poetry, too.

To readers who nevertheless do want something thematically worthwhile to take away, I suggest studying how these poems think through humanity's place in its world. On this topic, early poetry differs radically from the habits of thought standard in at least the wealthier parts of the globe today. Recent years have seen a growth in what might be called climate fiction, but also worries that contemporary writing struggles to grasp the dominating fact of human life in this century, climate change (e.g. Ghosh 2016, 3–84). Now, writers of the twelfth to the fifteenth centuries never knowingly wrote about climate change. Their work does, however, offer thought-worlds in which progress, growth, and comfort are not assumed, as they were for some rich people in some rich countries for a couple of generations around the twentieth century's end. Early poetry also frequently grapples with the unthinkable, and with ideas that resist language: a mentally-ill mind's distance from itself, the staggering emotions brought by good or bad fortune, the most admirable and the most evil of characters, and an inconceivably mighty God. Middle English and Older Scots poetry knows, as some of us must now re-learn, that humanity cannot always be trusted to act well, that a lifetime or longer can be defined by decline rather than progress, that wealth distorts the mind, that Nature has a certain authority, and that some things are so large they defy pen and mind.

Finally, the study of early poetry offers a firm defence against the calumny that reading and thinking about literature is lazy or easy. Someone handling early verse is obviously not 'just reading books', and that puts us in a better position to suggest that critics working on more recent works are also, perhaps, not just reading books, but are rather engaged in real, skilled, knowledgeable work. I turn now to the work itself.

2
Wording

A poet's choice of words is one of their most basic tools, what critics sometimes call their **lexis**. A sense for the layered meanings and associations of words plays a role in reading Middle English verse as it does in reading modern verse, and sometimes little differs at the level of method. Many ways of thinking about wording transfer quite smoothly across from any other period. If a present-day poet has a character say 'she was a decent wife', for instance, we can listen well to the resonances of *decent*; this example comes from a poem by Terrance Hayes (2010, 85, line 6). As often, one learns a lot by imagining a different word in the same place: if we imagine 'she was a *good* wife' instead, we can pick up the contrasting sense of 'passable', 'tolerable', 'good *enough*' that hangs around 'decent', and also the sense of the proper, the appropriate, the fitting—the earlier sense of the word *decent* in English. Much rests on the poet's choice of this one word. In practice, Hayes immediately makes the weight on the word overt, for the following words drape a pun across a stanza break:

> she was a decent wife. I know decent lives in the word
>
> *descent.*
>
> (6–7)

Hayes titles this poem 'Cocktails with Orpheus', and Orpheus is a poet-musician in Greek myth who descended into the underworld to take back his dead wife Eurydice, so these lines call upon potent associations. The adjective 'decent' matters, though, from the moment of its first arrival, as an important, understated choice which a critic might fruitfully discuss.

Middle English poetry rarely emphasizes the single word so much, partly because it was often written to be heard (see Chapter 11). Readers certainly can, though, make similar interpretative moves when reading it. Various Middle English reimaginings of the myth of Orpheus survive. *Sir Orfeo* presents a strange and enjoyable example (Laskaya and Salisbury eds 1995). Here, Orpheus has become Orfeo; his wife Eurydice is Heurodys. The poem introduces Heurodys as 'The fairest levedi, for the nones, / That might gon on bodi and bones' (53–54). This means something like 'the fairest lady, indeed, that could walk the Earth', but the poet's choice of words says more than a translation can. Unlike *womman*, in Middle English *levedi* is always, across its various shades of meaning, respectful. In this version of the story of Orpheus, as in Hayes's poem, the language used for women's status matters. One might pause, therefore, over the following line's 'bodi and bones'. As often in romances like *Orfeo*, this memorable phrase is not, in itself, the poet's invention: it is a stock pairing which crops up elsewhere (*Canterbury Tales*, III 1544; †Mannyng 1862, 5388; Langland 1995, XVIII.304). Really, the whole couplet delivers a routine description, for *Orfeo*, like other romances, makes ideals of its characters. This stock quality does not, though, weaken the phrase's force in this particular context: it crafts a contrast, suddenly foregrounding the fleshly mortality of the elevated lady of the previous line. This type of thought about words and the possible contrasts between them stretches across the experience of poetry from any period. It is a type of thought with uses beyond literary criticism (Williams 1983), and it deserves practice.

Readers new to Middle English might nevertheless feel that a greater gap separates us from *Sir Orfeo* than 'Cocktails with Orpheus'. However, although Hayes writes in modern English, neither I nor any other English-speaker can just walk into Hayes's poem and inhabit his own personal speech-history, or for that matter the exact context into which his publishers first unleashed his work. A fundamental gap separates poet, work, and readers here just as in Middle English: we forever read with the understanding that our bridging efforts will never fully work, though they might prove fruitful in other ways. Yes, there is a distance between a Middle English poet and me, but there is a distance between me and any poet writing today; there is even a distance between a poet and their own past self: just ask anyone who has returned in adulthood to poems they wrote in their teens. The difference in challenge between reading Middle English and reading present-day English is one of degree, not kind. Thinking otherwise overestimates the difficulty of Middle English and, just as importantly, underestimates the subtlety of present-day poetry.

Let me give another simple example, from a very early Middle English poem, one with much to offer readers in its very strangeness. Speaking directly to every reader or listener in the second person, it sets out to prompt reflection on life's brevity; not a comfortable topic, perhaps, but an important one.

> The wes bold yebyld | er the iboren were;
> The wes molde imynt | er thu of moder come.
>
> (For you a house was built before you were born; for you the earth was marked out before you came from mother. Conlee ed. 1991, 5, ll. 1–2)

In the first line, 'yebyld' means—and is the ancestor of—'built'. This poem has a riddling quality, and the 'bold' ('house') is a metaphorical way to talk, as the second line begins to explain, about a grave. From our time-bound point of view, a grave is made unpredictably, on demand. The poem prompts its audience to wonder whether if we could step outside time, the grave would seem foreordained. From an imagined timeless viewpoint, everyone already has a final end laid out, and in a society such as twelfth-century England, which regarded burial as the only accepted route for honouring the dead, that end is the 'molde imynt' ('earth marked out'). Modern critics have called this poem 'The Grave', but—like most early poems—it has no known title from its own time, and I held the title back till now to keep some of its riddling effect. To say that something is 'yebyld' implies construction and forethought, forethought reinforced when concrete image replaces metaphor in the second line and the poem speaks of earth being 'imynt', measured out. Labouring the point shows how wording can stay surprisingly accessible even in early poetry with a detached, ascetic view of life.

Etymology and register

All of that said, today we do sometimes lack instinctive access to earlier meaning and association. Take the word *aventure*, easily spotted as an ancestor of present-day *adventure*: its most common Middle English meanings are 'fate', 'event', 'accident', and 'risk', and only relatively rarely do we find it used to mean an 'exploit' or a 'questing journey'. The adjective *kinde* serves up another common example: Middle English writers definitely do use it to mean 'generous' or 'affectionate', as in its present-day senses, but they more often use it to mean 'natural' or 'innate'. When a Middle English poet saw the word *inspiracioun*, they sensed more strongly than we do the *-spir-* bit, which has to do in its origins with breath and is related to *spirit*; often in Middle English *inspiracioun* means not just the general sense of present-day *inspiration*, but specifically divine inspiration, from God. Speaking of spirits, the entity in Christian belief and theology today known as the Holy Spirit was known in Middle English as the *Holi Gost*, because *gost*, ancestor of present-day *ghost*, was used for spirits and souls in general; it could mean a dead person's spirit, or an evil spirit, but it had no automatic eldritch or spooky air.

To trace differences of this sort, one must unpick where words came from, and how they were used at the time. The value of knowing where words came from means that reading poetry from this time sometimes involves forays into etymology, the history of words. Happily, such forays hold a lot of interest for their own sake. The *Middle English Dictionary* (*MED*), which is publicly and freely available online, offers help with this; the *Oxford English Dictionary* (*OED*), which is available through many universities, can be even more helpful. Readers who look *etymology* itself up in the *MED*—under *etimologie*—or the *OED* will see that the word is first known in Greek but was borrowed into English from Latin and French. Expanding the *MED*'s list of quotations shows that the earliest recorded examples in English come from around 1400.

The word *etimologie* itself, then, hints at the range of other tongues that shaped Middle English vocabulary. Middle English borrowed many words from other languages, chief among them:

1. Latin, long present in England as the tongue of learning and of western-European Christianity;
2. Old Norse, a big influence on English thanks to extensive language contact during the Scandinavian settlement of northern and eastern parts of England and

the subsequent Danish conquest of England by the Cnut the Great in 1016 (see Dance, Pons-Sanz, and Schorn 2019; and Dance 2019); and
3. French, the tongue of England's Norman rulers after the Norman conquest of England by William the Conqueror in 1066, which continued to have influence throughout the period thanks to England's nearness to the greater cultural and political heft of France.

I discuss some of these connections at greater length in Chapter 10; what matters here are the varying forms, origins, and associations of the different layers of English's vocabulary.

Of course, Middle English also had many words which had already lived in English throughout its known history. These words exist in Middle English because they existed in Old English and usually, before that, in Old English's West Germanic predecessor tongues. Such words were probably either unmarked, or low in register, that is, either unnoticeable and transparent, or noticeably informal and simple. Words first witnessed in English around the time a work was written, meanwhile, are more likely to have been marked. If borrowed from a language with more prestige, such as French or Latin, they are also likely to have been higher in register. That said, there are some simple words which entered English from French or Latin and did so early, thereby becoming unmarked early. *Bishop* descends from the Latin word *episcopus*, but entered the language early in the Old English period, and had become wholly unremarkable even in early Middle English. Some other Christian terms—such as *angel*, *monk*, and *alms*—are similarly early loanwords. On the other hand, the adjective *episcopal*, 'having to do with a bishop', descended from related Latin words, but is first known in English in the fifteenth century, and then only rarely: the *MED* supplies just two quotations. This is a newer borrowing that might have sounded more marked to hearers.

Readers might well be thinking, 'What if I don't know any French or Latin?' Well, I know surprisingly little French myself, learned after my undergraduate days (it's never too late to learn something). For that matter, my Latin isn't all it could be. But I get by. An instinct for these things can develop through practice, and some simple tricks can help. Polysyllabic words ending in *-able*, *-aunce*, *-ence*, *-ize/-ise*, *-tion*, or *-cioun*, for example, are often arrivals from French or Latin. The simpler, shorter, and more everyday a word seems, the more likely it is to originate in Old English or Old Norse. It is worth checking after applying such rules of thumb, but they can help (Horobin and Smith 2002, 97–99).

After or during the application of rules of thumb, where should one check? The *MED* does offer brief etymological notes, but in the *MED*'s case these are gestures, and the *MED* also sometimes multiplies a word's senses perhaps beyond real distinctions. The most detailed and most judicious resource for etymology, when access is available, is the *OED*, where the entries revised recently, in the current millennium, are especially strong. The *OED* often serves best for detailed etymology, and sometimes it can moderate the *MED*'s distinguishing of senses.

The *MED* does, however, offer great help for understanding, and also the best, widest selection of example quotations from the evidence. These quotations sometimes implicitly reveal a word's usual contexts and associations. The quotations given in the *MED* don't grant a full or balanced survey of use: they come from a sample limited first by what survives, and second by what lexicographers have read. But the sheer number of quotations listed can inform. When the dictionary's researchers could find only three examples of a word in use, that word was less common and less familiar than one known from thirty examples. Often something can be guessed of a word's use from the types of work in which it appears. A word that the *MED* mostly quotes from medical prose, for instance, probably carries medical associations into poetry; similarly, if a word is only referenced in other poems, that might hint that speakers and writers of Middle English only used that word in verse, lending it a different air. This wealth of evidence makes the *MED* invaluable.

One further idea assists thinking about words: the division between **open-class** and **closed-class** words. Closed-class words exist in defined and restricted sets. English has a defined class of prepositions, for instance, and adding a new preposition to the language would be slow and difficult. The process can be glimpsed in Middle English in the case of the word *despite*. *Despite* was once a noun meaning something like 'contempt' or 'defiance', and so John Lydgate could write in the fifteenth century of someone acting 'In dispite of daunger and dispeyre' (1911–1934, *Complaint of the Black Knight*, 13). In the seventeenth and eighteenth centuries, in early modern English, the word came to be understood as a preposition, so that today we act not *in* despite of things, but merely despite them. This process happened slowly: being a closed class, prepositions don't admit new members fast or easily. The closed classes of words are auxiliary verbs, conjunctions, prepositions, pronouns, determiners, numerals, and interjections. Closed classes do change, but only very slowly.

Open classes change more quickly and easily, swallowing new words with little friction. English easily absorbs new nouns, adjectives, and adverbs, and verbs which aren't auxiliary verbs. There are fewer open classes, then, but most of the language's vocabulary sits within them. Often words from one of these open classes can also smoothly enter another open class: *access*, for example, was once only a noun and later became a verb. Some fields of study call open- and closed-class words 'content words' and 'function words', but this wording hinders literary criticism, where content and function don't neatly divide: for a critic, a small, seemingly functional word sometimes bears much meaning. The open–closed distinction sheds light on problems in and beyond the study of Middle English verse: we will need it in this chapter and in Chapter 5, and it will prove useful, too, to anyone studying works from later or indeed earlier periods.

A worked example

To explore how wording might be studied in practice, I take a fifteenth-century poem that, at least superficially, resembles what is often thought to be poetry today: a short first-person rhyming work expressing strong personal emotion.

Lettyr

	Myn hertys joy, and all myn hole plesaunce,	*whole desire*
	Whom that I serve and shall do faythfully	
	Wyth trew entent and humble observaunce,	*true intent; worship*
	Yow for to plese in that I can, treuly,	*what I can*
5	Besechyng yow thys lytell byll and I	*letter*
	May hertly, wyth symplesse and drede,	*heartily; humility*
	Be recomawndyd to your goodlyhede.	*generosity.*
	And yf ye lyst have knowlech of my qwert,	*if you wish to; health*
	I am in hele—God thankyd mot He be—	*well; must*
10	As of body, but treuly not in hert,	
	Nor nought shal be to tyme I may you se;	*until the time when*
	But thynke that I as treuly wyll be he	
	That for your ese shall do my payn and myght,	
	As thogh that I were dayly in your syght.	
15	I wryte to yow no more for lak of space,	
	But I beseche the only Trinité	*the Trinity*
	Yow kepe and save, be support of His grace,	*keep and preserve, by*
	And be your sheld from all adversyté.	
	Go lytill byll, and say thou were wyth me	
20	Of verey trouth, as thou canst wele remembre,	
	At myn upryst, the fyft day of Decembre.	*getting-up; fifth*

(Robbins ed. 1955, art. 189; *NIMEV* 2182 | *DIMEV* 3509)

This poem doesn't revel in imagery: only a few metaphors feature, and they are conventional. It lacks the heights and paradoxes of image that might be found in, say, Petrarch's sonnets. The poem is clearly loving, but just as clearly matter-of-fact. I suspect, though, that early modern love lyrics and overheated Victorian ideas have shaped our idea of earlier English love poetry more than exposure to the thing in itself. If this short poem fails to meet modern expectations, perhaps it tries to fulfil others; while I hunt for those, its lack of complex metaphors will make it easier to focus on the choice of words.

Various polysyllabic words populate the first stanza: 'faythfully', 'observaunce', 'recomawndyd', and 'goodlyhede'. 'Plesaunce' and 'observaunce', which form the poem's opening rhyme, are words with elevated associations: as the *-aunce* endings hint, both entered English from French, and the *MED* shows that the two words both have ranges of related secular and religious meaning which flow fruitfully into this poem. When the speaker begs to 'Be recomawndyd' in the stanza's closing line, he uses a word bearing some residual gravitas from its origins in the Latin word *recommendare* and possibly, as well, Old French *recommender*. The *MED* can also reveal that *recommenden* was probably a newer entrant to the language than *plesaunce* and *observaunce* at this time—its first known uses come in the late fourteenth century— and that, given its early appearances in Chaucer's works, it might bear particularly literary associations.

On their own, though, these details might mean little. Besides, the other words derived from French in this first stanza—*serve, symplesse, entent,* and *joy*—were all relatively normal in fifteenth-century Middle English. Yet the French and Latinate flourishes in the first stanza take on much more resonance when the lexical choices alter in the second. The second stanza contains not one word originating in French or Latin. It serves up seven lines of unremittingly Germanic wording: almost all of its words come from Old English, though 'qwert' comes from Old Norse. Single-syllable words dominate. All but two of the polysyllabic words in this stanza only have multiple syllables thanks to grammatical word-endings ('thank*yd*') or adverbial suffixes ('treu*ly*', 'day*ly*'); the two exceptions are 'knowlech' and 'body'. Single-syllable words hold all the rhyming positions, and the three *b*-rhymes (lines 9, 11, 12) are English's most basic verb ('be'), a very common verb ('se') and a pronoun, a closed-class word ('he'). Now, the poet did not write this stanza with an historical dictionary to hand; no such resources existed. But such a stark swerve away from French- and Latin-derived words surely originates in a choice to change tone and register.

Even the observation that this stanza hosts a distinct shift in word choice is in itself inert, though. In a reading of the poem it must inform a larger point. I propose the following larger point: when the second stanza turns to speak primarily of the speaker himself, with great humility—it is offered 'yf' the recipient would like to know how the speaker fares (8)—the shift in the poem's lexis, shorn of Latinate and French terms suggesting literary pretensions, conveys the speaker's diffidence. Like many effects of simplicity, the mechanics behind the humility stay hard to spot unless we peer closely at the language. Careful craft, itself anything but simple, creates the simplicity in the middle stanza of this seemingly mundane letter-poem.

Alongside its lexical simplicity, this second stanza conveys at least one conceptually complex idea, that the speaker 'wyll be he / That for your ese shall do my payn and myght, / As thogh that I were dayly in your syght'. The poet's choice of basic words here lets the audience focus on the proposal's oddness. The first part of these lines states a linguistically strange, out-of-body, out-of-self idea: the speaker *will be he*, someone else, who will work for the recipient's ease. This idea was not a new invention for this poem, but rather part of the common stock of wordings in the poetry of love-talk (compare *Troilus and Criseyde*, III.127–133). We shouldn't dismiss the idea on that account, though, since poets in this period recycled resonant phrases not out of laziness, but because they knew a good thing when they heard it. Matters become stranger still in a comparative conditional: the speaker promises that he will work for the recipient's ease *as though* he were in their sight (14). It is easy to think of comparisons always as devices of flowery imagery, the kind of flowery imagery which this poem pointedly does not display. This comparison eschews floweriness, but achieves something perhaps more fundamental. Any overt comparison, unlike full metaphor, is always a reminder that though A is like B, A is also—therefore—not B; this one asks readers to imagine the speaker and recipient together, and at the same time reminds us that they are apart. A quiet pathos rises through this counterfactual.

The effect of the sudden disappearance of high-register French- and Latin-derived terms continues a little into the third stanza, which begins with a line of neat monosyllables, mostly from Old English: 'I wryte to yow no more for lak of space'. True, 'space' is from French, but—and again here the *MED* guides us—the word had become entirely normal in English by the fifteenth century. It is the antithetical rhyme of 'Trinité' and 'aduersyté' which brings us back to high things—the highest things, in the case of the Trinity. The closing lines go on to achieve a kind of moderation. 'Remembre' and 'Decembre' are not originally English words, and create polysyllabic rhymes (**feminine rhyme**: see Chapter 6). Although 'trouth' is English through-and-through, 'very trouth' is a high and serious business, not invoked lightly: 'trouth' in Middle English means both present-day *truth* and the concept of faithful *troth* which is echoed in the present-day word *betrothed*. By contrast, 'uprist'—one's rising from bed—means, in its primary sense here, an everyday act, and brings in a sense of less serious business. This word is also, I suspect, a slightly intimate detail to mention in a poem which eschews flirtation in favour of devotion. That said, elsewhere in Middle English, 'uprist' can mean Jesus' resurrection, linking religious and romantic service here for any reader with a mind for puns. But to take the religious sense as prominent, rather than simply present, would be to read the poet as presumptuous. The seeming mundaneity of 'uprist' carries through in the closing of the final rhyme: except perhaps as a saint's day, the fifth day of December is not the most thrilling thing to remember. But it is this simplicity, this mundane quality, which fulfils the poem's appealing letter conceit. To a careful reader this poem displays artful artlessness, the quality of everyday commitment created through notable craft.

Further analysis might note the intersection of these words with rhyme. The *b*-rhymes of all three stanzas nearly **through-rhyme** together: the Middle English sound of 'I' sits close to the sound of 'he'. The fifth lines of all three stanzas rhyme on pronouns referring to the speaker (*I*, *he*, and *me*)—who is also rhymed with 'faithfully', 'treuly', and 'Trinité'. The speaker might put on simplicity, but he is also associated with consistency and constancy, in the meanings of the specific words chosen, in the way those words rhyme with each other, and in the consistent appearance of these lexical and rhyming effects as they build up across the poem. Yet further study might even turn to the poem's framing: it comes headed with the word 'lettyr' in its surviving manuscript copy, but the noun used in the poem itself for the imagined or real letter is 'byll'. This term has a formal air, being adopted from Anglo-Norman French and also used for legal documents. It is also, though, another word simple in its form, as the speaker and the poem claim to be. Notably, the fifth line unites the apparently simple speaker and the apparently simple letter-poem, 'thys lytell byll and I'. In the fifteenth and early sixteenth centuries a slew of such letter-poems personify the letter itself. Phrases of the 'Go lyttil byll' type frequently occur in letter-poems, but this wider tradition's existence should not obscure the oddness of the linguistic event. In these phrases, letter-poems technically address themselves, a decidedly unusual idea within the broader sweep of literary history.

I could say more on other aspects of this poem; I have said more on its wording alone than I would in normal literary-critical practice: the reader must judiciously select the features of a work that most call for comment relevant to the topic at hand. A fuller interpretation, built on some of these observations but perhaps labouring them less, might wonder what besides love is at play in the poem. At this time, elegant short love poems often deployed romantic love as a metaphor for other things. Such works had taken on many social functions for their authors, sometimes acting as shows of wit, or as tokens in homosocial power relations between men. I hope, though, the exercise has shown how much fruitful evidence can be dug out from a poem's wording using a little dictionary work. This is particularly the case for fourteenth- and fifteenth-century verse, which uses more words of French or Latin origin than early Middle English poetry does. In its extreme form, which I shall now turn to discuss, this tendency became aureation.

Aureation

Aureation is the name given to the use, in some Middle English and Scots works, of a high density of Latinate or French-derived words. Aureation usually involves some words then nearly or outright unknown in English. A few such words entered general usage and now seem unremarkable. We know the word *deception* today, for instance, even though it might have entered the language as a novelty in the verse of Thomas Hoccleve and John Lydgate. Most aureate words, however, lived short lives in the language and can now sound distinctly odd. For instance, Lydgate is, as far as we know, the only English writer ever to have called anything *flaskisable* ('changeable, unreliable'); when one of Lydgate's anonymous fifteenth-century successors wrote of the mythological sorceress Medea that 'if crafte fayled she usyde interfeccyon // With swerde or knyfe' ('if magic failed, she killed with a sword or a knife'), their choice of *interfeccyon* provided a grand, elevated rhyme word and created a pleasingly sharp contrast with the *swerde* and *knyfe* (Cowen ed. 2015, 1309–1310).

In enriching their vocabulary like this, fifteenth-century poets in part took inspiration from Chaucer, who did reach for abstruse Latin terminology at times, but they also elaborated and innovated beyond his writings. Many readers had some Latin and some French, making such words in and of themselves less strange; in some cases, it was their use in English which would have heightened and marked them out. 'Aureation' means 'gilding', covering with gold, and well conveys what poets felt they were doing to the language. Prose from the same time can show similar leanings.

Several factors might have driven aureation: a quest for grandeur and prestige; a wish to uphold the choice to write in Scots or English in the first place by showing how the language might take on Latin words; or even, perhaps (Gillespie 2008, 234–238, 254), as a response to debates over the orthodoxy of the English Church and the possibility of translation into English.

The Scottish poet William Dunbar, a brilliant writer active at the end of and just after our period, had a knack for sensitive aureation, exemplified in his *'Ballad of Our Lady', a poem praising Mary, mother of Jesus. Consider this brief sample:

Empryce of prys, imperatrice,	*empress; (great) worth; empress*
Bricht polist precious stane;	*polished stone*
Victrice of vyce, hie genitrice	*victor over; high mother*
Of Jhesu, Lord Soverayne;	
Our wys pavys fro enemys,	*wise shield*
Agane the feyndis trayne.	*against; fiend's guile*

(*in Dunbar 2004, 61–66)

Here Dunbar deploys three less familiar nouns imported from Latin: *imperatrice*, *victrice*, and *genitrice*. The shared *-ice* ending comes from *-ix* in Latin, and in that language, as Latinate readers of this poem at the time would have well known, it marks a feminine noun (in present-day English *victor* is gender neutral, but *victor* and *victrix* are masculine and feminine equivalents in Latin). Dunbar uses these words because they constitute the highest of high styles, appropriate to a subject he considers lofty.

On its own, though, an observation of the use of aureate diction for a high subject misses the main poetic effect of aureation in this poem, which lies in Dunbar's precise shifts in vocabulary, in the contrasts between gilded and ungilded moments. These lines don't, after all, contain only aureate words: nothing in the second, fourth, fifth, or sixth lines quoted would have challenged audiences. Dunbar concentrates the aureate terms in every other line, giving readers' minds short breaks. The *-ice* endings on his aureate words also serve the dense internal rhyme of the odd-numbered lines in his chosen stanza form, integrating with smaller, more familiar words such as *wys*, *pavys*, *vyce*, *enemys*, and *prys*. Meanwhile, *imperatrice* is both synonymous with *empryce* and, etymologically, is where *empryce* comes from: *emperess* entered English from French, and the French word descends from *imperatrix*. The first line therefore develops a rich reiterative quality. The whole poem displays similar cunning richness and repays careful study of its words.

The *MED* and *DOST* can assist in spotting aureation: words of French or Latin origin, introduced by fifteenth-century poets, and featured in few quotations, are likely to be aureate borrowings. As with any other local event in a poem, aureation should be examined for its effects rather than just identified. Perhaps the most immediate effect of aureation is an extra demand on comprehension, and often on readers' metrical abilities: they must discern, on the fly, how one or more fresh polysyllabic words fit the surrounding metre. The challenge also compliments an audience, though: by navigating the unfamiliar words, or words familiar from one language in another language, they match wits with the poet. Other effects become clearer when aureation is analysed in clusters. Local clusters of aureate diction within swathes of simpler wording, for instance, take on more significance through contrast. Equally, a poem generally given to aureation can contain blocks of less demanding lexis. Rhyme or syntax can relate aureate words to familiar words, either for reinforcement or for antithesis. Aureate lexis forms part of an array of rhetorical tools used to create the highest styles of poetry in the fifteenth century. As with any other aspect of wording, it becomes most interesting when varied, controlled, and contrasted with other types of vocabulary.

Aureation might sometimes read comically today. But the examples which have become normal in modern English might caution against that. If the language's history differed just a little, perhaps *deception* would now seem odd, while words we find *obnubilous* (obscure) would see common use. For us, aureation troubles the widespread post-Romantic assumption that poets should prefer ordinary language. One might equally suggest that poetry only is poetry because it isn't ordinary; calls for ordinary words in poetry, not unlike calls for common sense in politics, might collapse under close scrutiny. Perhaps, too, expert present-day users of English, living when the majority of speakers know English as a second language, should pause before judging what ordinary English is, and before dismissing the fifteenth-century desire to gild it with words from other tongues.

3
Phrasing

Poets choose words, but they also fit those words together in clauses, and then fit those clauses together in longer blocks of sense. This is the business of syntax. Syntax is the structuring of language: the ordering and linking of words, phrases, and clauses, and therefore also the ordering and linking of ideas. All written and spoken language has syntax, prose as well as verse, and an introduction to Middle English syntax in general lies well beyond my purview here (see guidance in Horobin and Smith 2002, 89–103; and literary discussion in Roscow 1981). I can, though, lay out some tools with which readers can grasp poets' choices.

Discussions of syntax in early verse must bear in mind that these poets didn't have the present-day concept of the sentence. Most seem to have thought about writing in rhetorical units, that is, in blocks of heard speech, rather than in the tight, punctuated, written parcels that schools train children to produce today. Phillipa Hardman has plausibly argued that efforts in printed editions to pin down fluid rhetorical units in rigid modern punctuation have hindered our appreciation of John Lydgate's poetry (2006), and the same might hold true for other writers. Indeed, something similar might hold true for much later verse too (Lennard 2005, 265–267): it was only in the nineteenth and twentieth centuries that a system of defined sentences and grammatical punctuation became fully standardized in English.

Middle English allowed freer word-order than modern English does, and in every stage of English's history poets have enjoyed more freedom in order than prose writers. The close attention with which readers might approach syntax in more recent verse often applies well to earlier poems. Consider the first stanza of Thomas Hoccleve's *Regiment of Princes*:

Musynge upon the restlees bysynesse	*worry*
Which that this troubly world hath ay on honde,	*troubled; ay: always*
That othir thyng than fruyt of bittirnesse	
Ne yildith naght, as I can undirstonde,	*yields nothing*
At Chestres In, right faste by the Stronde,	*Inn; the Strand*
As I lay in my bed upon a nyght,	
Thoght me byrefte of sleep the force and might.	*deprived; virtue; strength*
	(1999, 1–7)

The main clause here comes in the stanza's last line: the first main verb, 'byrefte', therefore comes even later than the famously delayed first main verb in the sixth line of *Paradise Lost*. All the preceding lines give contextualizing and positioning material. The syntax, and therefore the order of ideas, runs opposite to what might seem natural, and one can spend a fruitful minute rewriting and reordering the stanza into dull present-day English prose, marking the line numbers of its different parts. Readers can attempt this now, if they wish; here's what I make of it:

> Thought deprived me of the virtue and strength of sleep (7), as I lay in my bed upon a night (6), at Chester's Inn, very near the Strand (5), musing upon the ceaseless worry (1) which this troubled world always has on hand (2), that—as far as I can understand (4)—yields nothing other (5) than bitter fruit (4) (*or* 'the results [fruit] of bitterness'?)

Present-day translation and prosification show how Hoccleve has craftily organized the different clauses in the original Middle English verse. Translating a short, dense passage often clarifies its exact structure, and helpfully forces us to notice more of its details. Translating this made me spot the ambiguity of 'That' in line 3: is it the 'trobly world' which 'othir thyng than fruyt of bittirnesse / Ne yildith naght', or is it the 'restlees bysynesse'? We shouldn't expect to solve this question, but Hoccleve's syntactic creation of the question itself feels troublesome.

Looking more closely still, several individual clauses in this stanza contain their own smaller delays and reversals. Later Middle English, like present-day English, most prototypically prefers an order of grammatical subject, verb, and then object, that is, SVO. In this stanza, though, the order repeatedly varies. For instance, the verb 'yildith' hangs back until the fourth line, making the reader work through 'othir thyng than fruyt of bittirnesse' before finding out why that phrase is in the poem at all: the world does not ('Ne') yield anything else. This is a SOV structure, and it makes these lines reluctant to yield anything: once readers have the idea of the 'fruyt of bittirnesse' in their heads, they find that nothing else is coming. Similarly, in the stanza's final line, the object precedes the verb: 'Thoght [S] me [O] byrefte [V]'. Everyone has nights when their thoughts seem an outside agent determined to keep them wakeful, when they themselves feel out-of-place. Another reversal follows, flipping the usual word order for possession. Thought drives off not 'the force and might of sleep' but 'of sleep the force and might'. This serves up a rhyme on -*ight*, of course, but it also increases the effort demanded from readers or listeners. I'm cautious about mimetic readings of form—that is, interpretations which see literary form directly matching the shape of something represented in the text—but these lines seem so mannered that they probably do mimic restless thought. At the same time, the SOV structures might also recall Latin, a language in which SOV order is more natural. Even as Hoccleve's syntactic slalom conveys confusion, it might also show off his erudition, and compliment his readers by expecting them to keep up. For magnificent syntactic play achieving a different tone, readers might consult the beginning of the General Prologue to the

Canterbury Tales (I 1–18, especially 1–14), where an audience must navigate eleven lines of temporal clause to reach the verb 'longen'.

Syntax and verse form

Some other matters central to the reading of verse turn on the interplay of form and syntax. Unlike a prose writer, a poet had to distribute words, phrases, and clauses within set verse forms requiring arrangement in metrical lines, plus at least one type of ornamentation (rhyme and alliteration). I shall address the patterning of language in metrical lines, and then turn to some special matters relevant to the distribution of language in couplets.

Metrical lines of verse can **enjamb** or 'run on', or they can be **end-stopped**. Many of enjambment's effects in more modern verse work in earlier verse too. As in modern verse, enjambment opens up a wider gap between the words said and the set of formal rules regulating them, and clusters or patterns of either enjambment or end-stopping especially merit comment. In modern poetry, the poet's punctuation often shows whether lines enjamb or end-stop. But editors, not poets, add the punctuation in modern editions of Middle English and Older Scots works. Here is George Ashby's moment of self-naming in his fifteenth-century *Complaint of a Prisoner in the Fleet*:

> George Asshby ys my name, that ys greved   *grieved*
> By emprysonment a hoole yere and more.   *whole*
> (in *Mooney and Arn eds 2005, 29–30)

This is, at least, how these lines appear in the poem's most convenient edition. In the sole surviving manuscript copy, they run:

> George asshby ys my name that ys greued
> By enprysonment a hoole yere and more
> (Cambridge, Trinity College, MS R.3.19, folio 41 recto)

The 'a' of 'asshby' goes uncapitalized, and no punctuation sits where we might expect it today, after 'name'. (On editors' roles in general, see Chapter 9; on editors' punctuation see Butterfield 2016.) Indeed, most of this copy of the poem lacks punctuation in general; as I noted in my introduction, the period had a different set of punctuation habits, which scribes did not always follow in uniform ways. Consequently, and unlike in a present-day poem, we cannot read the presence or absence of enjambment simply by looking for punctuation marks at the ends of lines: we must take the editors' punctuation marks as expert suggestions and test those suggestions by reading the text. This is a good thing: it gives us a reason to read with care, and that process frequently leads to insights about other aspects of the work. Contact with early English raises the exercise of thinking about enjambment above the scutwork of merely spotting punctuation which poets have chosen to add themselves.

Alliterative verse has its own syntatic quirks. Lines of alliterative verse split into two halves, conventionally called the **a-verse** and **b-verse**:

> *a-verse* | *b-verse*
> Thus he passes to that port | his passage to seche
>
> *(Patience, 97)*

At the b-verse's end, alliterative verse lines usually favour end-stopping instead of enjambment, and usually end somewhere where a voice reading aloud would naturally pause, if only briefly (for further discussion, see Lawton 1980). The phrasing of alliterative verse displays a consistent pattern of distribution within lines. Key information, actions, or descriptions tend to appear in the a-verse, subsidiary information in the b-verse. When subordination occurs, a-verses tend to deliver main clauses, b-verses subordinate clauses. As an illustration, in this description of Jonah setting out on a journey in *Patience*—based ultimately on the biblical Book of Jonah—I italicize all the subordinate, modifying clauses:

> Thus he passes to that port | *his passage to seche,*
> Fyndes he a fayr schip | *to the fare redy,*
> Maches him with the maryneres, | makes her paye
> *For to towe hym into Tarce* | *as tite as thay myghte.*
>
> (Thus he goes to that port | *to seek his passage,*
> finds a fair ship | *ready for the journey,*
> meets with the mariners, | pays their fee
> *to take him to Tarshish* | *as quick as they can.*
> *Patience,* 97–100; compare Jonah 1:3 in the Bible.)

Four verbs, which all follow 'Thus', structure these lines: 'passes', 'Fyndes', 'Maches', and 'makes'. Three of the four b-verses contain subordinate clauses: the first is a purposive clause modifying 'passes', the second is an adjectival clause modifying 'shyp', and the fourth is an adverbial clause modifying 'towe'. Among the b-verses quoted, then, only the third contains a main verb ('makes'). The next modifying unit comes in the next half-line (100a), while the last half-line quoted, 'as tite as thay myghte' (100b), modifies 'towe' within the unit that is already modifying 'paye': it nests two layers deep. These lines display alliterative verse's tendency to push subsidiary information into the b-verse, and also alliterative verse's capacity to vary from that pattern.

Poets could also reverse normal syntax within a clause, rather than reversing the normal order of separate clauses. Here is an example from early in *Sir Gawain and the Green Knight*, probably written by the same poet as *Patience*:

> Forthy an aunter in erde | I attle to schewe.
> (Therefore a happening on Earth | I mean to reveal. *Gawain*, 27)

This line differs from normal Middle English svo order: it runs osv, object ('an aunter in erde'), subject ('I'), then verb ('attle to schawe'). The rules governing patterned alliteration might have encouraged the poet to write this, but the line's syntax also fits the topic at hand: by withholding the subject and the verb, the phrasing asks the audience's minds to work out what's going on, emphasizing the 'aunter in erde'. The specific place ('in erde') of poem, speaker, and audience in Britain has just been much at issue in the opening lines of *Gawain*. The word *aunter*—a shortened form of *aventure*—plays a role in the poem's generic self-positioning, and anyone trying to unpick how this poem describes itself ought to study the senses of *aunter* in the *MED*. I would hesitate to rest too much on such a reversal in just one line, but readers can certainly stay alert for sustained disruption of this sort at the level of the short passage. Other aspects of alliterative verse will return in Chapter 5.

Let us move out from the line to think about the unit of rhyme in rhyming verse, and specifically the couplet. Larger stanzaic rhyming structures are discussed in Chapter 7 but, as one of the period's dominant forms, couplet verse deserves a sustained treatment here. A couplet can be an **open couplet** or a **closed couplet**. A closed couplet is a self-contained syntactic unit, while an open couplet joins syntactically to other couplets at either or both of its ends. Here are three closed couplets in a row from the *Northern Passion* (the noun *passion* can mean Jesus' execution or, as here, an account of that execution):

Jhesu in the systyrn ley,	*Jesus; systyrn: [Jesus'] tomb*
And rose upon the thyrd dey.	*day*
The over-ston he pute besyde;	*stone on top*
No lenger he wold therine abyde.	*longer; abide*
He toke the wey to Galylé	*Galilee*
Ther men myght hym here and se.	*hear; see*

(in *Shuffelton ed. 2008, 1868–1873)

This *Northern Passion* was a persistent work, enjoying lasting attention. Although the poem originated in the thirteenth century, the edition quoted here uses a manuscript copy made around 1500. The *Northern Passion* swallows into itself much non-biblical material that had piled up around the four gospel accounts of Jesus' final days and crucifixion, adding whole scenes, substantial amounts of direct speech, and greater interiority for some of its figures; the poem also transmits an antisemitic portrayal of its Jewish characters as a conspiratorial mass. The long popularity of the *Northern Passion* provides one of the many pieces of evidence that early readers had more sympathy for runs of closed couplets, which to us may sound crushingly monotonous. That said, Middle English poets usually mixed both types of couplet, both open and closed. Even the author of the *Northern Passion* has open-couplet passages, and indeed begins with an open couplet (1–2).

A perception of closed couplets as monotonous should not make us think that they entail a lack of sophistication: some poets, such as Alexander Pope in his witty *Essay on Criticism*, have marshalled effective runs of closed couplets. Closed spells in couplet poetry can develop a laconic force, as in the just-quoted description of Jesus' resurrection, while a single closed couplet often achieves a pithy summing-up. Chaucer deploys strings of closed couplets in his Shipman's Tale, a story of double dealing in sex and coin. Closed couplets crop up when the merchant must travel, leaving his wife at home with his friend, the monk John. John bids the merchant farewell in a stilted, stagey series of closed couplets packed with rote good wishes and humdrum advice (VII 257–264). Then, when John begins to ask the merchant to lend him some money before departing, his speech suddenly becomes a fluid stream of open couplets, with frequent enjambment thrown in for good measure: a practised trickster's patter (VII 265–274). It is the preceding closed couplets, perhaps already funny for the plodding conventionality of their advice, that set this up. John's speech returns to closed couplets for his final reassurances (VII 275–280).

As the passage in the Shipman's Tale shows, some couplets also join into larger sequences with closed boundaries, so that the larger-scale syntactic unit begins with the first line of one couplet and ends with the second line of another. As a short, two-couplet example, here is part of the discussion of the relative sizes of astronomical bodies in the fourteenth-century *Prik of Conscience*, the early English poem that achieved the highest circulation:

> The sterres are shynyng fro us so fer   *shining from; far*
> That we se not howe mychel they er   *see; big; are*
> For the leste sterre that we on loke   *smallest; see*
> Is more then alle the Erthe, seyth the bok.   *the book, i.e. source*
> (*Morey ed. 2012, 181–184)

This statement runs across two couplets, but neatly begins where a couplet starts and ends where a couplet ends. One might say that these couplets are also at least slightly closed, for a subsidiary break occurs in the syntax after the second line quoted.

Couplet verse could also hold rhyme and syntax in counterpoint rather than matching them, in a practice called **rhyme-breaking**. Ruth Evans has usefully discussed this phenomenon (2018), with a focus on Chaucer. Poets adopted rhyme-breaking into English within this book's period, and examples convey rhyme-breaking better than explanation alone can. Consider the following passage from John Lydgate's *Siege of Thebes* (c.1421–1422), a kind of sequel to the *Canterbury Tales* in which Lydgate, a monk, imagines himself falling in with the pilgrims from Chaucer's earlier work. The Host invites Lydgate to join the company and their tale-telling contest on their departure for the return journey from Canterbury, offers some advice on sleep, and promises to wake his new companion in the morning. I've marked the rhyme-breaks with underlining:

    And lik as I power have and myght,
    I charge yow rise not at mydnyght,   *instruct*
    <u>Thogh it so be the moone shyne cler.</u>   *Even if*
    I wol mysilf be youre orloger   *clock*
    Tomorow erly, whan I se my tyme,
    For we wol forth parcel afore pryme;   *shortly before dawn*
    <u>A company, pardé, shal do you good.</u>   *par Dieu ('by God')*
    What? Look up, monk! For by kokkis blood,   *(L. was a monk); cock's*
    Thow shalt be mery who so that sey nay: *despite any naysayers*
    For tomorowe, anoon as it is day   *as soon*
    And that it gynne in the est to dawe,   *to lighten*
    Thow shalt be bound to a newe lawe.

                                                    (*2001, 119–130)

These lines contain much deserving comment. Playing on Lydgate's monastic identity, they mix blasphemy—'pardé', 'by kokkis blood'—and the language of religious life: 'pryme' means dawn because dawn was the time of the monastic service of Prime. For our present purpose, though, note how the Host's remarks tend to end major units with the first lines of couplets (third and seventh lines quoted) and begin units with the second lines of couplets (fourth and eighth lines quoted); there's a subsidiary pause after the ninth line quoted which is also a rhyme break, albeit a gentler one. Rhyme-breaking can have a variety of effects, but in these lines it contributes to the sense of flowing, unstoppable speech, and social pressure, from the Host.

    Lydgate probably learned to rhyme-break from Chaucer. Indeed, Chaucer's Knight's Tale shares a legendary Theban context with Lydgate's later *Siege of Thebes* and offers a masterclass in various uses of rhyme-breaking. A sharp instance accompanies the plot's final twist. In the first half of a couplet, a syntactic unit ends with Arcite looking up at Emily while riding a victory lap to celebrate winning the tournament for her hand, the reader being told that she 'was al his chiere, as in his herte' (*Canterbury Tales*, I 2683). The next syntactic unit, which modern editors tend to mark out with an indented first line, completes the couplet by beginning with 'Out of the ground a furie infernal sterte', and tells how the resulting riding fall kills Arcite (I 2684). This comes as the last of five couplets in the Knight's Tale rhyming *sterte* and *herte*, and so it suddenly introduces catastrophe in a rhyme pair which hitherto seemed safe. The first rhyme of these two words in the tale also describes someone coming off a horse, and is also rhyme-broken, but the rhyme-break there simply lends elegance to a transition out of speech (I 951–952). Here, by contrast, the rhyme-break reminds readers of cruel Fortune, who can lay someone low at the height of their triumph.

    Note that rhyme-breaking is not enjambment. The mismatch of syntactic breaks and *line* divisions produces enjambment, while the mismatch of syntactic breaks and *rhyme* divisions produces rhyme-breaking. Indeed, to create a rhyme-break, the first line of a couplet must not enjamb: end-stopping at the middle of a couplet brings the break to readers' attention. Nearby enjambment can, of course, sharpen rhyme-breaking's effect if it precedes or follows, as when Oedipus baffles and then kills the Sphinx in the *Siege of Thebes*:

> And so this Spynx, awapyd and amaat,   *amazed; overcome*
> Stood disamayed and dysconsolaat
> With chier dounecast, muet, pale, and ded.   *face; mute*
> And Edippus anon smote of the hed   *off*
> Of this fende stynkyng and unswete.   *unsweet*
> (*Lydgate 2001, 741–745)

The significant syntactic break that the editor marks after 'ded' seems very plausible and creates a stark syntax–rhyme disjunction appropriate to the Sphinx's death. Surrounding elements heighten the effect: the end of the preceding list at the word 'ded' clips neatly at the break, and the possessive at the start of the fifth line quoted ('Of this fende') pulls the reading voice on through the couplet's enjambed, open end, ensuring that the audience feels the syntactic continuity after the fourth line.

Although continuous couplets were a widespread, standard kind of verse in Middle English and Older Scots, poetry before Chaucer rarely featured rhyme-breaking. 'Rarely' doesn't mean 'never'. When the hero of *Sir Orfeo* drives a hard, deceptive bargain with the king of fairy land to retrieve his wife, two rhyme-breaks occur, one of them being a shift from direct speech to narration (*Laskaya and Salisbury eds 1995, 465–466, 471–472). Because this poem rhyme-breaks only occasionally, audiences might have found its rhyme-breaking more marked and distinctive. I think these examples add to the sense in this passage of wits pitted against each other. Later, in Chaucer, Lydgate, and other poets writing in the fifteenth century, rhyme-breaking became a widespread point of style. A single rhyme-break in such poetry might not merit mention alone, but its interaction with other aspects of the verse might earn attention. Insights can grow from a fuller study of a poet's control of the varying marriage or separation of rhyme divisions and syntactic divisions across a whole passage.

In such study, readers can combine knowledge of rhyme-breaking and of open and closed couplets. Though a simple closed–open couplet contrast serves as a useful tool and starting point, perhaps in reading long-form couplet poetry it might help to think of a range of options. In fully closed couplets, a syntactic unit begins when a couplet begins, and ends when the same couplet ends. Such writing feels quite restrictive and can prove hard to keep up for a long time. Poetry could have most or all units of syntax start at the start of a couplet and finish at the end of a couplet, but not necessarily the same couplet; this produces open couplets but no rhyme-breaking, and a sense of the couplet as a concrete building-block, more easily combined but not easily divided. A poet can loosen couplets yet further by rhyme-breaking often, by stopping

Phrasing 39

and starting syntactic units within lines, or by using both of these techniques at once. Such looser couplet verse can place syntax and couplet—or even line and couplet—in pleasing counterpoint. A poem might stick to one within this set of options, or it might shift through them at different points. Spotting shifts in style of this kind can be fun in itself and can also set up a good reading of a poem, moving beyond drily naming single features to seeing how different craft techniques pull together.

Zooming out further still from the line and the rhyme unit, lists also demand discussion as a larger-scale phenomenon making verse form interact with syntax and as a phenomenon beloved by poets. Lists might seem dry, simple, or even skippable—perhaps sometimes readers did skip them—but they proffer much for interpretation. The order of listed items can reveal priorities. Sheer accumulation also affects readers: quantity is itself a quality. These things hold true, however, in prose as well as verse, as anyone who has read Thomas Malory's list-strewn accounts of tournaments in his *Morte Darthur* will well know. But a verse list throws a special test at a poet: the list, already a form of language with syntax more restrictive than normal speech, must fit into the rules of the surrounding verse form.

If a poet allots one line to each list item, they create a simple structure which raises the metrical divisions between individual lines to prominence while playing down the significance of ties between lines, such as rhyme:

There men moun cal that day	*will call*
The day of grete delyveraunce,	
The day of wreche and of vengeaunce,	*retribution*
The day of wratthe and wrechednes,	*wrath*
The day of bale and bytturnes,	*pain*
The day of plente and accusyng,	*complaint*
The day of onswere and rekenyng,	*answer; reckoning*
The day of jugement and justyse,	*justice*
The day of sorow and angwyse.	*anguish*

(*Prik of Conscience*, Morey ed. 2012, V.1987–1995)

A full study of these lines on the Day of Judgement might remark on the repeated use of the same phrase ('The day of') at each line's start, the intermittent alliteration, and, less obviously but just as crucially, the consistent pattern of two nouns linked by 'and'. Such a study might also explore why the first item ('grete delyveraunce') varies from that double-noun pattern, and would examine the rest of the list: more listing lines follow 'sorow and angwyse', but—to help readers spend their time before Judgement Day efficiently—I have omitted them. Similar one-item-per-line listing occurs elsewhere in Middle English: Chaucer, for instance, uses it well in stanzaic contexts (*Troilus and Criseyde*, V.1828–1832; *Parliament of Fowls*, 176–182).

List syntax and metrical lines need not march in lockstep, however, and a poet can vary syntax fruitfully in a looser arrangement. Chaucer deploys such looser listing in his catalogue of birds in *The Parliament of Fowls* (323–371). There, readers can find several ways of matching list items to verse lines: Chaucer sometimes places multiple birds on one line (jay and heron, 346), sometimes uses multiple lines for one bird (goshawk, 334–336), and allows multi-line items to start mid-line (sparrowhawk, 338–339; nightingale, 351–352). All the while, he still has enough lines start with 'The [bird noun]' that a steady listing drumbeat lasts throughout. Chaucer could write longer, looser processions or progressions of figures (*Parliament of Fowls*, 211–294), and flexible pageant-lists of this sort occur too in fifteenth-century dream poems (Matthews 2016; Rust 2016).

Another poem, the violent and skilful *Alliterative Morte Arthure*, lists early in its progress places conquered and ruled by King Arthur (ed. Benson 1994, 26–46), and items served at a banquet that Arthur throws (176–204). Two such crafted lists in quick succession invite comparison. A joy in possession and power links both lists, and both lists also exhibit the typical syntactic distribution of alliterative verse, with list items usually occurring in a-verses and then being modified in b-verses. The lists do differ in some respects, though. The banquet list seems extravagant but not implausible for a fourteenth-century royal household, while the imperial possessions are partly fantastical: Arthur apparently rules, among other places, Norway (43), Denmark (45), Germany (44), and Greece (36). The feast list has a sense of time, being broken up by 'Then', 'Sithen', and 'Senn' (183, 187, 191, 195, 199), and the poet spends more space on details and appearance. The land list focuses more on the pleasure of arranging names. In the feast, Arthur attempts to overawe some hostile diplomats visiting his court. While the land list is—within the poem's imagination—just a statement of fact, the feast list describes a culinary performance that, the poem's audience know, Arthur stages for a purpose.

Lists can contain sub-lists, and such nested listing was a standard tool in academic writing in this period. Combined with the convenience of lists for memorization, nested listing could provide the large-scale form for a whole poem: lists and sub-lists shape the 16,000 lines of the popular instructional poem *Speculum Vitae*, a non-narrative work which probably invites dipping-in for passages on particular topics rather than sustained 'start-to-finish' reading (Hanna ed. 2008). What's more, lists furnish the material of some of the verse encountered first by Middle and modern English audiences, the nursery rhymes and educational memory aids (or **mnemonics**) encountered in childhood. Every list places its parts in parallel, but some lists contain more sophisticated syntactic structures than 'and ... and ... and', with some clauses subordinated to others. This thought brings us neatly on to this chapter's other topic: subordination.

Subordination

This chapter has already mentioned main and subordinate clauses. Poets' control of subordination and their choices about when and how to relate clauses offer much interest for analysis and deserve a section to themselves. I'll begin with two contrasting examples. The core plot of *Sir Orfeo begins when Heurodys, Orfeo's wife, has a nightmare:

As Ich lay this undertide	*morning*
And slepe under our orchard-side,	
Ther come to me to fair knightes,	*to me two*
Wele y-armed al to rightes,	*all correctly*
And bad me comen an heighing	*asked me [to]; in a hurry*
And speke with her lord the king.	
And Ich answerd at wordes bold,	*with*
Y durst nought, no Y nold.	*dared not and would not*
Thai priked oyain as thai might drive;	*rode back as fast as possible*
Tho com her king, al so blive,	*their; quick/joyful*
With an hundred knightes and mo,	*more*
And damisels an hundred also,	*ladies*
Al on snowe-white stedes;	
As white as milke were her wedes.	*their clothes*
Y no seighe never yete bifore	*yet*
So fair creatours y-core.	*excellent*
The king hadde a croun on hed;	
It n'as of silver, no of gold red,	*was not; nor*
Ac it was of a precious ston—	*but*
As bright as the sonne it schon.	
And as son as he to me cam,	
Wold Ich, nold Ich, he me nam,	*whether or not I wished it; took*
And made me with him ride	
Opon a palfray bi his side.	*palfrey: a type of horse*

(in Laskaya and Salisbury eds 1995, 133–156)

In these lines things simply happen, or simply are: Heurodys doesn't explain what she describes or indicate how any of the things and events she describes relate to each other. I think this quality implies that Heurodys cannot explain what she describes, and this inexplicability helps to create the passage's air of dreamlike menace.

Such simplicity has tangible causes in the language on the page. Combing through the passage again reveals that it has few subordinate clauses, and that such conjunctions as appear are almost all simply *and*, rather than conjunctions creating causal relationships such as *for*, *since*, and *because*. The passage doesn't use the simplest structures everywhere: its first lines are a temporal clause ('*As* Ich lay this undertide...'), and it contains eddies of reported speech ('And Ich answerd...') and simile ('As bright as the sonne'). But even its more complex moments stay short and restrained. The simplicity here does not mean a lack of sophistication: the passage should sound strange, unsettling, and hard to put together, and the poet achieves this by keeping things simple.

The king from Heurodys's dream later spirits her away to a hazily defined fairy land, prompting Orfeo to leave his kingdom to his steward and wander beyond civilization for years. He eventually finds his way to the fairy king's court, where he has the chance to rescue Heurodys—or to retrieve her, at least, for the poem keeps silent about her own wishes and her own view of fairy land. Although *Orfeo* implies origins for itself in a Breton lay (13–16), a narrative poem from Brittany, it ultimately descends from the Greek myth of the musician Orpheus and his wife Eurydice. In the myth, Orpheus pursues Eurydice to the Greek idea of the underworld but, in the end, fails to rescue her. In the Middle English period, readers could know the story from Ovid (*Metamorphoses* X.1–85), Virgil (*Georgics* IV.457–527), and, most influentially of all, Boethius (*Consolation of Philosophy* III, metrum 12, lines 5–55); Chaucer translated Boethius' version in *Boece* (III metre 12, lines 4–47). *Orfeo*, though, provides a radically altered version, with a different ending, and either little care for classical mythology or little knowledge of it.

Lydgate's *Siege of Thebes, to which I've returned throughout this chapter, is another Englishing of a Greek legend. After its introduction as an addition to the *Canterbury Tales*, the *Siege* retells the cycle of Greek myths about the ill-fated king Oedipus and his children, Polynices, Eteocles, and Antigone. Following the death of Oedipus—or rather, in Middle English, Edippus—his sons Eteocles ('Ethiocles') and Polynices ('Polymyte') fall out over who should inherit the throne of Thebes. The city's nobility tries to adjudicate and the two princes make their cases:

But for his part this Ethiocles	
Allegge gan that he was first yborn,	*started to claim*
For which he oght of resoun go toforn	*logically take precedence*
In the cité to be crowned kyng,	
Sith be lawe ther was no lettyng,	*by; obstacle*
For unto hym longeth the herytage	*belonged; legacy*
Be discent and be title of age.	*descent*
But Polymyte of ful hegh disdeyn	*high*
Al opynly gan replie ageyn	*began to*
And for his part seide, in special,	
Reson was non that he shuld have alle	*he: Ethiocles*
Regaly and domynacioun	*royal power*
And the lordship hooly of the toun,	*whole lordship*
And he right nought, out of the cyté	*he: Polymyte*
But lyve in exile and in poverté,	
Ful concludyng, withoute feer and dred,	
Rather than suffre that, he wil be ded.	*would rather*

(*Lydgate 2001, 1084–1100)

Two contrasted blocks of reported speech make up most of this passage. Ethiocles makes his stand on reason, and accordingly his speech can be broken down into a series of subordinate clauses introduced by conjunctions: he is (he says) the firstborn, *for* which reason he should be crowned, *since* there is no legal obstacle, *for* the throne comes to him by descent and his greater age. Each of these clauses is subordinated to the one preceding it. The nested arrangement suggested by the conjunctions does not, though, match the actual content of the clauses: Ethiocles goes from premise—he is older—to point—he should be king—in three lines (1085–1087), and then spends the next three lines simply restating his premise (1088–1090). Lydgate structures the report of Polymyte's speech more simply: he argues that there is no reason that two separate, parallel things should happen (1094–1098). Ethiocles' reasoning is not as logical as its structure might suggest; Polymyte has no reasoning at all, and presents no positive case, only negations. The narration of their dispute does neither claimant any favours and it is Lydgate's control of subordinate clauses that creates this impression.

As the contrast between these passages from *Orfeo* and *The Siege of Thebes* shows, a poem can feature language either more or less complexly arranged. Comparing these two quite different works, one might associate *The Siege of Thebes* with craft and subtlety, *Orfeo* with crudity. Lydgate's poem, after all, displays poised, organized rhetoric, longer lines of a type more familiar to the modern reader, and more elevated wording. Lydgate had a university education and has, significantly for the modern reader, a name, while the poet of *Orfeo* is anonymous and, knowingly or not, mishandles classical mythology. But to think that the *Siege* is careful and *Orfeo* crude would be to err. Simplicity is a choice too: Heurodys's dream would lack force if the poem delivered it through a carefully subordinated set of arguments.

'The king hadde a croun on hed' stands on its own and could be stated as one complete unit of sense, while 'Sith be lawe ther was no lettyng' does not: it is a sub-clause or a subordinate clause. Subordination is sometimes called **hypotaxis**, and writing in which elements are often subordinated to others is **hypotactic**. Conversely, writing with infrequent subordination is **paratactic**, and the absence of subordination is called **parataxis**. Polymyte's speech contains fewer examples of hypotaxis than does Ethiocles', but neither brother speaks as paratactically as Heurodys in the passage from *Sir Orfeo*. The balance between hypotaxis and parataxis has a relationship with the lengths of units of sense—short, clipped units are likely to be more paratactic—but not an absolute relationship: long units can be paratactic too. A close, but again not absolute, relationship also ties line length to grammatical complexity: choosing an overall form for a poem which entails short lines was likely to guide subsequent smaller-scale writing decisions towards shorter units of sense and less ambitious subordination.

Particular effects cannot be mechanistically associated with hypotaxis or parataxis. Such basic and widespread features of language do not create the same results every time. Broadly speaking, though, hypotaxis presents a chance to read verse for precise gradations of responsibility, causation, or chance. Parataxis, placing things in parallel, refusing to show the relations between them, forces readers to rule on such questions themselves, or to sit with the resulting ambiguity. Indeed, parataxis might train subtler readers, for where hypotaxis lays things out, parataxis demands thought.

Rather than mechanically reading a result from either feature of language, we might usefully consider the way a poet shuttles between the two. Most poems contain varying amounts of subordination at different points. A complex rhetorical unit with nested twists stands out much more in a poem which normally stacks one thing after another than in a poem wholly written in such whorls. Equally, parataxis in an otherwise intricate work or passage might constitute the slip of a mask, the blunt delivery of a home truth, or a point of particular emphasis. A return to *Orfeo* can further show how the control of subordination reveals things, even in a poem which might at first seem naïve set alongside the density of Lydgate's argumentation.

In *Orfeo*, outbreaks of syntactic complexity on a scale larger than the single line signal the story's heights. The poem's last sustained burst of complexity, an example I borrow and expand from G. A. Lester (1996, 125–126), occurs when Orfeo returns to his capital disguised as a minstrel. The steward whom Orfeo had appointed to run the kingdom in his place has honoured his absent lord's love of minstrels and music by harbouring musicians in the court. In a weird but delightful way, Orfeo's own delegated musical passion therefore gains Orfeo an audience on his disguised return. Orfeo tests the steward's loyalty and, finding that the steward has stayed true, reveals himself in a sustained display of cumulative subordination. Setting this passage up, Orfeo says 'Herkne now this thing', and although these words address the steward within the work, they might also be a prompt for a listening audience.

Yif Ich were Orfeo the king,	*If I*
And hadde y-suffred ful yore	*long ago*
In wildernisse miche sore,	*much pain*
And hadde ywon mi quen o-wy	*won my queen away*
Out of the lond of fairy,	
And hadde y-brought the levedi hende	*noble lady*
Right here to the tounes ende,	*town's*
And with a begger her in y-nome,	*lodged*
And were mi-self hider y-come	*come hither*
Poverlich to the, thus stille,	*in poverty*
For to asay thi gode wille,	*assay, test; good*
And Ich founde thee thus trewe,	*And = if*
Thou no schust it never rewe.	*should; rue*
Sikerlich, for love or ay,	*certainly; fear*
Thou schust be king after mi day;	
And yif thou of mi deth hadest ben blithe,	*joyful*
Thou schust have voided, al-so swithe.	*been exiled, at once*
	(558–574)

While the plethora of instances of *and* might make this sound paratactic, the opening 'Yif' applies to a remarkable six verb phrases in succession in lines 558–569, so that the text means '*if* I were King Orfeo, and *if* I had suffered, and *if* I had won' etc. The

'And' at the beginning of line 569 also means 'if', and explicitly restates the conditional for Orfeo's climactic point: if 'ich founde thee thus trewe, / Thou no schust it never rewe'. Tension builds up to line 570, where it is released by 'schust it never rewe', and listeners' patience finds reward in the steward's reward: 'Thou schust be king'. Then another 'yif' starts a (comparatively) much shorter unit, a single couplet's uneasy reminder of what the power of kings can be.

These detailed aspects of the poem's language come tied to its story and its themes, and a good reading will trace such ties. Orfeo's giant conditional retells, in miniature, the plot since he left Winchester. The telling comes inflected by Orfeo's own viewpoint: to say that he 'ywon' Heurodis 'o-wy' conceals a certain amount of begging and fast-talking at the fairy king's court (409–476). Through his story, Orfeo talks himself back into kingship. But these lines relate to more than just his identity. Like the description of his harping at the poem's start, they do something reflexive, having Orfeo the harpist narrate what has just happened in a work which conflates harping and narration. These lines also possess what would today be called dramatic irony, and that irony is bound up with the conditionality: the audience knows that these hypotheticals have been fulfilled; at the speech's start, at least, the steward and the others in the hall do not. By having Orfeo tell what has happened as though it *might* have already happened, the poet recalls the opening discussion 'Of old aventours that fel while' (8) and invites the audience to think on just what the telling of a lay is.

This final flourish in *Orfeo* stacks conditionals next to each other, but clauses can, of course, nest one within another. Readers can now, if they wish, return to the Hoccleve stanza with which this chapter began, and examine not just its order but its subordination too. They will see that the first six lines are one long adverbial unit, modifying 'byrefte', within which the first four lines are a smaller adverbial unit modifying 'lay' (how did Hoccleve lie? he lay *musynge*...). Those first four lines themselves contain two further relative clauses ('That...', 'Whiche...'). This type of deep, dense nesting of subordinate clauses offers a different type of bravura flourish. Both approaches exert powerful, determining forces on a poem's audience. A willingness to think through how exactly phrasing works aids the study of any verse from this period.

4
Metre (I): Alternating Metres

Metre is the measuring-out of line-lengths in verse. Not all verse uses measured lines, but Middle English and Older Scots verse does, and a little metrical knowledge brings much to the reading experience. If metrical study seems forbiddingly technical, thinking of it as a form of embodied time travel might help. Verse metre is embodied action: we interpret it using our lungs, throats, and mouths. In working with the rhythms of past forms of language, however imperfectly rendered today, one surrenders oneself—temporarily, in controlled, negotiated ways—to the demands of other times and the shapings of other bodies. Some aspects of learning about metre do involve technicalities, but in metrical work we also gesture across time: it's an area of study bolder and braver than is sometimes imagined.

In the close reading of verse, metre makes its greatest, most basic contribution by slicing text into metrical lines, offering a structure formed by language but also constraining language. Metre's core interest sometimes hangs, therefore, around the relationship—coordination or counterpoint—of metrical lines to syntax, which for convenience's sake appeared in Chapter 3. Other metrical observations can powerfully augment readings, though: it's often worth checking the metre of particular lines which have become interesting for other formal or thematic reasons. For the pleasure of reading poetry, meanwhile, grasping the rhythms that a poet crafted makes reading verse more satisfying.

Middle English and Older Scots metres ushered in subsequent metrical traditions, including the basic pattern of line that would dominate canonical verse from the later sixteenth century on, the pattern often called iambic pentameter. Studying the topic fills in that history. By placing things in history, though, we also help ourselves think on how those things could have gone otherwise. Studying metre puts later metrical traditions in perspective, and helps us see them as crafted options rather than as inevitable givens. This aspect of the topic has a particular importance because the Middle English period is the only time when English had no single prestigious set of metrical conventions, but rather multiple metrical systems happily coexisting. Old English verse had one settled metrical system (Terasawa 2011), broadly consistent despite differences from poet to poet and across time; modern English verse up to the twentieth century had an agreed prestigious metrical system too; today, free verse is in practice dominant. All of these periods saw plenty of dynamic variation within agreed systems, but none offer the total variety found in Middle English and Older Scots, when multiple different approaches to metre rubbed shoulders amicably. The middle of metrical history helps us imagine literary style with less inevitability.

Metre (I): Alternating Metres   47

The metre of early poetry is a lively topic. Researchers sometimes disagree. It's not the case that no one knows what they're talking about, or that problems can't be solved. Rather, disagreements happen because the problems are complex, and work on them continues: we know more about the topic than we used to, but research proceeds through debates over the evidence. Most researchers can, though, agree on some things about metre in this period. First, verse followed metrical rules—it was **regular**—though the particular rules that it followed did vary. Second, metre matters: it sits at the core of Middle English verse-craft. Third, distributions of stress and numbers of syllables both mattered in Middle English metrical systems, though they mattered differently in different systems.

In researching beyond these points, experts face some problems specific to the period. Almost no remarks on early English and Scots metre survive from the period itself, so researchers must reverse-engineer metre from verse. Scholars propose competing theories to explain how aspects of metre at this time worked. They also use competing vocabularies and systems of description. Very few Middle English poems survive in books copied by the poets themselves—**autograph** manuscripts—leaving us reliant on the variable copying of scribes. Scribes didn't always grasp what poets had in mind, and sometimes they worked while separated from the poets they copied by time's passage, or by differences between regional types of English, or by both (*Troilus and Criseyde*, V.1793–1798). Present-day editions sometimes use metrical knowledge to improve the text they offer; scholars can justify this process (see Chapter 9), but it means that the editions themselves—especially the accessible sort prioritized in this book—will not uncomplicatedly serve as material for primary metrical research. Moreover, many Middle English poems were probably sung or read aloud (see Chapter 11), and performance practice might not always have matched manuscript presentation (Zaerr 2005; Putter 2018): as anyone who's paid attention to pop music or hymns can attest, song stretches and squashes words in ways that wouldn't come through on the page.

Despite these challenges, some approaches to Middle English metre do suit beginners, and can usefully sharpen reading experiences and close readings. This chapter focuses on such useful routes in, and it delivers basic models that might be refined in further study. Poets writing in Middle English experimented with and adopted a considerable range of metrical systems, and that range makes giving a full accounting of the period's techniques here impossible. Readers can chase references up to learn more. Though Donka Minkova has written a fine multi-author, multi-tradition overview suitable for students who already have some basic grounding in linguistics (2007), most past studies have tended to orbit this or that poet in particular, usually Chaucer. I cover Chaucer here, but this chapter should also guide readers into thinking about the metres of at least some other poets. More so than most formal matters, the appreciation of metre benefits from practice. Readers who wish to develop a serious facility with Middle English metre will want to try out the techniques discussed here, to return to this chapter and Chapter 5, and to pursue further reading.

Crudely speaking, Middle English poems fall into two metrical traditions. One was **alliterative verse**. We lack a good name for the other, because it birthed the types of regular metre familiar to us in modern English poetry, and so it seems normal to us, like water to fish. Sometimes scholars call it 'syllabic', 'stress-syllabic', or 'accentual-syllabic', but I shall call this tradition **alternating metre**, because it relies on predictable alternations, and I begin with it, since it is likely to be more familiar to most readers.

Natural stress, metrical beat

To discuss metre, I'll borrow the rudiments (not the refinements) of Derek Attridge's approach to the topic (1995). We can understand alternating metres as metres which structure lines through the regular, predictable alternation of two elements: **beat** and **offbeat**. Beats and offbeats are created by, but are not the same as, stresses in words.

In spoken English, some syllables are stressed, and some are not. The distribution of stress can be marked using (say) 'S' for stressed syllables and 'u' for unstressed syllables. One way of delivering this paragraph's opening sentence has the following pattern of stressed and unstressed syllables:

u   S u S   u   S   S u u u   S   u   S   u S
In spoken English, some syllables are stressed, and some are not.

In English, most multi-syllable words have a usual stress pattern, called lexical stress: a lexical stress usually falls on the first syllable of *spoken* and not the second. The surrounding phrasing can influence stress patterns too, in what is called phrasal stress: in this example, the sentence as I tend to say it, *some* and *not* take on phrasal stress. Both lexical stress and phrasal stress are sub-types of natural stress.

Natural stress itself in Middle English often worked as in present-day English and, therefore, present-day readers can stress many phrases correctly by reading them aloud using current English assumptions about stress. Some words did have different lexical stress layouts. Words borrowed into English from French often carried natural stress on a later syllable in Middle English but changed over time: we tend to say 'náture' today, but Middle English speakers probably said 'natúre'. Some words could have diverse stress patterns, such as *godesse*, for example, and, amusingly, *diverse*; in a traditional example, a line from the *Canterbury Tales* encourages readers to stress the first syllable of this word at its first occurrence, but the second at its second: 'In dívers árt and ín divérse figúres' (III 1486). This flexibility extended even to some closed-class words, so that, unlike in present-day English, *after* and *under* could sometimes take stress on their second syllable.

In alternating verse, poets arrange most natural stresses in an alternating pattern. In the audience's minds, this relatively predictable pattern of natural stresses creates an even more predictable alternating pattern of *perceived* **beats** and **offbeats**. Once established in the audience's mind, the alternating pattern develops a life of its own. I shall mark beats with a stroke ('/') and offbeats with a lower-case 'x'. A **single offbeat** is created by one syllable perceived as not prominent (x), and a **double offbeat** is created by two adjacent syllables perceived as not prominent (x x); not all alternating metres permit double offbeats.

An audience will have their metrical expectations shaped by lines in which the syllables which would probably take natural linguistic stress all form a neat pattern, such as

> x / x / x / x / x / (x)
> Of twenty yeer of age he was, I gesse
>
> (*Canterbury Tales*, I 82)

With their expectations thus developed, the audience's minds will impose the same pattern of alternating beats and offbeats on elements in a line which might not carry natural stress, but which can be promoted into a beat's position. Therefore, in a line such as the one immediately following, 'Of his stature he was of evene lengthe', the word *his* forms a beat even though it might not take natural stress in normal speech:

> x / x / x / x / x / (x)
> Of his stature he was of evene lengthe
>
> (*Canterbury Tales*, I 83)

Incidentally, this line offers another good example of a French-derived word with a lexical stress pattern different to its standard pronunciation today, 'statúre'. Some inflections at the ends of words also formed beats more easily than they can in modern English verse, and so poets could rhyme on, for example, the *-yng/-ing* ending:

> x / x / x / x /
> Envie hath kinde put aweie
>
> x / x / x / x / (x)
> And of malice hath his steringe,
>
> x / x / x / x / (x)
> Wherof he makth this bakbitinge.
>
> ('Envy has driven out nature, and is motivated by malice,
> which makes him gossip maliciously'. Gower, *Confessio
> Amantis*, II.3140–3142)

'Envíe' and 'malíce' here offer yet further examples of French-derived words with lexical stress on their second rather than their first syllables. Although poets generate alternating metre initially using natural stresses, it is a *perceived*, unnatural pattern of beats. Therefore, readers shouldn't try to work out a line's metre by considering each word alone, but should rather consider each line as a whole, within the context of the preceding lines and a poem's general metrical habits. One often works out a line's pattern most easily by taking a run up, reading the preceding lines aloud first, to catch hold of the pre-existing metrical pattern and see how it affects the line in question.

Alternating verse therefore sometimes involves beats placing occasional unusual emphases on words which would in normal speech rarely receive natural stress—such as *his* in the example above. Such verse generates a background friction between natural stress and the imposed pattern of beats, a friction which waxes and wanes as the poet desires. Short lists can present extreme, and consequently useful, examples of such friction. Chaucer begins Book III of *Troilus and Criseyde* with an address to Venus, fruitfully conflating, first, the mythological Roman goddess of love, second, the planet with its supposed influence on human affairs, and, third, the feeling of love itself. Venus' power is felt everywhere, he writes,

> In hevene and helle, in erthe and salte see
> Is felt thy might, if that I well discerne:
> As man, brid, beest, fissh, herbe and grene tree
> Thee feele in times with vapour eterne.
>
> (III.8–11)

The surrounding metrical template established by earlier lines is x/x/x/x/x/, with an optional eleventh syllable single offbeat (x), and this well describes the experience of hearing or reading lines 8–9 and 11; in line 11 the word 'with' offers another small example of a word that normally matters little but rises to prominence here thanks to a metrical beat. But the natural lexical stresses of the first five monosyllabic items listed in line 10 fiercely resist any alternating metrical pattern of beats and offbeats:

```
 u   S    S    S     S     u    S u  S
As man, brid, beest, fissh, herbe and grene tree
```

Lexical stresses make it tough to read this line aloud as any x/x/x/x/x/(x) offbeat-beat pattern, and the results of any attempt to do so sound weird. The surrounding metrical scheme stays robust enough to absorb this momentary friction as the following lines go on, but the friction is an appreciable effect. Such moments of high friction between metrical beats and natural stresses demand negotiation by individual readers encountering the work. Sometimes no single rendering demonstrably works best. Close reading can note the friction itself, though, and make use of it: at minimum, it creates moments of emphasis.

Some linguistic quirks

A few extra quirks of language help in understanding Middle English metres. The modern names for the three most important are **elision**, **syncope**, and **synizesis**. A fourth matter, the pronunciation of *-e* at the ends of words, also demands treatment here.

In **elision**, an unstressed vowel at the end of a word immediately followed by a vowel at the start of the next word became absorbed by the following vowel, producing a single sound. This also often happened when a vowel at a word's end was followed by a word beginning with *h-*, because speakers of Middle English often dropped word-initial *h*. In my notation here, a line above the writing shows elision:

> x / x / x / x / (x)
> Bot he the betre his mouth assaie
>
> (Gower, *Confessio Amantis*, VI.642)

In this example, 'his' is to be pronounced *'is*. Readers might use this pronunciation of *his* naturally in many positions in everyday speech; I certainly do. Elision was not a special licence granted in verse. It was and is a normal feature of language which remains with us today. Poets merely took advantage of it.

In **syncope**, an unstressed syllable is dropped inside a word or phrase. Some examples also occur very often in present-day English: *medicine*, for instance, can be three syllables or can syncopate to two (*med'cine*). Middle English *every*, like present-day English *every*, could have three or two syllables, and frequently manifested in speech as 'ev'ry':

> x / x / x / x / (x)
> In every place, in every stede.   *location*
>
> (*Confessio Amantis*, IV.1123)

The following couplet in Chaucer's General Prologue to the *Canterbury Tales* features syncope in both lines:

> x / x / x / x / x / (x)
> And specially from every shires ende   *shire's*
>
> x / x / x / x / x / (x)
> Of Engelond to Caunterbury they wende.   *travel*
>
> (*Canterbury Tales*, I 15–16)

The place-name *Caunterbury* was routinely pronounced with syncope: *Caunterb'ry*. The present-day English do this to *Canterbury* too. The *-y* in this line also offers another good example of a syllable which wouldn't necessarily take natural stress in normal speech, but gets promoted to a beat in this metrical context. Syncope, like elision, is not some kind of special rule invented for old poetry. These are mundane events in language which poets have naturally folded into their practice.

Synizesis similarly refers to a normal feature of present-day as well as Middle English, despite its intimidating name. In synizesis, the vowel sound of *y* and *i*—the same vowel, in this period—can, when it is followed by another vowel, become the consonant which is represented by word-initial *y-* in the present-day phrase 'yes, yoghurt yields youth'. So, for example, when Gower writes 'Ful many a soubtiel craft of kinde' within a set of eight-syllable, four-beat lines (**Confessio Amantis*, V.1026), the surrounding metrical pattern of beats and offbeats encourages an audience to read the line as

> x / x / x / x / (x)
> Ful many a soubtiel craft of kinde   *subtle; nature*

Not

> x / x x / x / x / (x)
> Ful many a soubtiel craft of kinde.

This second option is discouraged by the metrical context, because Gower has consistently avoided double offbeats. Like elision and syncope, synizesis doesn't apply to every word in all circumstances, but is encouraged or discouraged by the surrounding metre and context. Gower liked the phrase *many a*, but he was perfectly capable of using *many* in places where its *-y* would sound as a vowel, contributing a normal single offbeat:

> x / x / x / x / (x)
> The Grecs of Trojens many slowe.   *Greeks; Trojans; slew*
> (*Confessio Amantis*, V.7211)

Minkova (2007, 184–186) and Thomas G. Duncan (2005, 22–24) offer further, fuller discussions of these and of related phenomena.

Finally comes final *-e*. In Middle English spelling, *-e* at the ends of words usually represents an unstressed schwa sound: in present-day English this is the sound of the first *a* of *banana*, or the *e* of *petition*. The use of final *-e* is probably the most famous thing about Middle English spelling, fossilized today in mock-archaic signs announcing the sale of souvenirs in Olde Gifte Shoppes. In later Middle English pronunciation, in the later part of this book's period, final *-e* was already disappearing from most types of spoken English. Chaucer's verse nevertheless features a meaningful final *-e*, and final *-e* persisted as a metrical feature in the work of some poets, notably Hoccleve and Lydgate, in the fifteenth century; the available evidence also suggests that it retained metrical significance in alliterative verse. These continuing metrical functions don't necessarily mean that people continued to use final *-e* in normal speech. English-speakers might, possibly, have carried on pronouncing or at least perceiving it for a while in poetry as an elevating archaism, which they felt sounded formal and refined. That might seem odd but, as with **aureation** in the same century (see Chapter 2), if people did this then they revealed an implicit belief that verse could sometimes deserve a distinct, markedly different kind of language.

When, then, should one consider sounding final -*e*? A crude but workable first rule of thumb for alternating verse is this: sound it if its presence makes the line resemble the pattern of beats and offbeats in surrounding lines. Most often, this will be because it provides a single offbeat separating two beats in verse which generally keeps beats separate from each other rather than letting them abut. A second rule of thumb is to pronounce it at the ends of lines. A more advanced reason to sound final -*e* in Chaucer's verse is that it has appeared at the end of an adjective modifying a plural noun or at the end of a so-called 'weak' adjective (see Appendix section 16). Readers might also see mention of 'etymological final -*e*', when a scribe has written a word without the final -*e* but the poet might nevertheless have pronounced the word *with* a final -*e*. We can guess at etymological final -*e* when the *OED* tells us that the word concerned descends from an Old English or Old Norse ancestor ending in a syllable that would have reduced to final -*e* by the later Middle English period.

Armed with this information, the time has come to discuss some specific poets and poems. Alternating metres came in many arrangements, more than can be discussed here, but I can cover a core set: four-beat lines, septenaries, and five-beat lines.

Four-beat lines

Four-beat lines were the default type of alternating English metre from the thirteenth century to the early fifteenth century. They have remained a vital template beyond this book's period, up to the present day. In the fourteenth century, they formed the mainstay of Gower's English poetry and structured Chaucer's earlier works. Four-beat lines served in many major poems, including romances, histories, and widely read religious guides. They got started early: possibly the earliest surviving regular four-beat alternating poetry in English—and also perhaps the earliest known substantial English poem in couplets of even length—is a rhyming guide to Christianity's most prototypical prayer, the Paternoster, from around 1200 (*NIMEV* 2709 | *DIMEV* 4305; Morris ed. 1898, 55–71). This poem, which I shall call by its first words, *Ure Feder*, shows no overt interest in its own form, and though it could be a first surviving example it is probably not the first example written. Metrical studies of Middle English have often centred more on Chaucer, his later fourteenth-century contemporaries, and his successors, leaving the metrical qualities of many preceding poems as something of a scholarly hinterland, even though such poems were culturally vital in their own time. A few works have explored these topics, but they can be specialized and difficult to track down (e.g. Solopova 1994; Fulk 2002; Duffell 2008). The landscape of much alternating metre before Chaucer presents a bit of a wilderness which, like the wildernesses in Middle English romances, prompts caution.

Even making allowances for changes during manuscript transmission, many earlier Middle English poems in four-beat lines seem to allow the following options between their four beats:

1. no offbeat, so that beats abut; or
2. a single offbeat; or
3. a double offbeat.

Here, for example, are some lines describing the impartial justice of the titular hero of *Havelok the Dane*, written in the late thirteenth century:

```
/   x / x x / x  /
To the faderles was he rath:

/  x /  x    / x /
Wo so dede hem wrong or lath,

/ x / x  / x  /
Were it clerc or were it knicth,

x  /  x   / x x / x /
He dede hem sone to haven ricth,

x   /  / x / x   /
And wo dide widuen wrong—

/   x / x   /   x /
Were he nevre knicth so strong,

 x  / x  /   x / x / x
That he ne made him sone kesten

x / x   /   x  / x /  x
In feteres and ful faste festen.
```

(He was a mentor to orphans: whoever did them wrong or harm, whether it was a cleric or a knight, he quickly gave them justice, and whoever wronged widows—there was never a knight so strong that he [Havelok] didn't quickly throw him into fetters and most securely lock him up. *Herzman, Drake, and Salisbury eds 1997, 75–82)

The poem of *Havelok* seems unconcerned about keeping the number of syllables per line fully regular, or about ensuring that only single offbeats intervene between beats. The poet also felt fine about lines beginning with a beat rather than an offbeat, if the first, second, third, and sixth lines quoted offer anything to go by. While, as we shall see, some later writers used this **headless** arrangement as an occasional tool, this poet deploys it frequently as a normal pattern. Despite its freedom in other respects, though, this excerpt and the rest of the poem display a commitment to four beats per line.

Such verse differs from the regular syllables of some more modern English poetry. When I met this kind of Middle English verse for the first time, I found it awkward and challenging. My view changed with more experience, and we should entertain the idea that such writing was skilled in its own way. Most types of English speech don't assign each syllable an even amount of time, but rather keep the timing of naturally stressed syllables steady by varying the speeds of intervening unstressed syllables, pushing rapidly through clusters of unstressed syllables and drawing out lone unstressed syllables. This type of verse, counting beats but relatively unbothered about the distinction between single and double offbeats, therefore seems appropriate enough to the language: in reading aloud, the voice naturally smooths over the differently shaped events between beats. This type of verse also has its own interesting effects, and it lets spells of greater regularity stand out themselves. In some cases, works that survive as inert texts displaying confusing metre on the page might have come to life in performance aloud, with lost performance habits perhaps the absent key that might wholly explain a poem's metre.

On the other hand, some earlier four-beat verse paid more attention to syllable count and tended to avoid double offbeats between beats. This preference for single offbeats made sense, for maintaining it brought English alternating metre a little closer to prominent metrical systems in the two most prestigious of the tongues in contact with Middle English and Older Scots: Latin and French. It is sometimes suggested that Chaucer and Gower brought a habit of avoiding double offbeats into English poetry in the late fourteenth century. But some earlier poets showed similar care. The early Middle English *The Owl and the Nightingale, for instance, already has few abutting beats, has few double offbeats, and achieves syllabic regularity in a line of four beats and eight syllables, or nine when the line closes with an extra offbeat. Here, as an example taken more or less at random, is the Owl coming up with a nickname to fling at the Nightingale:

    x / x / x / x / (x)
    Theos ule luste swithe longe

    x   / x / x / x / (x)
    And wes ofteoned swithe stronge.

    x /   x / x   / x / (x)
    Heo quath, 'Thu hattest "nihtegale",

    x / x / x   / x / (x)
    Thu mihtest bet hote "galegale"!'

(The owl listened a long while
And grew extremely angry.
She said, 'You're called "nightingale",
But a better name is "gabblegale"!'
*Fein ed. and trans. 2022, 253–256)

The metre holds quite steady here, assiduously providing single offbeats between beats. *The Owl and the Nightingale*, a marvellous gem of a poem, combines witty debate across a breathtaking range of general knowledge—the law, morality, music, not to mention bird lore—with knockabout insults. The Nightingale is merrier (perhaps too merry), the Owl more serious (perhaps too serious). Despite her po-faced characterization, the Owl can still slip, as she does here, from argument into name-calling.

One of the earliest identifiably Scots poems, John Barbour's *Bruce* (or *Brus*), makes fine use of the four-beat couplet. The poem relates, in sometimes bloodthirsty detail, the struggles of Robert the Bruce and his fellowship against English power. Its metrical norms can be found in sustained regular passages, as in the following description of Robert's brother Edward, with a small troop of horsemen, stumbling on a larger English army on a misty day:

> x / x / x / x /
> The myst wox cler all sodanly
>
> x / x / x / x /
> And than he and his cumpany
>
> x / x / x / x /
> War nocht a bowdraucht fra the rout.
>
> x / x / x / x /
> Than schot thai on thaim with a schout,
>
> x / x / x / x /
> For gyff thai fled thai wyst that thai
>
> x / x / x / x /
> Suld nocht weill feyrd part get away;
>
> x / x / x / x /
> Tharfor in aventur to dey
>
> x / x / x / x /
> He wald him put or he wald fle.

(The mist cleared up very suddenly, and then he [Edward Bruce] and his company were less than a bow-shot away from the [English] army. Then they [the Scots] charged them with a shout, for they knew that if they fled, no more than a quarter of them would get away; therefore he [Edward Bruce] wished to put himself at risk of death rather than fleeing. Barbour 1997, IX.588–595)

The poem in general orbits the regularity in syllables as well as alternating beats that this particular passage displays, and Barbour's verse makes itself pleasurable within that regularity: note for instance the gentle **rhyme-break** between the third and fourth lines (see Chapter 3); the lexical flow from 'bowdraucht' to the verb 'schot', which describes a cavalry charge but takes on, coming after 'bowdraught', an impression of arrow-like speed (see the senses of 'schute' in *DOST*); and the pointed promotion of the third and final closed-class 'thai' in the fifth line to a beat and a rhyming position.

Both Chaucer and his contemporary and acquaintance John Gower wrote in four-beat lines: Chaucer did so early in his career, and Gower did so for his longest English poem, *ature; and his *Confessio Amantis*. Both poets wrote careful, controlled verse, but their uses of the four-beat line varied, usefully showing how even related poets have their own metrical personalities. Gower's four-beat lines are highly consistent, and his *Confessio Amantis* delivers a four-beat masterclass. He kept to the same number of syllables in each line: either eight or, in lines with a two-syllable rhyme including a closing offbeat (**feminine rhymes**: see Chapter 6), nine. Gower avoided double offbeats and didn't let beats abut. Among many other stories, in his poem's fifth book Gower tells the legend of Jason and Medea, an eye-popping tale of magic, sex, betrayal, and other similar distractions (V.3247–4242). Readers can compare other tellings in Chaucer's *Legend of Good Women* (1368–1679), in John Clerk's fifteenth-century alliterative-verse †*Destruction of Troy* (1869, books I–IV), and in the anonymous fifteenth-century English translation of Boccaccio's *On Famous Women* (Cowen ed. 2015, 1289–1386). Here, Gower describes Medea's first meeting with Jason:

```
x  /  x  /  x  / x   / x
Forthi sche gan hir yhe impresse        therefore; eye

x /  x /  x    / x  /
Upon his face and his stature,

x    /  x  /  x  /   x  /
And thoghte hou nevere creature         how

x  /  x  /  x  /  x  /
Was so wel farende as was he.           handsome

x  / x  /  x  /   x  /
And Jason riht in such degré            just as much

x  / x  /   x  /   x  /
Ne mihte noght withholde his lok.       couldn't; look
                                        (*V.3378–3383)
```

These lines stay metrically very predictable, and such metrical predictability is typical of Gower's four-beat metre. It might threaten monotony, but Gower wards that off with enjambment and flexibly placed syntactic breaks, frequently splitting pairs of rhyming sounds: the *he:degré* rhyme splits across a major syntactic division, creating a rhyme-break that joins Medea and Jason across a shift in perspective. Gower's playful syntax sustains expansive, varied storytelling in a very steady metre.

Chaucer began his career with four-beat lines, in which he wrote *The Book of the Duchess* and *The House of Fame*. Chaucer's four-beat line is not, however, Gower's four-beat line. True, his lines avoid double offbeats, and many lines could be Gowerian:

    x / x / x / x /
    I have gret wonder, by this light,

     x / x / x / x /
    How that I lyve, for day ne night   *neither day nor night*

    x / x / x / x /
    I may nat sleepe wel nygh noght.

                                      (*The Book of the Duchess*, 1–3)

We might note in passing Chaucer's flashy maintenance of consonance (*-ght*) across two rhymes—the fourth line, not quoted, ends in 'thoght'—with the consonants on both sides of the vowels in 'night' and 'noght' also matching up. Metrically, these are predictable lines. Then, as *The Book of the Duchess* goes on, an occasional oddity surfaces:

    x / x / x /   x / x
    And I ne may, ne nyght ne morwe   *cannot; morning*

     / x / x / x /x
    Sleepe, and thus malencolye   *melancholy*

    x   / x / x / x /x
    And drede I have for to dye.   *for to: that I might*

                                               (22–24)

The first of these lines stays conventional—the metre permits the additional offbeat at its end in feminine rhymes, such as *morwe:sorwe*—but the second is **headless**. A headless line lacks the normal starting offbeat, forming a /x/x/x/ pattern, or /x/x/x/(x) if we include the optional final offbeat for feminine rhymes. Chaucer's four-beat line, unlike Gower's, turns headless on occasion. Headless lines were not new to English in Chaucer's work. Some earlier four-beat verse, as the example of *Havelok* showed, went headless so often that a single headless line in them lacks interest as a metrical event, though a close reading might still find value in a run of headless lines, or a switch from headless lines to lines starting with offbeats. Ad Putter has argued that Chaucer uses headless lines not just for variety but purposefully, sometimes to surprise and emphasize, and sometimes to make complex syntax, grammar, or speaker relations clearer (2017). We can certainly divine a purpose in this example. 'Sleepe' is the verb set up by the modal 'may' in the previous line, but readers or listeners must wait through the adverbial phrase 'ne night ne morwe' to get to the verb, which comes later than its most natural syntactical position. Perhaps Chaucer has a bit of fun with the idea of waiting for 'Sleepe' here, and more certainly his metre strongly emphasizes what the poem's speaker lacks. Other headless lines appear, often to achieve similar emphases or to begin speech, as *The Book of the Duchess* continues (e.g. 56, 74, 539, 720). Chaucer's four-beat line differs from Gower's, then, involving a different range of techniques.

I have tackled four-beat lines first because they were the default from which the better-known verse of Chaucer and the Chaucer tradition emerged. They were also probably the default to which many other metrical setups in Middle English related, or from which they stemmed. Consider the start of a song of unrequited love (*NIMEV* 1330 | *DIMEV* 2222) scribbled in a fifteenth-century grammar notebook:

    x/   x   x   /   x   /   x   /
    Y lovede a child of this cuntré,   *young man; country*

    x   / x   /   x   / x   /
    And so Y wende he had do me;   *thought*

    /   x /   x   /   x   /
    Now myself the sothe Y see: *truth*

    x   / x   /
    That he is far.

    x   / x   / x   / x   /
    Were it undo that is y-do   *undone; done*

    x   /   x   /
    I wold be war.   *wary*

                          (Duncan ed. 2013, art. II.107, ll. 3–7)

This poem's half-length fourth and sixth lines are two beats long, and their effect develops through contrasts to the surrounding four-beat lines. The four-beat line is the verse's backbone even though the metre varies away from it in some lines. Perhaps in performance a singer might have drawn out the short lines to fill the same duration as the four-beat line.

Septenaries

Septenaries offer a similar case of a metre related to the four-beat model. These are seven-beat lines, made up of a four-beat unit followed by a three-beat unit. Septenaries look very much like pairs of four-beat lines with the second line's fourth beat left implicit (Attridge 1995, 148). The three-beat unit might sometimes have been sustained in performance to match the four-beat unit's duration; twenty-first-century evidence needs careful handling, but the third beat of the three often doubles its length in my own readings of septenary poetry, seemingly without any conscious choice on my part. For accessible examples, one might turn to some of the *'Harley lyrics', so-called because they are preserved in London, British Library, MS Harley 2253. Some of the Harley poems have an alternating-metre septenary line, and here are two lines from one example:

>   /   x   / x   / x/ | x   / x   /   x   / x
>   Ich have loved al this yer | that Y may love namore;
>
>   /   x   / x   / x / | /   x   /   x / x
>   Ich have siked moni syk, | lemmon, for thin ore.
>
>   (All this year I've loved [so much] that I can love no more; I have sighed many a sigh, darling, for your mercy. *Fein ed. 2014–2015, art. 65, ll. 5–6)

One might note in passing the fruitful promotion of 'for', which would have little natural stress, to the prominence of the sixth beat in the second line quoted, just in case the audience was in any doubt about why this song's singer has been upset. Although this is a stock phrase in a conventional love song, its handling here works well.

The twelfth-century poets who introduced septenaries to English—figures likely lost to history—probably modelled them on a similar Latin metre, the *septenarius*. *Poema Morale* is the one of the earliest surviving English poems using septenaries. It offers austere afterlife advice, in rhyming septenary couplets:

>   x / x / x   /   x / | x / x / x   /   x
>   Tho sulle habben hardne dom | the here waren hardde,
>
>   x   / x / x   /   x / | x   / x /   x /   x
>   Tho the evel hielden wreche men | and evel laghe arerde.
>
>   (Those who were harsh here [i.e. in this life] will receive a harsh judgement, those who ruled poor people cruelly and raised up evil laws. Treharne ed. 2010, 171–172)

Early Middle English septenaries also occur in the work of Orm (or Orrm), an idiosyncratic churchman writing around the end of the twelfth century. Orm wrote unrhymed septenary lines which avoided double offbeats: he counts as another example of an early, pre-Chaucerian poet who held to the single offbeat and counted syllables fastidiously. His *Ormulum*—titled for its maker—is a set of verse sermons for different Sunday gospel readings. The sermons are arranged chronologically in the order of Christ's life, and the collection has lost material, making it incomplete today. Orm's septenaries rigorously end each four-beat portion with a beat and each three-beat portion with an offbeat. Here is Orm's retelling of the biblical account of an angel announcing Jesus' birth to some shepherds (Luke 2:10):

>   x /   x /   x   /   x / | x   /   x   / x / x
>   Ne beo ye nohht forrdredde off me, | acc beo ye swithe blithe,
>
>   x   / x   /   x   /   x   / | x / x   /   x   /   x
>   Forr Icc amm sennd off heoffness aerd | to kithenn Godess wille,
>
>   x / x   /   x / x   / | x /   x   / x   /   x
>   To kithenn yuw that all follc iss | nu cumenn mikell blisse.

> (Do not be afraid of me, but be very glad, for I am sent from the region of heaven to tell God's will, to tell you that a great joy is now come for all people. 2023, 3348–3353)

In various ways, Orm was an outlier. We have no signs that he influenced any other works. Even in its present, incomplete form, the *Ormulum* is a long poem, but it was probably written to be experienced in small chunks. And Orm is an interesting figure. He invented and painstakingly applied his own spelling system to help readers pronounce his verse sermons correctly. Very unusually, the sole surviving copy of the *Ormulum* is an **autograph**, a manuscript in Orm's own hand (Oxford, Bodleian Library, MS Junius 1). His choice to write with neither regular rhyme nor regular alliteration also anticipates later blank verse, a quirk of literary history to which Chapter 6 returns.

Poets elaborated on the grounding idea of the septenary, playing on the hazy boundary distinguishing one seven-beat line from two four-beat lines with the last beat in the second left implicit. The romance †*Sir Ferumbras* exemplifies a common variation on the septenary. This work is another unusual survivor. We have a copy in its author's hand, wrapped, even more unusually, in what appears to be a draft or part of another version of itself (Oxford, Bodleian Library, MS Ashmole 33). The author laid it out in long lines for the first 3,410 lines of verse. In this long-line section, the fourth beats of each pair of septenary lines rhyme with each other, as do the seventh:

> x /   x   / x / x / | x   / x x   / x /
> For if thou yknewe me aright— | my doyinge and my creaunce—
>
> x   / x   / x / x / | x / x   / x   /
> Thou noldest profry me no **fight**, | for al that gold of **Fraunce**.
>
> (For if you knew me properly—my doings and my reputation—you wouldn't offer to fight me, even for all the gold in France. †Herrtage ed. 1879, 358–359)

In other words, by rhyme—especially important when more people would hear such works than would read them by eye—each of these septenary couplets becomes an *abab* quatrain, or, including the number of beats per line in the notation, $a_4b_3a_4b_3$. Like septenary verse as a whole, this $a_4b_3a_4b_3$ model echoed some sub-types of *septenarii* in Latin verse, which could feature similar internal rhyme. We can even lineate the verse that way, in defiance of the original poet's manuscript layout:

> For if thou yknewe me aright—
> My doyinge and my creaunce—
> Thou noldest profry me no fight,
> For all that gold of Fraunce.

Other examples of $a_4b_3a_4b_3$ stanzas occur from the thirteenth century on, in short anonymous verse (e.g. *Fein ed. 2014–2015, arts 35, 61) and in more self-conscious poetry: the later fifteenth-century hymn to Mary by William Dunbar quoted in Chapter 2 as an example of aureation deploys $a_4b_3a_4b_3$ stanzas. Middle English poems in this form are the ancestors of the common metre or ballad metre $a_4b_3a_4b_3$ pattern frequently used in more recent Scots and English verse, including numerous modern ballads and hymns:

    x / x / x / x /
    Amazing grace, how sweet the sound

    x / x / x /
    That saved a wretch like me.

    x / x / x / x /
    I once was lost, but now am found,

    x / x / x /
    Was blind, but now I see.

Many of Emily Dickinson's poems can be read in this four-plus-three septenary pattern. Here's a short, complete example:

    / x / x / x / x
    Surgeons must be very careful

    / x / x /
    When they take the knife!

    / x / x / x / x
    Underneath their fine incisions

    / x / x /
    Stirs the Culprit - *Life*!

(1999, art. 156)

Though Dickinson laid this poem out as four lines rhyming $x_4a_3x_4a_3$ in her own manuscript copy, an editor could choose to print them as two long septenary lines, aa_7, much like *Poema Morale*. Long tendrils of transmission link all these later works back to poets working in septenaries from roughly eight hundred years ago.

An $a_4b_3a_4b_3$ pattern is the most common development from the septenary, but others occur. For instance, intermittent three-beat lines within a four-beat framework create many of the **tail-rhyme** structures discussed in Chapter 7, such as $aa_4b_3cc_4b_3$ stanzas (e.g. *'In Erth It Es a Litill Thing', Dean ed. 1996; *Fein ed. 2014–2015, art. 60). We don't know whether septenaries and these examples of tail-rhyme share related origins, but both relate to a four-beat norm. More sophisticated accounts can unpick distinct traditions within the verse grouped here under the four-beat and septenary headings (Cornelius 2022, 109–112), but for now I shall turn to five-beat lines.

Chaucer's five-beat line

In the later fourteenth century, Chaucer invented a new, five-beat line. His innovation had far-reaching consequences. Though by the sixteenth century ignorance of Chaucer's sounded final -*e* made his verse seem jolting, the lineage of five-beat lines that he started flowed on into the sixteenth-century development of five-beat blank verse as a self-conscious style, and on into Shakespeare, and on to Hutchinson, Bradstreet and Milton, still on to (say) John Dryden, Sarah Fyge Egerton, Mary Leapor, and Alexander Pope, and thence to the Romantics and the Victorians. The five-beat line still echoed through free verse in the twentieth century: as T. S. Eliot must have known, the sixth and tenth lines of 'Prufrock' invite reading as orthodox five-beat shapes, and so descend from Chaucer's work. Although four-beat lines have probably served in more verse overall through the whole history of English letters, in the centuries after Chaucer five-beat lines appear in many poems which had, or sought, prestige. The heyday of the five-beat line lasted less long than the career of alliterative metre, which predated English itself and lasted, in changing forms, into the sixteenth century, but it still had a good run for one poet's idea.

Such continuity helps: readers who know something about metre in the early modern period are closer to understanding Chaucer's five-beat practice. But continuity hinders, too. Poets after Chaucer picked up his line and developed it in different directions, melding in other influences. In the long run, some of these different directions petered out, but in their own time they were lively and viable. Accustomed to see Chaucer's metre as a precursor to the metres of (for instance) Shakespeare, scholarship has sometimes judged these growths as failures to move towards (for instance, again) Shakespeare rather than as experiments worthwhile in their own right. I shall describe the basics of Chaucer's five-beat line, and then consider, as an example offshoot, John Lydgate's practice. I close this chapter by noting some other interesting avenues of fifteenth-century innovation in five-beat lines. Like alliterative verse, Chaucer's metre and other metres used after his death form a live and lively field of study (e.g. Barney 1993, 77–114; Chaucer 1995, 112–123; Duffell 2018; Myklebust 2022). My discussion won't wade into questions such as the presence or absence of metrical feet in Chaucer's work, or the suitability of the phrase iambic pentameter; on the latter point, I think it sufficient and useful here to speak only of five-beat lines (Barney 1993, 85; Fulk 2012, 128–129).

Chaucer did not pluck the five-beat line from thin air. He developed the line drawing on French verse-craft, and also on Italian models that were closed to some of his contemporaries. Nothing in either French nor Italian verse-craft exactly matches the result, which unites continental European strains of practice with aspects of earlier English verse. Chaucer's five-beat lines have the following basic features:

1. beats and single offbeats alternate, so that beats do not abut;
2. double offbeats are usually avoided;
3. rhyme comes at the fifth beat, which is usually the tenth syllable; and
4. the typical rhythm is rising—that is, the pattern tends to begin with an offbeat followed by a beat (x/) and to keep moving from offbeat to beat thereafter.

These features together produce a basic pattern of x/x/x/x/x/:

        x / x / x / x̄ /   x /
        For with that faire cheyne of love he bond   *chain; bound*

        x /   x /   x / x /   x /
        The fyr, the eyr, the water, and the lond   *fire; air; land*

        x / x /   x /   x / x /
        In certeyn boundes, that they may not flee.   *certain borders*
                                          (*Canterbury Tales*, I 2991–2993)

As in four-beat lines, the line also permits an additional final single offbeat in a feminine rhyme:

        x   /   x / x /   x / x   / x
        And on his pitous face he gan byholden.   *piteous*

        x   /   x / x /   x / x / x
        But Lord, so ofte gan his herte colden.   *to grow cold*
                                            (*Troilus and Criseyde*, IV.361–362)

To account for the possibility of feminine rhyme, the basic pattern of Chaucer's five-beat line could be written out as x/x/x/x/x/(x).

Plus, just like in his four-beat line, Chaucer could begin his five-beat line with a beat rather than an offbeat. He could do this using a headless line, but headless lines seem rarer in his five-beat lines than in his four-beat verse. More commonly, he inverted the first beat and offbeat for a /xx/x/x/x/(x) pattern, in a move sometimes called **initial inversion** (a point of debate: Putter 2017; Myklebust 2022, 34–35). An emphatic set of initial inversions occurs at one point in the Nun's Priest's Tale, in one of the cockerel Chauntecleer's (many) departures into comically grand rhetoric:

        /   x x   /   x / x / x /
        Mordre wol out, that see we day by day.   *Murder will*

        /   x x   / x /   x   / x / x
        Mordre is so wlatsom and abhominable   *loathsome*

        x /   x / x /   x / x / x
        To God, that is so just and resonable,

        x   / x / x   /   x̄ / x /
        That he ne wol nat suffre it heled be,   *hidden*

        x   / x / x / x   / x   /
        Though it abide a yeer or two or three.

        /   x x   /   x / x   / x /
        Mordre wol out: this my conclusioun.
                                                     (VII 3052–3057)

Initial inversions in the first, second, and last lines emphasize *Mordre*, which forms the topic. The first and last lines quoted hammer home the phrase 'Mordre wol out', which could well have been proverbial even in the late fourteenth century, though its earliest known appearances occur in Chaucer. The second line delivers a metrically matching initial inversion in different words. The initial inversions here are not, alone, a dramatic event, but they combine with other elements. This passage forms part of a sophisticated debate over the interpretation of dreams. The debate derives much comic energy from the tension between, on the one hand, impressive, elegant rhetoric and a serious topic of genuine interest to readers—then and now—and, on the other, the fact that the two speakers are chickens. To sustain that tension, the rhetoric needs to fly high. Various aspects of these lines help. Chauntecleer deploys, for instance, the Germanic-and-Latinate doublet of 'wlatsom and abhominable', two words which mean nearly the same thing but come from different origins and registers. A related lexical choice happens at the end, in 'conclusion', a word associated in Middle English with logical academic argument. As often, a metrical observation alone takes us only so far, but it can draw our attention to other important things and can, with them, open up a route into a passage.

Five-beat lines also stand out from four-beat lines in their imbalance. Four-beat lines have a strong tendency to split into balanced halves, with a predictable and regular pause—a **metrical caesura**—between the second and third beats. Five-beat lines have no built-in dividing point that can give balanced halves: the closest they can get to an even split is a break between the second and third beats, or between the third and fourth, but in either case one part of the line always outweighs the other. This built-in imbalance and unpredictability offered poets another way to craft contrasts or consistencies across lines: shifting the positions of pauses within lines. Since Chaucer's five-beat line has no set, obligatory pausing point, no regular metrical caesura, we can speak of a local **rhetorical caesura**, a caesura of choice, when a syntactic pause breaks the line up. This flexibility opens up scope for more variation. In studying Chaucer's five-beat poetry readers might want to keep an ear open for patterned variation between lines which pause after the second beat and lines which pause after the third, especially if that variation coordinates with other notable effects. While the five-beat line could never have balanced halves, it could develop a regular metrical caesura in another poet's hands; it is worth considering how other poets worked with the basic metrical idea of five beats. Other poets got started early, for Gower experimented with five-beat lines. He used them for one set-piece poem inside *Confessio Amantis* (8.2217–2300) and in one shorter free-standing work, *In Praise of Peace* (in *Forni ed. 2005), an elegant advice poem written after—and obliquely addressing—Henry IV's 1399 usurpation of the English throne from Richard II.

Five-beat lines after Chaucer

Many poets took on the five-beat line from Chaucer, but they fostered it in different ways. I shall explore one example here, that of John Lydgate. Lydgate's metrical fingerprint differs from Chaucer's, but, accepted on its own terms, his metre achieves feats just as interesting. Lydgate usually wrote in five-beat lines with an optional closing offbeat for feminine rhymes: x/x/x/x/x/(x). So far, so Chaucerian. Unlike Chaucer, though, he placed a regular, obligatory pause, a true metrical caesura, between the second and third beats. Chaucer could pause within a line, but did not feel obliged to, so his pauses are optional rhetorical caesuras; Lydgate's caesuras come as an obligatory metrical fixture. Not all are major syntactic breaks: they can be fairly brief pauses. But pauses they usually are, and some become more than brief. When a major syntactic break occurs within a line, Lydgate routinely places it here, after the second beat. Lydgate thus brought the five-beat line closer to a French model, the *décasyllabe*, which had ten syllables and a regular metrical caesura after its fourth syllable.

By adopting this metrical caesura after two beats, Lydgate won himself other options for regular variation besides techniques such as headless lines and initial inversion. With the caesura between the second and third beats established as a regular feature onto which readers could grapple, Lydgate had freedom to play with the exact arrangement of syllables at this point in the line. His most common line would have—I mark the caesura with '|', a vertical bar—either a x/x/|x/x/x/(x) pattern or a x/x/x|/x/x/(x) pattern. But he could permit himself an extra offbeat around the caesura, making a x/x/x|x/x/x/(x) pattern, as in the middle line here:

       x / x   / | x   / x /   x   /
       As I gan neigh this grisli dredful place,   *as I neared; grisly*

       x / x   / x | x /   x / x   /
       I wex astonyed: the light so in my face   *grew astonished*

       x /   x   / |
       Bigan to smyte.

                                           (*Temple of Glas*, *2007, 23–25)

Neither a listening audience nor someone reading this poem from the page would have had the aid of a present-day colon, and the extra offbeat probably helped Lydgate's public grasp the implied causal link between the speaker's surprise and the light that's mentioned next, despite the lack of any overt causal word.

Lydgate could also write lines without any offbeats between the second and third beats at all, a pattern of x/x/|/x/x/(x). Among the features of Lydgate's metre, these **broken-backed lines** have proved the most divisive. They undoubtedly challenge present-day ears. Before readers absorb Lydgate's metrical caesura as a persistent feature, they often find the adjacent beats clash together. But the caesura does still conceptually separate the beats, even without an offbeat. Maura Nolan has explored the possible beauties offered by reading broken-backed lines (2013). She points out that in the prologue to Lydgate's *Siege of Thebes* (2001), broken-backed lines occur especially often, indeed characteristically often, in the loud, boisterous dialogue of the Host. For example:

> x / x / | / x / x /
> Thogh ye be soul, beth right glad and light (97)
>
> x / x / | / x / x /
> To ben a monk, sclender is youre koyse (102)
>
> x / x / | / x / x /
> Be now wel war—stody wel tonyght! (143)

Cases such as these, in which Lydgate dealt broken-backed lines out mindfully, aiming at a specific literary-linguistic characterization, suggest that his broken-backed lines don't emerge from sloppiness. Such mindful writing licenses readers to look out for craft when broken-backed lines occur elsewhere. Lydgate also wrote headless lines, and might have had a greater tendency than Chaucer to use these to raise closed-class words to prominence.

Consider the closing stanza from Lydgate's deliciously admonitory *Dance of Death*, in which he explains that the work translates a French one displayed in Paris. I mark the caesura in each line:

> x / x / |x / x / x / x
> Out of the Frensshe I drewe it of entente,   *with purpose*
>
> x / x / |x / x / x /
> Not worde by worde but folwyng the substaunce.   *sense*
>
> x   / x /|x / x / x / x
> And fro Paris to Engelonde it sente
>
> x / x / x |/ x / x /
> Oonly of purpos yow to do plesaunce.   *please*
>
> /   x x / |x / x / x /
> Rude of langage (I was not born in Fraunce),   *Crude*
>
> x   / x / x | x / x / x /   *if no syncope pre-caesura*
> Have me excusid; my name is John Lidgate;   *Pardon me*
>
> / x / x|x / x / x /   *if no elision pre-caesura*
> Of her tunge I have no suffisaunce   *their tongue; not enough*
>
> x   / x   / x | x/ x / x /   *if synizesis in* corious
> Her corious metris in Englisshe to translate.   *crafty verses*
>
> (*Cook and Strakhov eds 2019, A version, 665–672)

Metrical variation significantly increases in this stanza's final lines: the seventh is headless, and characteristically lands the headless beat on a closed-class word, while the sixth, seventh, and eighth can all have a Lydgatean extra syllable between the second and third beats. The fifth line makes readers choose between perceiving a beat on the important open-class word at its start, or on the following *of*. Lydgate might play here with his own competence, metrically crafting his own signature even as he claims a lack of the right expertise: 'I was not born in Fraunce' perhaps alludes not to a lack of French, but to the possession of an English—and so less prestigious—type of French (see Chapter 10). Yet in its regular caesura after the second beat, Lydgate's metre is more Francophile than Chaucer's. This end to the poem achieves a witty mix of humble withdrawal, assertive self-naming, and distinctive metrical play.

Lydgate made his metrical practice individual, but most of his individualisms didn't pay off in posterity: Shakespeare and Marlowe are not known for their Lydgatean broken-backed lines. One can, though, imagine in a parallel universe a Shakespeare who wrote Lydgatean lines, and Lydgate's practice reminds us that not all aspects of versecraft's history are inevitable. Had metrical history played out differently, later poets could have taken to Lydgate's obligatory metrical caesuras. And Lydgate is just one among the many poets who adopted Chaucer's five-beat line and developed it in different directions. While four-beat lines and their derivatives continued to dominate in much popular and folk verse, five-beat lines gradually proliferated in polite writing as the fifteenth century wore on, underpinning works by, among others, *James I of Scotland (in Mooney and Arn eds 2005), Osbern Bokenham, John Capgrave, *Robert Henryson (2010), Charles d'Orleans, *Richard Roos (in Symons ed. 2004), *William Dunbar (2004), together with many anonymous poems such as *The Assembly of Ladies*, *The Floure and the Leafe* (both in Pearsall ed. 1990), *The Assembly of Gods* (Chance ed. 1999), *Generydes*, *The Romans of Parthenay*, and short lyrics. Most of these have received less metrical study than Chaucer or Lydgate. As with Lydgate's verse, they might well contain intricacies and innovations.

In which connection, it seems worth closing this section with a few words on Thomas Hoccleve, who provides an instructive example of innovation in five-beat lines. Born roughly contemporary with Lydgate, Hoccleve died about a quarter-century earlier (1426). He stands as another prominent poet in the first generation of people writing southern English verse for the well-connected after the career of Chaucer, whom he may have known personally. We have **autographs**, surviving copies of some of Hoccleve's poems in his own hand. Yet his metre has challenged readers in its variation from Chaucer's. Hoccleve appears to have prioritized keeping a regular count of syllables over keeping a steady $x/x/x/x/x/(x)$ offbeat–beat pattern (Myklebust 2022). This is not to say that Hoccleve ignored beat patterns: his lines still orbit a $x/x/x/x/x/(x)$ model, they simply vary more from that pattern in their beat alternation while varying less in their syllable counts. Compared to Chaucer's work, Hoccleve's lines changed the quality they weigh most. They admit abutting beats and more inversions in more places, while their interest in maintaining a regular syllable count discourages headless lines. This approach broke away from what Chaucer had achieved. We respect syllable-counting in some other contexts, though—critics don't judge it a problem in Marianne Moore, who was much more purely a syllable-counter—and we should approach Hoccleve's metre as Hoccleve's metre, rather than as a failed attempt to ape Chaucer.

Even around just one idea, a five-beat line, then, poets found much variety. They found at least as much variety as in subsequent centuries, when five-beat lines had become a wholly settled default for prestigious poetry. Alternating metres form a family of approaches marked by variation and experimentation, and often looking to surrounding languages for inspiration. Each poet and poem requires an individual approach in reading, but this chapter has laid out some basic tools and models. The variation found across different alternating metres was, though, only variation within one facet of metre in this period. Coexisting with alternating metres was a whole other metrical approach: alliterative verse.

5
Metre (II): Alliterative Verse

> Herkenes me hendely | and holdes you stille,   *Listen to; politely*
> And I shall tell you a tale | that trew is and noble   *true*
> Of the real renkes | of the Round Table.   *royal warriors*
> (*Alliterative *Morte Arthure*, 15–17)

Reading these lines aloud swiftly shows that their metre isn't predictable or explicable as an alternating system. They are lines of **alliterative verse**.

This name is slightly awkward, for at least two reasons: first, the defining feature of alliterative verse is at least as much a particular approach to metre as it is regular alliteration; second, any verse can contain alliteration, and so poets writing in alternating metres could use regular alliteration too. For instance, *Pearl* displays alliteration in most of its lines, and other poems in the same manuscript use alliterative verse, but *Pearl* itself uses alternating four-beat lines, not alliterative metre. Similarly, a number of the *'Harley Lyrics' contain frequent ornamental alliteration but are composed in alternating metres (e.g. *Fein ed. 2014–2015, arts 27, 29, 30, 33). Scholarship on Middle English usually reserves the phrase 'alliterative verse' for verse in half-lines of alliterative metre, of the sort exemplified by the quotation from the Alliterative *Morte*. This chapter also includes two related topics, the special wording used in some alliterative poems, and the tradition of alliterative-stanzaic verse.

The earliest surviving form of English, Old English, had a vibrant tradition of alliterative verse. Although some details differed, this tradition sounds recognizably similar to Middle English alliterative verse:

> Wraetlic is thes weal-stan, | wyrde gebraecon;
> Burg-stede burston, | brosnath enta geweorc.
>
> (Wondrous is this wall-stone; disastrous events have shattered it; the fortified cities have broken apart, the work of giants decays. *The Ruin*, in Bjork ed. and trans. 2014, 1–2)

A few early Middle English poems display metrical affinities with Old English alliterative verse, though scholars debate whether any of these examples qualify as the direct kin of later alliterative verse; the early Middle English poet crucial to the problem is Layamon, and this chapter will discuss him later. Poetry uncontroversially written in strict alliterative metre re-emerges in the written record around the middle of the fourteenth century, around 1350. This later Middle English alliterative verse resembles, but does not precisely match, the verse-craft used in Old English. The patchy written record of early Middle English poetry makes it difficult to work out whether alliterative metre survived to the fourteenth century through written transmission, oral tradition, or both.

Whatever the mechanism, though, some kind of continuous history of practice probably did run from Old English verse to later Middle English alliterative verse. This scenario most efficiently explains their metrical similarity, and the preservation in Middle English alliterative verse of some words derived from Old English and not found elsewhere in Middle English. This continuity makes alliterative metre in half-lines the family of metrical methods that lasted longest in English, one that persisted for at least a millennium. Alliterative verse dwindled slowly away during and after the fifteenth century, partly because of changes in the English language itself (Weiskott 2016, 148–167; Cornelius 2017, 130–146; Russom 2017, 259–260). When we read alliterative verse from the fourteenth and fifteenth centuries, then, we read the final flowering of the continuous living tradition of English's original verse form—though modern poets such as W. H. Auden, Richard Wilbur, and Carter Revard have drawn on alliterative metre as models for new forms which might work in modern English (Phelpstead 2004).

Many surviving alliterative poems share more than just metre, chasing related topical interests: politics, history—in the broad sense assigned to the word 'history' at the time—and virtue. They might have formed a tradition in more than just metrical ways. Chaucer hints that, from his viewpoint, alliterative verse was a Northern phenomenon (*Canterbury Tales*, X 42–43), but we shouldn't uncritically accept the opinion of a southerner with his own different verse tradition. In any case, this opinion comes not from the poet's mouth but in the voice of the Parson, a character sceptical about all verse (X 44). Despite the Parson's view of alliterative verse as something Northern, William Langland's alliterative-verse *Piers Plowman* seems, from its manuscript distribution, to have found plenty of readers in the south of England, while *St Erkenwald* is an alliterative-verse poem all about London's deep past. What's more, alliterative and alternating metres cohabited in the same physical manuscripts, and the poet of *Sir Gawain and the Green Knight* used alliterative and alternating metres in different parts of the same stanza (Chapter 7). Middle English alliterative verse might have orbited particular themes and might have flourished in the Midlands and the North, but it didn't stay penned-up in particular areas.

Research investigating the workings of alliterative verse continues, and so do debates over the best ways to describe and explain those workings. This doesn't mean that anything goes in alliterative metrics, or that research travels in circles: we know more than we did four or five decades ago, and researchers agree on some key points. Grasping these points of consensus, I aim here at a working description of mainstream

Middle English alliterative metre for enjoyment and study, not a full model of its mechanics. Readers should feel encouraged to investigate further, for alliterative verse has many charms, and needs future experts.

Alliterative metre

Every line of alliterative metre comes in two parts, called **half-lines**. An obligatory pause, a **metrical caesura**, separates the two half-lines. We can distinguish the first and second half-lines by calling them the **a-verse** and **b-verse**. At least a small syntactic break separates the two. I shall print a vertical bar ('|') between the a-verse and b-verse. Here, for instance, is the first line of *Wynnere and Wastour*:

> a-verse | b-verse
> Sythen that Bretayne was biggede | and Bruyttus it aughte.
> (Since Britain was built and Brutus ruled it. *Ginsberg ed. 1992, 1)

And here is the Green Knight demanding that King Arthur's court play his game early in *Sir Gawain and the Green Knight*:

> a-verse | b-verse
> Forthy I crave in this court | a Cristemas game.
> (Therefore I crave in this court a Christmas game. 283)

Reading these lines aloud with their meanings in mind makes the syntactic break at the caesura obvious.

As noted in Chapter 3, a-verses tend to run longer than b-verses and tend to deliver more main clauses. The b-verse often contains a grammatical object, a modifying phrase or a subordinate clause. In 'Sythen that Bretayne was biggede | and Bruyttus it aughte', the whole line is a subordinate clause, but the b-verse is notably shorter and relies on the a-verse through a parasitic pronoun reference ('it'). In 'Forthy I crave in this court | a Cristemas game', the subject ('I'), verb ('crave') and an adverbial phrase ('in this court') all come in the a-verse, while the b-verse delivers only the object. B-verses also have, as we shall see, more metrical constraints, and therefore tend towards more unnatural word order.

Normal English speech, outside of verse, possesses natural stresses (Chapter 4), and contains both **open-class** and **closed-class** words (Chapter 2). It is a crude approach, but one helpful for beginners, to say that in alliterative verse the beats are the naturally stressed syllables of the line's open-class words:

> x   xx / x   x   / |x / x x / x
> Forthy I **crave** in this **court** | a **Cristemas game**

All syllables in *forthy, I, in, court* and *a* go unstressed, because they are closed-class words. The only syllables of *crave* and *court* are stressed, because they are single-syllable open-class words. The individual syllables which would naturally be stressed in *Cristemas* and *game* are stressed—these are open-class words too. This arrangement gives us, in this line, four beats, or **lifts**, as scholars often name the beats of the alliterative line; I shall prefer the word 'lift' as it distinguishes alliterative metre from alternating metres. Note that within an open-class word, only the specific syllables which receive natural stress count as lifts. 'Bretayne', as a whole, is not a lift: the syllable *Bret-* is a lift, while the syllable *-ayne* isn't. Similarly, the *gam-* of 'game' is a lift, but the *-e* is not. Natural lexical stress in English normally falls on a given word's first syllable, but sometimes comes later: in the line 'And then repreved he the prince | with mony proude wordes' (*Gawain*, 2269), the second syllable of *repreved* supplies the a-verse's first lift. Likewise, in 'That evere he dide dede | that deere God displesed' (*Piers Plowman* B, XIV.325) the fourth lift is the *-ple-* of 'displesed'; the extra *d*-alliteration of the word's naturally unstressed first syllable adds a stylish extra flourish beyond the required structure, but does not signal that that syllable is stressed.

I called the use of the open-classed and closed-class distinction to identify lifts crude. A slightly more sophisticated description would say more specifically that nouns, most adjectives, participles, and infinitives usually supply lifts; that adverbs and open-class verbs sometimes supply lifts; that auxiliary verbs and the verb *have* usually don't supply lifts; and that all other types of word also usually don't supply lifts. Even this account collapses the subtlety of the metrical rules absorbed by alliterative poets and their audiences, for which see the more developed, and sometimes diverging, models of experts (Putter, Jefferson, and Stokes 2007; Cable 2009; Weiskott 2016; Cornelius 2017; Russom 2017).

Aside from the lifts, the rest of a line of alliterative verse is made up of **dips**. A dip is a **short dip** if it contains one and only one naturally unstressed syllable. In the b-verse 'and Bruyttus it aughte', both *and* and the *-e* of 'aughte' are short dips. A dip is a **long dip** if it contains two or more naturally unstressed syllables. In the b-verse 'a Cristemas game', the *-emas* of 'Cristemas' is the only long dip. Long dips can also form across the boundaries between words: in the half-line 'Forthy I crave in this court', 'Forthy I' is one single long dip of three unstressed syllables; in the half-line 'Sythen that Bretayne was biggede', 'Sythen that' is one long dip of three unstressed syllables. Long dips cannot, under any circumstances, form across the boundary between half-lines, at the metrical caesura. One long dip is metrically equivalent to any other long dip, even if they contain different numbers of syllables: 'Forthy I', 'Sythen that', '-emas', '-ayne was', and 'in this' are metrical equivalents, of equal metrical significance, because they contain multiple syllables. They are metrically equivalent even though some contain three syllables, the others two. The discrepancies in exact syllable count do not matter: it is the *plurality* of the unstressed syllables that matters, because that is what makes these dips long rather than short. Scholars have not yet reached a consensus on whether very long dips of over four syllables occurred (see, for instance, Inoue 2023).

These, then, are the three components which go to make up any line of alliterative verse:

1. **lift**, the or a naturally stressed syllable in an open-class word: /
2. **short dip**, a single naturally unstressed syllable: x
3. **long dip**, a sequence of two or more naturally unstressed syllables: x...x

The line 'Forthy I crave in this court | a Cristemas game' can be understood metrically as follows:

    x   x x / x x /
    Forthy I crave in this court
    (xxx/xx/ = long dip, lift, long dip, lift)

    x / x x / x
    a Cristemas game.
    (x/xx/x = short dip, lift, long dip, lift, short dip)

Alliterative verse looks anarchic when analysed using the concepts appropriate to alternating metres: it doesn't build a predictable alternation of perceived beat and off-beat. When readers approach it as an arrangement of lifts, short dips, and long dips, however, a set of rules emerges. These usefully divide between rules for the a-verse and rules for the b-verse.

Researchers have agreed on fewer rules for the a-verse than the b-verse. But the a-verse typically contains two lifts, and frequently contains more than one long dip. This tendency reflects the a-verse's role in delivering more words and more meaning. We think, too, that the a-verse avoids patterns which would count as legitimate b-verses, so that lines of Middle English alliterative verse have an asymmetric quality. Or, to put it another way, poets kept up asymmetry by doing in a-verses those things banned from b-verses: including multiple long dips, ending the a-verse in a lift, or ending the a-verse in a long dip.

Scholars disagree over whether or not the a-verse could also contain more than two lifts. There are, at least, lines which might tempt us to think so:

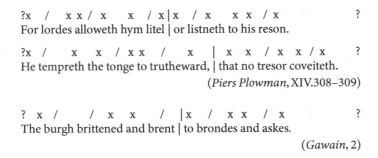

(Gawain, 2)

Experts must decide whether they think such lines are permissible or were reduced in practice to two real lifts by the suppression of one of the potential lifts in the a-verse. Debate on the question of possible three-lift a-verses continues (e.g. Putter 2012). In close reading, we can temporarily sideline the problem of possible three-lift a-verses and look out for such lines anyway: even if, ultimately, they had only two real lifts, their greater length holds potential interest.

The b-verse follows a tighter set of rules, and scholarship understands it better. The b-verse contains exactly two lifts and ends with the second lift followed by a short dip (/x). The b-verse must contain one long dip and can only contain one long dip. The long dip occurs either *before* the first lift or *between* the two lifts. The long dip cannot occur after the second lift because, as just stated, the b-verse ends with its second lift followed by a *short* dip (/x). When the long dip precedes both lifts, the two lifts can either be separated by a short dip or can just abut.

A poet composing in strict alliterative metre therefore has one big choice to make for any given b-verse: does the long dip sit *before* or *between* the lifts? Taking these rules together, a typical b-verse can have one of only four metrical arrangements, two with the long dip before the first lift, and two with the long dip between the two lifts.

1 and 2: long dip before first lift

1. x...x/x/x: long dip before first lift, short dip between lifts

   x   x /   x /   x
   bi the tymes ende

   ('by the time's end', *Gawain*, 1069b)

   x   x   / x   /   x
   undere stelen bowndes

   ('under steel bands', *Wynnere and Wastoure*, Ginsberg 1992, 252b)

2. x...x//x: long dip before first lift, lifts abutting

   x   x   / /x
   to the flod hyes

   ('hurries to the water', *Cleanness* 538b)

   x   x   x /   /   x
   and of the Pount Tremble

   ('and of Pontremoli', *Alliterative Morte Arthure*, Benson ed. 1994, 352b)

3 and 4: long dip between the two lifts

3. x/x...x/x: long dip after first lift, initial short dip

   x / x x   x / x
   of floures and of herbys

('of flowers and herbs', *Wars of Alexander*, Duggan and Turville-Petre eds 1989, 4508b)

x　　/　　x x　　/　　x
and breekless him seemed

('and he seemed to lack trousers', *Alliterative Morte Arthure*, 1048b)

4. /x...x/x: long dip after first lift, no initial short dip

　/　　x　　x　/　x
payntid of silvir ('painted with silver', *Wars of Alexander*, 3155b)

　/　　x x　/　x
wordes ynewe

('words enough', *Wynnere and Wastoure*, 282b)

This is a lot to absorb, but rereading these points carefully and applying them to some b-verses will bed the knowledge in.

A working knowledge can enhance close reading. Consider the following passage, taken from the climax of *Sir Gawain*. At the Green Chapel, Gawain glances at the Knight's long axe, his 'giserne', and shrinks back:

>Then the gome in the grene | graythed him swythe,
>Gederes up his grymme tole | Gawan to smyte;　　　　　2260
>With all the bur in his body | he bere hit on lofte,
>Mynt as maghtyly | as marre him he wolde.
>Had it driven adoun | as drye as he attled,
>There had ben ded of his dint | that doghty was ever;
>Bot Gawayn on that giserne | glyfte hym bysyde,　　　　2265
>As hit com glydande adoun | on glode hym to schende,
>And schrank a little with the schulderes | for the scharp yrne.
>That other schalk with a schunt | the schene wythhaldes,
>And thenne repreved he the prynce | with mony proude wordes:
>'Thou art not Gawan', quoth that gome, | 'that is so good holden'.　2270

(Then the man in the green swiftly readied himself, raises his grim weapon to smite Gawain; with all the force in his body he bore it aloft, planned [the stroke] as mightily as though he would destroy him. Had it driven down as strongly as he had in mind, then he who was ever strong [i.e. Gawain] would have died from his blow; but Gawain glanced aside at that long axe, as it came gliding down to destroy him on the ground, and shrank a little with his shoulders because of the sharp iron. The other man withheld the bright [weapon] with a jerk, and then he reproved the prince with many proud words: 'You're not Gawain,' said the warrior, 'who's reckoned so good'. 2259–2270)

In this stanza, 'for the scharp yrne' is the ninth b-verse, but it is the very first b-verse of the stanza in which the long dip precedes the first lift (2259–2266; 2267 scans xx//x), after a full eight b-verses in a row with long dips between their lifts. This contrast doesn't mean that the metre mimics Gawain's shrinking back—how would language do that?—but the sudden contrast, with lifts abutting for the first time in this stanza, does put extra weight on the 'scharp yrne'. Like many metrical observations, this means only a little on its own, but it combines well with other aspects of the poetry: a reader might point out, for instance, that the alliteration in the 'scharp yrne' line continues the consonant sound of the previous line's final lift ('schende', 2266), which then runs on into the first three lifts of the following line ('schalk', 'schunt', and 'schene', 2268), so that 'scharp' sits within a larger flourish. This *sch*-alliteration runs across a syntactic break after 'yrne', at the end of line 2267, which shifts the grammatical subject. Along with that shift of subject comes a perspectival shift in the perception of the axe: for the Green Knight the axe might be a bright object, 'the schene', yet—understandably!—Gawain's attention rests not on the axe's beauty, but its *edge*.

These observations can inform a broader grasp of this passage, which tests Gawain's virtue and identity ('Thou art not Gawan'). He shows courage in coming to face beheading in the first place, but also flinches in a human way, pointed up by the metre, at the Green Knight's weapon. This small failing fits a pattern in which the poem questions Gawain's understanding of virtue: in his view even the slightest slip-up, the smallest flinch, might destroy his virtue forever (2382–2383, 2512), yet both the Green Knight and the court to which Gawain returns judge his performance exemplary. These competing conceptions of virtue might, in turn, have something to do with gender. In romances more generally, the virtue and reputation of knights can rise and fall with their accomplishments, while the virtue of women usually seems binary: women either keep or lose it (Flannery 2020). Gawain imagines his own goodness in much the same binary way that other romances imagine female goodness, and one might want, with this thought in hand, to consider his blaming of women (2414–2428), his devotion to Mary, and for that matter his exchanges of kisses with his host at Hautdesert. Past critics have discussed these topics. Now, though, I would go to read criticism armed with at least one observation that is my own thought, however small, and so might form the kernel of useful writing.

This line of thought is, though, only one of many which might integrate my observation about the 'scharp yrne' b-verse into broader patterns of work on the poem. Readers need not agree with it, and in literary-critical practice one wouldn't need to quote the whole stanza or to lay out an explanation at this length: this example has run on to show that metrical quirks and larger questions do relate to each other. It's rarely efficient to work out the metre of long stretches of alliterative verse for no reason, but when a short passage already seems notable, checking the metre can reveal extra enhancements. Often multiple features work together, or sit in tension, to achieve an effect.

Like a model of an atom for novice physicists, this working account of alliterative metre could grow more accurate. I heartily encourage anyone who finds alliterative metre interesting to pursue the topic further. Actually-existing alliterative verse works will sometimes break these rules, and scholars must decide whether such departures from the norm come from poets' choices or the hazards of transmission through hand copying, and whether in such places editors can and should try to fix the text. Readers might at this point, though, reasonably wonder how alliteration itself fits into alliterative verse.

Alliteration

How does the alliteration in alliterative verse work? The topic offers a useful chance to consider, briefly, alliteration in alternating verse too, and the ties between the two traditions. In Middle English alliterative verse, the lifts in the a-verse normally alliterate with each other and with the first lift of the b-verse—and *only* the first lift in the b-verse. The b-verse's second lift, the fourth lift in the whole line, usually does not alliterate with the other three: 'crave ... court | ... Cristemas ... game'. This pattern can be written out as AAAX or, marking the caesura between a- and b-verses, AA|AX. Lifts which begin with vowels alliterate with all other lifts which begin with vowels, regardless of the vowel sounds. Thus in *Wynnere and Wastoure* the first three lifts in the line 'The **or**dire of the **Au**styns, | for **ough**te that I wene' alliterate together in an orthodox AA|AX pattern (*Ginsberg ed. 1992, 186). As far as the verse form is concerned, only syllables which are lifts alliterate. In 'Forthy an aunter in erde | I attle to schewe', for example (*Gawain*, 27), 'an', 'in', and 'I' are all words beginning with vowels, but they aren't lifts; as far as the verse form is concerned, the meaningfully alliterative syllables are *aunt-*, *erd-*, and *att-*. Because lifts are the naturally stressed syllables of words, not always the first syllables, poets could achieve alliterative patterns such as that in the line 'And eftersones of the same | he served him there' (*Gawain*, 1640). Most poets seem to have felt that the initial consonant of a consonant cluster could legitimately alliterate with an instance of the same consonant alone: thus 'crave' and 'Cristemas' (*cr-*) match up with 'court' (*c-*).

Alliteration's ubiquity in this style of verse makes it a tempting topic for comment. As with regular rhyme, however, the obligatory nature of basic AA|AX alliteration and its high frequency lessen its significance. Alliteration often tempts students into comments on onomatopoeia. But for a statement such as 'the harsh *k*-alliteration of this line conveys the moment's danger' to be true, *all* lines of English verse alliterating on a *k* or hard *c* sound would have to relate to danger, which they obviously do not. If—keeping the same imaginary example—a line sounds threatening, don't assume that its alliterative sound is responsible. Look harder: perhaps some combination of syntax, metre, and lexis cause the effect. Onomatopoeic readings of alliteration can sometimes work, but require knowledge and careful justification (Turville-Petre 2018, 141–147). Similar health warnings come attached to the links between words established by alliteration. Anyone listening to typical alliterative verse normally hears a triple alliterative link in every line. Within one line, therefore, no especially profound insight can come from the links of meaning between three words connected by obligatory alliteration, just as the mere linking of two words by couplet rhyme in a long sequence of rhyming couplets doesn't—on its own, at least—reveal some grand poetic device.

Alliteration stands out when it diverges or extends from this basic pattern. Lines therefore demand more notice when they alliterate in any pattern *other* than AA|AX. In the AA|AX pattern, the reliable delivery of a non-alliterating lift followed by the b-verse's final short dip perhaps helped audiences perceive line-breaks. However, later Middle English poets did sometimes write lines with alliterating final lifts, that is, lines patterned AA|AA. This happens in the very first line of *Piers Plowman*: 'In a somer seson, | whan softe was the sonne' (Prologue, 1). Such AA|AA lines almost certainly stuck out for contemporaries as heightened moments. Other variations were possible. In *Sir Gawain*, for instance, 'At the soper and after, | many athel songes' appears to be a line in which all four lifts alliterate in two pairs, AB|BA (1654).

Alliteration could also run over more than one line, incorporating the fourth lifts of surrounding lines or simply maintaining the same sounds in the first three lifts of consecutive lines, and this type of flourish sometimes deserves comment; it crops up especially often in the *Alliterative Morte Arthure* (Benson ed. 1994). A shift from a run of one alliterative sound to a run of another sound deserves note, as it might match and highlight a contrast in the text's meaning; Howell Chickering points out an effective example of this in *Sir Gawain*, at lines 504–515, which works not because the alliterative sounds engage in onomatopoeic mimicry, but rather because the sounds contrast with each other (1997, 13–14). For useful advice on alliterative patterning, readers might consult A. V. C. Schmidt on its use in Langland (1987, 29–79); scholarship has since superseded Schmidt's metrical remarks, but, for readers taken by the topic, his commentary on the patterning of alliteration remains a handy guide with applications in verse beyond *Piers Plowman*.

Present-day readers are probably more familiar with alliteration as a voluntary ornament rather than as an obligatory structural feature, and Middle English poets writing verse in alternating metre used this kind of alliteration too: such local moments of alliteration appear in many poems which have no obligatory alliterative commitments, and elective alliteration deserves a mention here. If alliteration in alliterative verse often offers little interest to the close reader on its own, since the poet had to include it in every line, then alliteration beyond alliterative verse must, by the same token, more often deserve notice for its own sake.

Sometimes the use of alliteration in alternating metres seems deliberately to invoke the tradition of genuine alliterative verse. This is probably what Chaucer is up to when, without abandoning his rhyme scheme or his alternating metre, he deploys alliteration for a battle scene in the Knight's Tale:

Up spryngen speres twenty foot on highte;	*in height*
Out goon the swerdes as the silver brighte;	*like*
The helmes they tohewen and toshrede;	*hew and shred*
Out brest the blood with stierne stremes rede.	*violent*

(*Canterbury Tales*, I 2607–2610)

The larger alliterative passage here sustains itself for some time (2605–2616); Chaucer similarly reaches for alliteration for a naval battle in the *Legend of Good Women* (635–647). These are set-pieces, though, and many other deployments of alliteration probably do not look to the tradition of alliterative verse. Consider the close of Chaucer's *House of Fame*, when Fame gives 'Every tydynge' instructions and sends them out into the world (2111). Here readers can find a line of two alliterative pairs: as the tidings depart, 'Ther mighte I seen / Winged wondres faste fleen' (2117–2118). This offers quite a different effect to those found in fully alliterative verse, sharply contrasting the two halves of line 2118—a headless line, we might note—and it heightens the dazzlement in the prospect being described rather than calling on an external tradition.

John Lydgate wrote at least one poem which uses frequent alliteration, alongside aureate diction of the sort discussed in Chapter 2, to praise Mary (*NIMEV* 99 | *DIMEV* 176; 1911–1934, vol. 1, art. 49). Numerous lines in this poem alliterate: Mary is the 'Cristallyn welle of clennesse cler consigned, / Fructifying olyve of foilys faire and thicke' (37–38), for instance. Nevertheless, the metre remains Lydgate's normal alternating practice (Chapter 4), and Lydgate happily included lines without alliteration: only rhyme stays regular throughout. Some readers valued the poem, for someone painted its fourth stanza on the wall of a church in Suffolk, underneath an image of Mary (Griffith 2011); other quotations from Lydgate appear elsewhere in the church, and such survivals show how people displayed Middle English poems in places well beyond books (Wakelin 2018, 164–183). Other notable, accessible examples of alliteration used as ornamentation in alternating metres occur in some of the *Harley lyrics from the first parts of the fourteenth century and in Robert Henryson's excellent *Fables* (2010). All such moments of elective alliteration hold potential interest; since they were not forced on poets by over-arching formal choices, they might merit more comment than some examples of structural, obligatory alliteration.

Special wording

Another aspect of alliterative verse not strictly metrical but most easily treated together with metre is its distinctive vocabulary. Poets writing alliterative verse tended to convert adjectives to nouns more often than poets writing in other traditions did. In *Sir Gawain*, the adjective *schene* (bright) is converted into a noun referring to the Green Knight's axe when the poet writes that the Green Knight 'with a schunt | the schene withholdes'. If it helps comprehension, imagine adding '[one]/[ones]' or '[thing]/[things]' after the adjective: the axe is a *schene* [*thing*]. Modern English retains this ability to make nouns of adjectives, or to *substantivize*: in *A Woman of No Importance*, Oscar Wilde has Lord Illingworth describe fox-hunting as 'the unspeakable in full pursuit of the uneatable' (1909, 23).

More challengingly, most alliterative verse also uses some specialized vocabulary. Readers meeting the opening events (say, lines 1–466) of *Gawain* for the first time will rapidly encounter some unfamiliar words. A *tulk* and a group of *tulkes* are both mentioned early on (3, 41), and the poet also uses *gome* (151, 178, 179, 405), *hathel* (221, 234), *segge* (226, 394, 437), *freke* (241, 430), *renk* (303, 432) and *wye* (314, 384). All of these words mean 'man'. All apart from *segg* also carry shades of meaning suggesting a warrior, and a knightly or noble warrior at that. Most alliterative poems draw on an inventory of words not generally found elsewhere, and these synonyms for 'man' are just one cluster of examples. Some of these words, such as *tulk*, probably originate in Old Norse (see Dance 2019). Some, such as *gome*, originate in words which were mainly restricted to poetry even in Old English. This poetic-lexical continuity provides some of the evidence for genealogical ties between Old English verse and later Middle English alliterative poetry, despite the mysterious period between them.

Although the use of some of these words seems to have been geographically distributed, these words weren't restricted to regional varieties of English: if they were simply spatially distributed, they would appear with similar frequency in a range of non-alliterative and indeed non-verse works. Instead, they probably constituted a set largely restricted to alliterative verse, and therefore marked as poetic, or indeed as alliterative-poetic. Poets also used such words in alliterating positions disproportionately often, often enough that it might be helpful to think of these words not just as words markedly characteristic of alliterative verse, but as alliterative words. Obligatory alliteration encouraged poets to arm themselves with as many open-class words as possible, to allow for the maximum range of alliterative possibilities, and so fostered the retention of older words not used elsewhere which might serve as synonyms for common concepts such as 'man'. But the presence of these words must also have sent a strong signal about style.

The choice of words in alliterative verse doesn't somehow possess more antiquity or authenticity and doesn't constitute a kind of writing either more traditional or less sophisticated or learned. Alliterative poets also delighted in novelties and used much specialized French- and Latin-derived vocabulary for armour, horses, architecture, and military action. Their verse displays as much erudition as any other body of writings. The legendary story of Troy, for example, regarded as a kind of history during this period, was translated three times into long Middle English poems, two in alternating metres, John Lydgate's *Troy Book* and the anonymous 'Laud *Troy Book*', and one in alliterative verse, John Clerk's †*Destruction of Troy* (1869–1874). Fragments of an alternating-verse *Scottish Troy Book* also survive. All four of these poets sought to transmit a weighty and (to them) historical matter transmitted in a Latin work. Clerk was no less ambitious or outward-looking than his peers in his attempt to tell the story of the Trojan War, a story which Chaucer picks out in his *House of Fame* for its special weight (1464–1474). The *Pearl* Poet, meanwhile, seems to have read the Bible in Latin, a range of French literature, and possibly also Dante.

In using special, alliterative-poetic words, then, alliterative poets did not simply transmit an older or somehow more truly English tradition. Rather, alliterative poets perhaps chose from among a greater number of separate reservoirs of high style than other poets, summoning an array of short synonyms probably associated in hearers' minds with alliterative verse, but also conscripting the same Latin and French linguistic resources available in other sorts of poetry. (For further accessible guidance, see Lester 1996, 101–105; Turville-Petre 2018, 19–36.) The *MED* can help with identifying specialized alliterative-verse vocabulary and other types of terminology.

In close reading, the trick is to take care before resting too much interpretative weight on single words, and instead consider cumulative effect, working at the scale of the passage. Think on the order in which ideas, and words with different shades of meaning, are introduced, especially bearing in mind that self-contained lines in largely unrhymed verse could be flexibly re-ordered, making the poet's control of syntax in some ways freer at the passage scale even as the demands of alliteration required greater care at the scale of the single line. All such elevated lexis takes on more weight when found in groups or clusters rather than singly.

Early Middle English alliterative verse

The basic contours of alliterative verse known from around 1350 onwards have some clarity. A few early Middle English poems in half-lines with nearly systematic alliteration survive, and their relationship to alliterative metre presents more problems. Chief among these stands the *Brut* of Layamon (2001). At some point in the few decades around 1200, Layamon—or Lawman—composed a mythological history of Britain. His *Brut* transmits legends about Britain before and during the coming of the disparate groups speaking Germanic languages which would become English. We have no way of knowing historically in what manner the English language and its first speakers came to Great Britain, and neither did Layamon. However, drawing on earlier myths, especially the tradition spread by Geoffrey of Monmouth, he imagines them as an invading force. Despite writing in English, though, Layamon did not make the earlier proto-English his heroes. Following pre-existing histories of Great Britain, he took the earlier British as protagonists. He devotes several thousand lines to the life of King Arthur, whose reign forms the long poem's large-scale climax—and about whom, I emphasize again, Layamon had no historical evidence.

Here is part of Layamon's rendering of one of Merlin's prophecies, looking forward to Arthur's lifetime:

> Of him scullen gleomen | godliche singen;
> Of his breosten scullen aeten | athele scopes;
> Scullen of his blode | beornes beon drunke.
> Of his eyen scullen fleon | furene gleden;
> Aelc finger an his hond | scarp stelene brond.
> Scullen stan walles | bivoren him tofallen;
> Beornes scullen rusien, | reosen heore maerken.
>
> (Minstrels shall sing beautifully about him; noble poets shall eat of his breast; heroes shall be drunk on his blood. Sparks of fire shall fly from his eyes, each finger on his hand [shall be] a sharp steel blade. Stone walls shall fall before him; heroes shall shudder, their banners collapse. 2001, 9410–9416)

This moment in the poem achieves an unusual density, not least because it contains a doubled reflexive mention of its own making when it promises that 'scullen gleomen | godliche singen / Of his breosten scullen aeten | athele scopes'. The passage also contains a detail original to Layamon and absent from his source, a heroic echo of Christianity's defining ceremony, the Eucharist, in 'Scullen of his blode | beornes beon drunke'; it might be relevant that Layamon says he was himself a priest. Layamon calls back to this passage later in the poem, repeating some elements and changing others (2001, 11489–11499).

Layamon evidently did write half-lines: they can be heard as soon as his verse is read aloud. But his poetry follows neither the specific rules of later Middle English alliterative verse, nor the specific rules of Old English alliterative poetry. Scholars have found various ways to place him inside metrical history but haven't yet achieved a consensus on which placing works best. Readers can, though, attend closely to his inventive use of the ornamentation of both alliteration and rhyme. No overarching theory of metre is needed to see that he plays with alliteration: his lines can alliterate XA|AX or AX|AX, patterns unusual in later Middle English alliterative verse but permitted in Old English verse, and they can also alliterate AX|XA, XA|XA, AA|XA, or AA|AA, patterns generally avoided in both Old English and later Middle English verse.

More adventurously still, the a-verse and b-verse can rhyme instead of alliterating, as in 'Aelc finger an his *hond* | scarp stelene *brond*', and the two half-lines can rhyme imperfectly, as in 'Scullen stan *walles* | bivoren him to*fallen*'. Although Layamon uses rhyme between half-lines, he avoids rhyme between full lines—or in other words, rhyme between adjacent b-verses—which suggests that for him the relationship of a-verse to b-verse takes priority, and that the two halves of the full line seemed in his head two parts of a whole, not unlike the way we perceive the two lines in a rhyming couplet today. Some lines contain no rhyme or alliteration, while a few combine both features, as in 'Feowerti thu*sunde*, | ifeolled to than *grunde*' (10328).

Overall, alliteration remains more common than rhyme in Layamon's *Brut*, but with no strict rule requiring one of the two in every line, the use of either becomes more interesting as a choice. At points alliteration and rhyme might interact fruitfully, as in Layamon's version of the story of King Lear, or rather Leir. Here he describes Cordelia—Cordoille, virtuous and heroic in Layamon as in Shakespeare—overhearing her sisters flattering their father:

> Heo was alre yungest, | of sothe yaer-witelest,
> And the King heo lovede more | thanne ba tueie the othre.
> Cordoille iherde tha lasinge | the hire sustren seiden thon kinge;
> Nom hire leaf-fulne huie | that heo lighen nolden.
>
> (She was the youngest of them, the most keen-witted about truth, and the King loved her more than both of the other two. Cordoille heard the lying that her sisters spoke to the king; she swore a faithful oath to herself that she would not lie. 1963–1978, 1512–1515)

Two rhyming lines (1513–1514) are followed by an alliterating line (1515) in which the previously incidental *l*-words 'lovede' and 'lasinge' find sudden prominent echoes in the pairing of 'leaf-fulne' and 'lighen'. These lines show how alliteration within one line, normal and unremarkable in itself, can engage the latent force of open-class words from adjacent non-alliterating lines. Layamon doesn't want the audience to miss the following conversation's collisions of loyalty, lying, and love.

Layamon's rhymes might also, sometimes, imitate his main source, the rhyming Norman French *Roman de Brut*, written by a man known to us only as Wace. But rhymes also appear at points when Layamon departs from the French, showing that he did not simply follow Wace. What's more, despite adapting French material, the *Brut* also uses few French-derived words. The final result is often richly engaging verse. Here is Layamon's description of one of Arthur's battles against the Romans (another ahistorical myth):

> Tosomne heo heolden | swulc heovene wolde vallen.
> Aerst heo lette fleon to | feondliche swithe
> Flan al swa thicke | swa the snau adun valleth,
> Stanes heo letten seoththen | sturnliche winden.
> Seoththen speren chrakeden, | sceldes brastleden,
> Helmes tohelden, | heghe men vellen,
> Burnen tobreken, | blod ut yeoten;
> Veldes falewe wurthen, | feollen here-maerken.
> Wondrede yeond that wald | iwundede cnihtes overal;
> Sixti hundred thar weoren | totredene mid horsen;
> Beornes ther swelten, | blodes aturnen;
> Straehten after stretes | blodie stremes.
> Balu wes on volke; | the burst wes unimete.
> [...] at than laste | nuste nan kempe
> Whaem he sculde slaen on | and wham he sculde sparien,
> For no icneou na man other there | for unimete blode.

(They engaged together as if the heavens were falling. First they let fly arrows with terrible speed, thick as snow falls down, then they launched fiercely-flying stones. Next spears crashed together, shields broke up, helmets shattered, high men fell, armour broke, blood flowed out; the plain reddened, battle-banners fell. Wounded soldiers wandered all through the woodland; six thousand were trampled there by horses; fighters died there, blood ran; bloody streams followed the paths. Ruin came upon the people; the devastation was beyond measure. [...] At the end, no warrior knew whom he ought to slay and whom he ought to spare, for no man there could recognize another due to the profusion of blood. 13703–13715, 13718–13720)

After a few lines, in a common feature of battle poetry, weapons and armour become the grammatical subjects in depersonalized, general descriptions of an inhuman brawl. Interested readers can compare the battles in the later *Alliterative *Morte Arthure* (Benson ed. 1994) which tells another version of the Arthurian story. Part of the impact of this passage's core comes from a repetition not of particular words but of a syntactic pattern: ten consecutive half-lines end in a verb (13706–13710). Despite Layamon's indulgence elsewhere in the exoticized othering of a variety of pagan foes of Arthur, in this description he makes no effort to distinguish the two sides, or to say that one side fought heroically. He focuses instead on the disastrous result.

I have noted that Layamon adapted his *Brut* from a Norman French poem, Wace's *Roman de Brut* and, as is often the case when dealing with adapted works, checking what was added reveals much. There is a helpful edition of Wace with a parallel English translation (1999); the relevant lines of Wace's work are 12539–12575. Comparing these shows that Layamon has added many of the stranger, more haunting and vivid elements, such as the reddening earth, the two similes of falling heavens and snow, and the startling line about bloodstreams flowing along the forest paths, 'Straehten after stretes | blodie stremes'. This kind of enhancement is characteristic of Layamon's adaptive process (Ashe 2017, 313). Wace does describe a hard-fought battle, with pitiless elements, 'the living trampling on the dying' ('Les vifs les muranz defuler'; 1999, 12572; trans. Judith Weiss). It is Layamon, though, who leaves every fighter in horrifying, bloodied isolation, adding the detail that 'nan kempe' could tell whether anyone else, covered in gore, was friend or foe. The idea of bloodied unrecognizability wasn't new, but Layamon chooses to insert it, and gives it some vim. With its cycles of violence and its strange prophecies, Layamon's *Brut* sits a long way from ideas of a comic, urbane, or courtly 'Middle Ages'. That makes it salutary reading, though, and it does have its interests, its engagements with history and politics, and its formal beauties (Allen, Roberts, and Weinberg eds 2013).

Some other early Middle English survivals suggest that Layamon's verse-craft might represent a tradition rather than one poet's eccentricity. These works include 'The Grave' (*NIMEV* 3497 | *DIMEV* 5543; Conlee ed. 1991, 3–6), the *Soul's Address to the Body* (*NIMEV* 2684.5; Moffat ed. 1987) and *The Proverbs of Alfred* (*NIMEV* 433 |

DIMEV 714; not actually written by Alfred the Great). I take the poem scholars have named 'The Grave' as an example; this poem has already had a mention in Chapter 2. 'The Grave' begins, as noted there, in the past tense:

> The wes bold yebyld | er the iboren were
> The wes molde imynt | er thu of moder come.
>
> (For you a house was built before you were born; for you the earth was marked out before you came from your mother. Conlee ed. and trans. 1991, 1–2)

Then, though, it drags its audience into the future so that it can deliver a set of statements along the lines of 'Swa thu scealt on molde | wunien ful calde' ('Thus you shall dwell, quite cold in the earth', 11). 'Swa thu scealt on molde | wunien ful calde' lacks alliteration and instead has internal near-rhyme. Something similar happens two lines earlier, when the poem says that in the grave 'The helewaghes beoth laghe, | sidwaghes unheghe' ('the endwalls are low, the sidewalls un-high [i.e. low!]', 9). This line also lacks alliteration and uses near-rhyme instead. The rhymes strengthen the case that these are choices rather than lapses or copying errors.

It is all too tempting to see such verse forms, with their irregular mixes of alliteration and rhyme, as merely waystations between more regular Old English verse before them, on the one hand, and, on the other, the larger body of Middle English verse with either regular rhyme or regular AA|AX alliterative lines. These poems sometimes attract an acute version of the attitude lavished on Middle English verse in general, the attitude which sees works as necessary but uninteresting developments on the road to later, worthier writing. In their own time, however, such poems probably represented a normal, understood strain of verse. If historical perspective makes them sound transitional, probably few at the time heard them that way. Moreover, what tends to be read as looseness in their style might more fruitfully be framed as freedom. As in Orm's refusal of regular rhyme or alliteration, these poems reveal early Middle English poets licensing themselves to reduce, vary, or abandon certain formal constraints. And only certain formal constraints. Others were retained, and though from the great height of a European survey these lines might seem chaotic, the poems remain **regular**, in that they obey some observable rules: the half-line system remains, for instance. Freedom in verse is not naturally good—or bad—but the fact that such freer variation in ornament was thinkable makes literary history more exciting. It shows how changes in verse-craft didn't march inexorably towards one end, towards rhymed verse, blank verse, or free verse, but could pause, digress, or simply plough their own furrows.

Alliterative-stanzaic poetry

One other body of verse requires mention here. A group of later Middle English **alliterative-stanzaic** poems feature obligatory alliteration within the line, and some distinctive alliterative verse vocabulary, combined with obligatory end-rhyme, most often marshalled into rhyming stanzas of about thirteen lines (on these stanzas, see Chapter 7). Alliterative-stanzaic poems often achieved a dense and demanding level of obligatory formal patterning. As a discernible lineage rather than just any one poet's isolated experiments, they might reach the pinnacle of such patterning in the whole history of English and Scots verse-craft. Accessible examples include *Three Dead Kings* (Audelay 2009, art. 38), *The Pistil of Swete Susan* (Peck ed. 1991), and *The Awntyrs off Arthur* (Hahn ed. 1995). This last poem, *The Awntyrs*, probably dates from the first part of the fifteenth century and might originate in Scotland or northern England. Scholarship's inability to settle the question of the poem's origins shows how cultural and linguistic distinctions between England and Scotland in this period could be hazy. A later flourishing cluster of descended poems innovating on this tradition certainly survives from Scotland: *Sir Golagros and Gawain* (Hahn ed. 1995), Richard Holland's *Buke of the Howlat* in the late fifteenth century (2014), and *Ralph the Collier* (Lupack ed. 1990), which is probably from the sixteenth century. The surviving evidence makes it hard to say when and how the alliterative-stanzaic tradition got going, though one might perhaps see precedents in some gnomic, barely-studied short poems of the 1270s, brought to light by O. S. Pickering (1992).

Alliterative-stanzaic verse relates to orthodox unrhymed alliterative verse: examples frequently draw on the same special vocabulary. Having a relationship doesn't make two things the same, however, and alliterative-stanzaic poems differ from true alliterative verse in various ways (Weiskott 2016, 103–106). Most obviously, end-rhyme orders them into stanzas, something orthodox alliterative-verse poems avoid. End-rhyme provides a new point of focus, sharply signals the divisions between metrical lines, and probably weakened the metrical caesura separating a-verse from b-verse. With rhyme marking the ends of lines, the non-alliterating fourth lift in the standard AA|AX pattern lost its role marking the line's close for the reader's ear. This loss of purpose for the non-alliterating fourth lift might help to explain why these poems depart more often from the AA|AX norm towards AA|AA patterns.

The metre of alliterative-stanzaic poetry, meanwhile, sometimes shows signs of shifting into alternating beats and double offbeats, losing its metrical caesura:

    x / x x / x x / x x / x
    Of palaies, of parkes, of pondes, of plowes,

    x / x x / x x / x x / x
    Of townes, of toures, of tresour untolde,

    x / x x / x x / x x / x
    Of castelles, of contreyes, of cragges, of clowes.

                         (*Awntyrs off Arthur*, 148–150)

This cluster of lines, alliterating AAAA, delivers a list of royal possessions. They are internally symmetrical: the first halves and second halves of each line have the same metre, thereby departing from another alliterative-verse norm, the tendency of a-verses to avoid legitimate b-verse patterns. (The manuscripts disagree on some points in these lines, but only two of their disagreements would affect the metre, and on those points I think the text printed here correct: Gates ed. 1969, 108–109.) The three lines also resemble each other metrically more than is common in true alliterative verse. In the first and third lines quoted there is little reason to hear caesuras in the middle. After all, syntactically speaking, both lines are four units separated by three pauses of equal significance, marked in modern punctuation by the three commas within the line. These features taken together represent a push towards alternating metre dominated by regular double offbeats and lacking sharp distinctions between a- and b-verses, and this push would intensify in the later-fifteenth- and sixteenth-century Scots alliterative-stanzaic works. Alliterative-stanzaic poems were, then, a slightly different kettle of metrical fish from orthodox later Middle English alliterative verse.

Of all this book's chapters, this one has dealt most with a definable tradition rather than just a formal feature: though metre is key, other things—such as topics, themes, and wording—also mark alliterative verse out as a distinctive field. Yet that space had fuzzy edges. Alliterative-stanzaic poems unite a number of tools found separately elsewhere. Present-day instincts might slice Middle English verse up into distinct traditions tied to named, canonical authors: alternating and alliterative, Chaucer and Langland, say, or perhaps alternating *versus* alliterative, Chaucer *versus* Langland. Alliterative-stanzaic poetry resists such slicing. As I outlined earlier in this chapter, though, despite its roots in Old English poetry, alliterative verse wasn't a parochial, isolated holdout (and indeed Old English poetry too had cosmopolitan sources and interests). Rather, alliterative verse had ties stretching out to other forms. It changed in different poets' hands and over time, too: for instance, fifteenth-century alliterative lines might have become more tolerant of b-verses ending not in a short dip, but directly at the second lift (Weiskott 2023, 79). The hybrid alliterative-stanzaic poems and the freer types of alternating four-beat lines discussed in Chapter 4 perhaps sit at different points on a spectrum between true alliterative metre and the rigorously controlled alternating metre of Chaucer and Gower. I shall say more on the stanza forms of alliterative-stanzaic poems in Chapter 7. For now, though, alliterative-stanzaic poems have brought us to Middle English poetry's other prominent ornamental feature: rhyme.

6
Rhyme

When asked to define poetry, non-expert interviewees today often point to rhyme as a key feature. Yet plenty of modern English poetry doesn't rhyme; the power of not rhyming prompted a rich tradition of early modern worrying about rhyme's vice or virtue (Stagg 2022, 103–136), and a famous note from Milton at the start of *Paradise Lost*. If we consider all the world's tongues, many verse traditions don't indulge in **regular** rhyme, that is, rhyme as a structural, obligatory feature. As a technique in European vernaculars, regular rhyme arrived rather recently, within the last 1500 or 1600 years (Gasparov 1996, 96–102). Regular rhyme has older roots elsewhere: Classical Chinese, for instance, has a rhyme tradition at least a millennium longer.

Old English poets used occasional one-off rhymes for local effects but, almost without exception, not as a regular feature. The hazy figure of the Old English poet Cynewulf wrote a few passages using rhyme as a local ornament, while *The Battle of Maldon* and a handful of short Old English works of the tenth and eleventh centuries intermittently draw on rhyme and related types of aural chime (Stanley 1988; Atherton 2022). The one exception, inevitably called by modern scholars the 'Rhyming Poem', rhymes assiduously, though in inconsistent groupings (Bjork ed. and trans. 2014, 90–97). Regular rhyme appeared in late-antique Latin poetry, and then proliferated in Latin verse during and after the ninth century, so later Old English poets would have met the idea. The survival of one, but only one, exception to the lack of regular rhyme in Old English verse therefore suggests that later Old English poets could imagine regular rhyme, but didn't care to do it; fair enough, for their sophisticated verse already had great beauty.

This rhymelessness changed in the twelfth century. Brief rhyming snatches possibly—only possibly—from around 1100 survive in accounts of the life of a saint, Godric of Finchale (e.g. *NIMEV* 2988 | *DIMEV* 4701, *NIMEV* 3031 | *DIMEV* 4734; see Butterfield 2022, 45–58). The earliest English works I know with full-fledged, regular, sustained rhyme, though, are the later twelfth-century *Poema Morale (septenary couplets; one version in *Fein ed. 2022) and *Ure Feder*, a guide to the Paternoster from around 1200 (four-beat couplets; *NIMEV* 2709 | *DIMEV* 4305; Morris ed. 1898, 55–71). In unleashing sustained, regular rhyme in English, these poets imitated Latin and French models. These particular poems probably aren't the earliest composed examples of sustained English rhyme, for two reasons: first, they seem comfortable with rhyme in English, and, second, many twelfth-century poems have disappeared, so it would be odd luck for the very first rhyming examples to survive.

Despite being relatively new to English verse, regular rhyme found success. The majority of Middle English poems have obligatory rhyme at the end of each metrical line. All but two of the other poems known to me contain obligatory alliteration instead. Alliterative-stanzaic poems, discussed in Chapter 5, employ both types of ornament at once. (The remaining two poems receive some discussion at the present chapter's end.) Surviving manuscripts show that readers thought rhyme very important, and took pleasure in it (Sawyer 2020, 110–143). Those making books sometimes spent much labour time highlighting rhyme visually on the page. When rhyming verse was copied in prose lineation, scribes used punctuation to signal rhyme structures instead. The visual highlighting of English rhyme peaked in these centuries (Fein 2019b, 44), and the graphic presentation of English verse form has never since asserted itself so much. Today, this tendency towards the visual pinpointing of form survives only in more self-conscious traditions, such as concrete poetry.

Though rhyme's presentation has changed, many other aspects of rhyme have stayed consistent across the last eight centuries. To classify how rhyme works, we can break down what a syllable is. Every syllable has a vowel sound at its core; it might also have consonant sounds at its start, at its end, or at both its start and its end. In the most typical type of rhyme, two syllables agree in their vowel sounds and any following consonants but disagree in what precedes their vowels. (Technically, in normal rhyme the nuclei and codas of two syllables match, but their onsets differ; I refer curious readers to Ferber 2019, 58–74.) Thus, in present-day English, *slight* and the second syllable of *unite* rhyme, because their vowel sounds and following consonant sounds match, while their starting consonant sounds differ, and because lexical stress falls on the second syllable in *unite*. To indicate a rhyme pair, I shall italicize the rhyming words and link them with a colon, thus: *slight:unite*. A rhyme can involve multiple syllables, if they keep matching—as in *slighted:united*—and I shall discuss this type of multi-syllable rhyme in more detail later in this chapter.

All of these aspects of rhyme hold true for Middle English as well as for modern English. Most poets writing rhyming verse in Middle English matched the vowels of the final beats of rhyming lines, and any sounds which followed those vowels. Just like present-day English, Middle English offered fewer chances for rhyme than words in Latin and the Romance languages descended from Latin. Chaucer says as much when closing one of his shorter poems: since 'rym in Englissh hath such scarsitee' (scarcity), he says, 'it ys a gret penaunce' to translate his French source closely (*Complaint of Venus*, 79–82). His comment really, of course, makes a boast, for he has just successfully rhymed his way through the problem.

Because many features of rhyme haven't changed, Middle English rhyme often rewards the kinds of reading applied to rhyme from later periods: it invites readers to seek an implicit connection between words, whether through similarity or contrast. So, as a simple example, when Hoccleve turns during his *Regiment of Princes* to attack the vice of avarice—that is, greed and miserliness—he laments the lack of charity among the great:

>   Allas, thogh that a man deskevere and pleyne   *reveal; show*
>   To many a lord his meschevous miserie,   *wretched misery*
>   The lord nat deyneth undirstonde his peyne;   *doesn't deign to*
>   He settith nat therby a blakberie.   *doesn't give a damn*
>   (4712–4715)

Misery and *blackberry* do not rhyme as neatly in present-day English as they did for Hoccleve, but one needs no special historical knowledge to grasp the pairing's force. In moving from 'miserie' to 'blakberie' the audience descends through at least two significant distinctions: abstract to concrete, and (recalling Chapter 2) French derivation to originally English vocabulary. The descent prompts bathos: what's a blackberry set against human misery? Unlike many examples of the bathetic, though, this moment of bathos produces not comedy, but rather anger at the lord's unconcern. The bathos invites resistance: readers might well demur at the descent to the blackberry. Hoccleve's choice of another seemingly happy, English-derived word for the third and final instance of this rhyme sound, in the next line, confirms the indignant, bitter contrast drawn:

>   He settith nat therby a blakberie.
>   Welthe in the lordes sail blowith ful merie,   *lord's*
>   But the needy berith his sail so lowe   *needy one bears*
>   That no wynd of confort may in it blowe.   *comfort*
>   (4715–4718)

Again, if readers listen to the poetry they will need no particular Middle English expertise to unpick rhyme of this sort. They can have the courage to attend to such rhymes much as they would read rhyme in later poetry, without feeling that they need a special toolkit.

Just as in later poetry, this reading will often entail thought about rhyme's interaction with other aspects of verse, most prominently **enjambment**. Just as in later poetry, too, readers should stay alert for subtleties such as the relaxation of the normal expectation that adjacent rhymes should differ. For example, *Sir Orfeo consists, in its standard text, of 302 couplets, and in only two instances do two adjacent couplets rhyme on the same sound to create a four-line chain of **through-rhyme**. Both points matter to the story: the first is a moment of high emotion (325–328), the second a moment of high tension (453–456). These moments reward close study, but one need not know anything specific to this period to grasp them.

The most crucial shift necessary in reading rhymes from this period involves attitude, not technique. In reading Middle English rhymes we must, as much as possible, unthink the common twenty-first century sense that rhyme always amuses. The glut of couplet verse in the eighteenth century left the English couplet, in particular, sounding pat, and the twentieth century brought further challenges to rhyme's reputation. Rhyme's persistence in popular song and advertising jingles has probably done it no favours among the sorts of people who look down, perhaps unwisely, on popular songs and advertising jingles. Middle English poetry challenges readers to think themselves back into a context in which obligatory rhyme could carry grief as easily as comedy. This shift of attitude matters more than any knowledge of the details of rhyme's use, and in truth a good number of modern poets have proved the point themselves. Anyone doubting rhyme's power can try reading the sorrowing couplets of Thom Gunn's 'Lament' (2017, 167–171); while doing so, readers familiar with the Middle English poem *Pearl (Stanbury 2001) can ponder the resonance between these two works (Sawyer 2021b). To relearn rhyme's value is the main thing. Some other specificities of rhyme in the period do, however, deserve comment.

Masculine and feminine

I have already noted that a rhyme can last for multiple syllables, as in the rhyme *slighted:united*. Critics conventionally call single-syllable rhyme **masculine rhyme** and multi-syllable rhyme **feminine rhyme**. These words don't mean that poets and readers thought there was something feminine about multi-syllable rhyme; they just make a distinction. Present-day and recent English poets have tended to prefer masculine rhymes, but poets writing in Middle English enjoyed using both; a pleasing Hocclevian example of feminine rhyme is *assaillid:faillid:entaillid*. Although masculine rhyme involves matching one syllable with one syllable, the words involved need not be monosyllabic. All matches between monosyllabic words, such as *nam:cam*, produce masculine rhymes, but so can matches in which one or both words have multiple syllables, such as *contree:see*, *innocence:apparence*, *conquerour:honour*, *chivalry:worthy*, or *mariage:corage*. Due to changes occurring between Middle and present-day Englishes, readers today might need to rejig their sense for where beats might fall in some of these words to grasp the rhyme.

The distinction between feminine and masculine rhymes rarely fires an entire reading on its own, but it can take on significance in concert with other features, or if rhyme of one type occurs in a passage or poem which sticks in general to the other. As a simple example, note the slight extra emphasis achieved by the masculine rhyme on 'wo' following two feminine rhymes when Gower has a speaker complain that he suffers in love

such a passion		F
That men have gret compassion,		F
And everich be himself merveilleth	*every one by*	F
What thing it is that me so eilleth.	*ails*	F
Such is the manere of mi wo		M
Which time that I am hire fro.	*when; from*	M

(*Confessio Amantis*, VI.169–174)

Chaucer appears to have preferred feminine rhymes for the closing couplet of his **rhyme royal** stanza (see Chapter 7), so much so that a masculine rhyme at the end of one of his rhyme royal stanzas stands out slightly. A noted philosophical passage in *Troilus and Criseyde*, in which Troilus agonizes over the problem of free will, includes some examples (IV.953–1078). Chaucer created three important masculine rhymes in this passage by rhyming the stanza's closing couplet on *necessité* (IV.958–959, 1042–1043, 1056–1057). Anyone questioning free will might mention the concept of necessity, but we might also reasonably suspect that Chaucer was playing games here. *Necessité* makes the stanza-closing rhymes vary from their usual feminine pattern just when the concept of necessity troubles Troilus most, pushing questions about who controls the story and the poetry into the reader's consciousness. A couplet earlier in the poem presages the link (II.622–623). Similarly, a slightly unusual masculine rhyme at the end of a rhyme royal stanza in the Clerk's Tale marks a disjunctive moment of travel in the story (*Canterbury Tales*, IV 783–784). Most later poets using the rhyme royal stanza do not display the same firm preference for feminine rhymes in the closing couplet; this is not an aesthetic failing on their part, merely a difference in practice.

Sometimes poems adopt the contrast between feminine and masculine rhyme as a structuring feature. The hymn 'Stond wel, moder, under rode' (*NIMEV* 3211 | *DIMEV* 5030), for instance, imagines a dialogue at Jesus' crucifixion between Jesus and his mother Mary in stanzas rhyming *aabccb*, and in most stanzas the *a*- and *c*-rhymes are feminine while the *b*-rhymes are masculine. Jesus speaks each stanza's first three lines, Mary the fourth, fifth, and sixth, while the masculine *b*-rhymes tie the two units of speech together:

'Moder, now tarst thou might leren	F	*first; learn*
What pine thole that children beren,	F	*pain [they] suffer; bear*
What sorwe have that child forgon'.	M	*sorrow [they]; have lost*
'Sone, I wot, I can thee telle,	F	*I know*
Bute it be the pine of helle,	F	*Unless; pain*
More sorwe ne wot I non'.	M	*sorrow I do not know.*

(Duncan ed. 2013, art. I.91, 37–42)

This stanza, like the poem as a whole, might make for strange reading today, but it has a humane breadth: Mary's suffering joins with the pain of all those who have lost children, no small topic for listeners in a time of high youth mortality rates. The hymn survives in various forms, occasionally with music, in six manuscripts. I quote here from an edition based on a copy with attached music, and which intervenes in the text in an attempt to reconstruct metre (Duncan ed. 2013); readers can compare another text from the Harley Manuscript (*Fein ed. 2014–2915, art. 60, 37–42).

Perfect and imperfect

Rhyme can also be **perfect** or **imperfect**, and in Middle English writing this distinction might map onto a distinction between different types of poetry. In a perfect ('true' or 'full') rhyme, the rhyming vowel and all following sounds match exactly; in an imperfect ('half', 'near', or 'slant') rhyme, sounds match in a variety of less exact ways. As with masculine and feminine rhyme, these terms don't imply a judgement of quality. That said, Gower and Chaucer stuck to perfect rhymes, and the later lineage of poets who saw themselves as writing poetry in the same tradition—for example, Lydgate, Hoccleve, Ashby, Skelton, the poet of *The Assembly of Ladies*—usually followed them in this. An imperfect rhyme wasn't a solecism in any absolute sense, but some poets clearly preferred perfect rhymes.

However, the evidence suggests that other poets, in certain contexts, did use imperfect rhymes (Jefferson, Minkova, and Putter 2014). In one group of such rhymes, dubbed **feature rhymes**, the consonants after the rhyming vowel differ, but are related to each other in the manner in which the mouth produces them. In the examples *Rome:one, tyme:pyne* or *everychone:among*, for instance, the consonants are all nasals. In another group, **subsequence rhymes**, one of the rhyming words has a plural word-ending which the other lacks: in the **Sultan of Babylon*, *songes:amonge* and *knyghtes:light* are both subsequence rhymes (in *Lupack ed. 1990, lines 1992–1994, 2087–2089). Both types of rhyme might have ties to performance aloud, and occur particularly, though not exclusively, within a set of romances in quatrains rhyming *abab* (Jefferson, Minkova, and Putter 2014, 632–634). Both types also occur in modern pop music, and modern poetry: Elizabeth Bishop could rhyme *long* and *Babylon* (2004, 'The Burglar of Babylon', 38, 40). One should not regard all imperfect rhymes as mistakes, but rather ask what they might do for the poet, and whether they align the work with Middle English verse romance.

Autorhyme and punning rhyme

Normal perfect rhyme involves agreement between the vowels of two syllables and all sounds which follow those vowels, but disagreement between the preceding consonants. A poet can, though, abandon the difference entirely, and write rhymes which sound too perfect, rhyming elements which sound wholly identical. (Technically, in these rhymes not just the nuclei and coda of the syllables but their onsets too all match.) There are two ways to create identical rhymes: rhyming a word with itself—**autorhyme**—and rhyming a word with a different word that happens to sound the same—**punning rhyme**.

Autorhyme is, on its own, a simple technique. Poets can, however, work well with simplicity. When Dante Alighieri uses the name *Cristo* (Christ) for rhyme in his fourteenth-century Italian *Comedy*, he only ever rhymes it with itself: from his point of view, what other word would be worthy? Although the poet of *Ure Feder*, the earliest known sustained English poem in four-beat couplets, was no Dante, the poem displays some effective uses of autorhyme joined with through-rhyme:

> Hwaswa ne forgefeth heore hating,
> Ne God ne forgeveth him na thing;
> Gode men, lusteth to me: ower hating
> Forgeve ye thin sunful efenling,
> Luve him for Godes thing.
>
> (Whoever doesn't forgive others' hatred, God will definitely not forgive him any deed; good men, listen to me: forgive your sinful peer for your own hatred, love him for God's sake. Morris ed. 1898, 219–223.)

The autorhyme on *hating* pointedly switches from a distancing pronoun—'heore [*their*] hating'—to a nearby one—'ower [*your*] hating'—so that hatred comes closer to home. Early in the history of English rhyme, autorhyme found some appreciation, then. However, later Middle English and Older Scots writers seem to have avoided autorhyme, possibly regarding it as too simple.

The other route to a fully matched rhyme is **punning rhyme**, in which a poet rhymes words with different senses that sound the same. Punning rhyme invites readers or listeners to tease out differences from the seemingly identical. Such rhymes were (and are) a feature of French verse-craft, where the technique is sometimes called *rime equivo(c)que*. Example teaches punning rhyme better than description. Gower had a knack for this rhyme technique, and in one virtuoso passage describing the Lover's desire his *Confessio Amantis* delivers six punning rhymes in a row:

And in this wise, taketh kepe,	*matter; take note*
If I hire hadde, I wolde hire kepe;	*keep her*
And yit no Friday wolde I faste,	*fast, i.e. abstain from meat*
Thogh I hire kepte and hielde faste.	*held secure*
Fy on the bagges in the kiste!	*Fie; [money] chest*
I hadde ynogh, if I hire kiste.	*enough; kissed*
For certes, if sche were myn,	*surely; mine*
I hadde hir levere than a myn	*I'd rather have her; mine*
Of gold. For al this worldes riche	*riches*
Ne mihte make me so riche	*Could not*
As sche, that is so inly good.	*inwardly or very*
I sette noght of other good,	*set no store by*
For mihte I gete such a thing,	*if I could get*
I hadde a tresor for a king.	*I'd have a treasure [fit]*

(V.79–92)

Poets could pun in rhyme in several ways. They could rhyme related words in different parts of speech. When Gower rhymes *riche:riche*, the two words are related, but the first is a noun while the second is an adjective. This pattern reverses, adjective coming first, in the *good:good* rhyme: as in present-day English, 'good' as a noun in Middle English could mean virtue—'try to see the good in people'—or a possession—'overpriced goods'—and so the second *good* here introduces an ambiguity. Through that ambiguity the rhyme might remind us that romantic love can raise someone's attention from worldly goods but can also distract them from moral goods. Sometimes the plural and singular forms of the same noun could create feminine punning rhyme when *is* followed the singular instance: Chaucer rhymes *placis* with *place is* (*Canterbury Tales*, III 1767–1768). Another form of punning rhyme arises from homophones: otherwise unrelated words which sound the same by chance. Thus Gower's *myn:myn* rhyme, in which the possessive pronoun *mine* and the mineral noun *mine* are unrelated, yet sound the same. Note how Gower reveals the meaning of the second *myn* across a line-break, with 'Of gold' beginning the next line. In a similar manner, Chaucer can rhyme the month 'May' with the verb 'may' (*Canterbury Tales*, I 1461–1462, 1511–1512).

Punning rhyme had a history in English before Gower and Chaucer in the fourteenth century. The earlier **The Owl and the Nightingale* uses it, for instance, at one point deploying an emphatic rhyme on *thought* as two different parts of speech:

> The nyhtegale in hire thouhte
> Atheold al this and longe thouhte
> Hwat heo tharafter myhte segge,
> Vor heo ne myhte noht alegge
> That the ule hedde hire iseyd.
>
> (In her mind the nightingale
> Pondered all this and focused on
> What she might say next
> Because she couldn't rebut
> What the owl had said to her. *Fein ed. and trans. 2022, 391–395)

Punning rhymes crop up repeatedly in *The Owl and the Nightingale* (e.g. 285–286, 339–340, 367–368). The *Ure Feder* poet might have liked autorhyme, but *Ure Feder* uses punning rhyme well too. For instance, the poet writes that God created humanity with upturned faces for a reason:

> Neb upwardes He him wrohte;
> He walde thet he of Him thohte,
> Thet He lufede him mid thohte
> Al swa the lauerd thet him wrohte.

> (He [God] made him face upwards; He wished that he would think of
> Him, so that he would love Him in his mind, as the lord who had made
> him. Morris ed. 1898, 95–98)

These lines ask listeners to pick carefully through pronouns to track whether God or man is meant, an effect I have tried to point up by anachronistically imposing uppercase H in pronouns referring to God; the one surviving manuscript offers no such help. Speakers of early Middle English, used to a more complex pronoun system and more flexible syntax, would have had an easier time here, yet not, I think, an outright easy time. Perhaps the pronoun thicket might have challenged even a first-language audience. The verse puts a heavier load on its listeners' attention to make them work out the human–divine relationship described. The poet achieves not just through-rhyme but also a chiastic (ABBA) pattern of rhyme words. The *wrohte:wrohte* rhyme is pure autorhyme, preceded by the same word in each case, with only the slight tweak that the second *wrohte* occurs inside a relative clause rather than as a main verb. The *thohte:thohte* rhyme, however, works across different parts of speech: *thohte* appears first as a verb, then as a noun, nestling punning rhyme at the structure's heart.

Some examples of punning rhyme defy both easy classification and straightforward judgement of tone. The most verbally mobile character in *Troilus and Criseyde* is the go-between Pandarus, a figure capable of fellow feeling and magnificent rhetoric, but also of creepy manipulation. Pandarus often provides pithy proverbs, which grow less and less comforting as the story's tone darkens. Near the most joyous point in the poem, before things begin to collapse, he advises the heroine Criseyde that she must shore up her relationship with Troilus rather than waste time wondering what is making Troilus worried. When a building burns, he says, firefighting takes priority over finding out:

> How this candel in the strawe is falle.
> A *benedicite*! For al among that fare   *bless us!; amidst that business*
> The harm is don, and fare-wel feldefare!   *farewell thrush!*
> (III.859–861)

'Fare-wel feldefare' seems from context here to mean something like the idiom 'the horse has bolted'. Is *fare:feldefare* a punning rhyme? It appears to qualify: the consonants before rhyming vowels match, and *feldefare* is in origin a compound noun, so its second part independently matches in rhyme. And who wouldn't succumb to a wit that fits *fare* into one couplet three times, twice as a rhyme word and in three distinct senses? In the context of Pandarus' all-too-persuasive advice to Criseyde, though, the punning rhyme's ease feels untrustworthy. Bird images crop up repeatedly in *Troilus and Criseyde*, and here the image of the departed thrush presages Criseyde's future, which holds a departure from Troilus and Troy both. The burning building invoked earlier in the stanza foretells Troy's future too. While Chaucer does not describe the city's destruction, foreknowledge of its coming sack hangs over the whole poem for both the audience and those among the characters, who are blessed—or cursed—with prophecy (I.64–84, V.1520–1526). As with many things Pandarus says, this punningly rhymed proverb can leave an audience at once impressed and queasy.

Filler rhyme

The types of rhyme discussed so far seem fairly crafty. Like poets at other times, though, writers in Middle English also sometimes deployed **filler rhymes** (or 'rhyming tags'): stock words or phrases which can fill out a line with a rhyme sound the poet otherwise needs and lacks. Filler rhymes often take the form of intensifying or validating asides, suiting a wide variety of semantic contexts. For some examples, we can turn to *The Prik of Conscience, a storehouse of knowledge about life and the afterlife mixed in with brisk ethical advice, and the early English poem that circulated most widely. Describing the heavenly city inhabited by the saved after the world's end, the text says that

<blockquote>

Aboute the cyté shal nought be seen	*city; naught*
Bot bryght bemes oonly, as I ween,	*but; beams; think*
The whiche shul shine fro Goddes face	*shall; from*

(*Morey ed. 2012, VII.1563–1565)
</blockquote>

Here the phrase 'as I ween' was probably adopted by the poet to provide a rhyme for 'seen'. This phrase and other convenient filler phrases are scattered through the poem: things are known 'withouten dout' (VII.5) and facts are offered 'as the book tellus' (*tells*; V.1346). One thing marking these out as filler material is their isolation within the surrounding syntax: if the demands of rhyme were relaxed, these fillers could be removed without disruption. Indeed, when people rewrote Middle English verse into Middle English prose, they often stripped out the filler rhymes, showing that readers at the time could recognize them—although we don't know what they called them.

Scholarship sometimes associates the use of filler rhymes with verse romances in particular, or with the utilitarian style of teaching poems such as *The Prik of Conscience*. Certainly, in the context of rough-hewn romances and teaching poems, modern experiments in performance suggest that filler rhymes offered a flexibility absent in the more precise works of Chaucer and Lydgate (Zaerr 2005, 197–198). However, Chaucer, Gower, and their successors did use filler rhymes too. Chaucer wrote them throughout his career: the opening rhymes of his early *Book of the Duchess* rely on them (1, 3), and anyone who reads his late-career *Canterbury Tales* will learn the seemingly firm but rather empty phrase *for the nones*, which Chaucer rhymes with *at ones, but ones, noon is, Amazones*(!), and, most often, *bones*. Chaucer also rhymed fillers such as 'I wene' (*Troilus and Criseyde* III.499, V.1088) and 'as the storie telleth us' and its equivalents (*Canterbury Tales*, V 655, VI 622, IX 128). In Middle English, a filler rhyme seems not to have been, in and of itself, a failing, and such rhymes had no associations with a particular genre, or with works lacking prestige.

Readers should, then, hold back from resting too much interpretation on one of these rhymes. However, while some authorities would tell students simply to avoid writing about filler rhymes, and while critics have sometimes ruled them out of craft analysis in the past, I think we can find use and pleasure in them. True, filler rhymes resist, in their emptiness, the kind of intense local scrutiny that propelled close reading in the middle and later parts of the twentieth century (Spearing 1964, 9–10). Yet scholars have traditionally cut Chaucer's filler rhymes, at least, some slack (Lumiansky 1951). While Chaucer undoubtedly wrote well, I suspect a circularity in this granting of leeway: because they already trust in Chaucer's brilliance, critics have more willingly laid aside their existing aesthetic assumptions for his poetry. Present-day criticism is perhaps better placed to appreciate ostensibly empty things, and also to consider how the individual phrases in filler rhymes, bleached of meaning, as linguists metaphorically describe them, might work in aggregate.

One can, after all, read a pattern of such filler material together. The intermittent tags in *The Prik of Conscience* lend a more personal air to a poem that otherwise feels dense in information. The poet seems to have expected the work to be read aloud, and the brief first-person filler remarks about the truth and authority of its contents would then have become asides for the person reading to inhabit. The same is probably true for the filler tags in many other instructional poems in Middle English, such as *The Prik of Conscience*'s nephew-poem *Speculum Vitae* (Hanna ed. 2008), and in many romances; perhaps it holds for tags in Chaucer's works and those of his successors too.

Rhyming tags also have a role in the anticipation of verse form. A central feature of regular rhyme is foresight, or perhaps more truly fore-hearing. Without even trying, someone experiencing the beginning of a unit of rhyme will find themselves anticipating what might match and complete the structure. This effect undergirds the pleasures we feel both in rhymes which feel fated, and in rhymes that surprise and pique us. It also drives the comic force felt when verse veers toward taboo words in second or third rhyming positions. Filler rhymes affect expectation, for if the audience have heard a filler before, they might fill it in faster than the text, or someone reading the text aloud, can deliver it. When the filler rhyme provides the first part of the rhyme unit, its presence gives readers time to anticipate what might follow; when a filler rhyme closes a rhyme unit, the audience might have guessed it already. In both cases the filler rhyme offers a moment's cognitive rest, and that rest perhaps makes filler rhymes more significant within passages which otherwise tend towards surprising rhymes.

When genuinely empty, meanwhile, filler rhymes perhaps function as form-for-form's sake. In prose, they wouldn't exist. Since form alone brings them into being, they let poetry display its bones, its construction. Therefore, something counterintuitively modernist hangs about them. They invite thought on rhyme in general: don't all rhymes possess, in a smaller degree, the same kind of artificiality?

Elective rhyme

Rhyme occasionally appears in alliterative verse. In some ways, rhyme holds more interest, and stands out more, when it appears optionally in unrhymed works. At one point in William Langland's long, searching examination of self and society, *Piers Plowman*, the figure Anima, a personification of the soul, discusses the fourteenth-century church and its problems. Worldly wealth, he argues, stops priests doing their jobs; let the authorities take that wealth away and have priests live by their tithes:

> If possession be poison, | and inparfite hem make,   *imperfect them*
> Good were to deschargen hem | for Holy Chirches sake.   *It'd be good;*
>   *unload*
>   (Langland 1995, XV.564–565)

This is a pithy end rhyme, thumping home Anima's radical point all the more forcefully in its unrhymed context. Or at least, a mostly unrhymed context: within this short passage, before and after these two lines, two other lines occur which both extend the poison metaphor and both end-rhyme on *-alle* (XV.560, XV.566). Langland's use of rhyme offers a useful starting point for readers interested in the deployment of rhyme in other alliterative poems (Schmidt 1987, 67–79). Elective rhyme provides one point of consonance between earlier verse-craft and twenty-first-century writing: as unrhymed verse has become more common, sudden rhyme has returned as a technique for contemporary poets (e.g. Hayes 2018, 23, lines 13–14).

Early blank verse

Even Middle English alliterative verse is not free of ornament, however: regular alliteration counts as a kind of recurring ornamentation, and a restrictive one too. Just two Middle English poems known to me are **blank**, that is, metrically regular but displaying neither regular rhyme nor regular alliteration. The existence of these two examples matters. We associate blank verse, as an idea and a phrase, with the sixteenth century: it holds a place alongside the sonnet as one of that century's most prized and prestigious formal legacies. Various factors, such as the posthumous fame of Shakespeare's plays and the canonical position of John Milton's *Paradise Lost*, have cemented blank verse into literary history as a major innovation. Blank verse implicitly splits off the sixteenth and following centuries from Middle English. We should, therefore, pause over the fact that at least two poets writing in Middle English invented blank verse, independently and at different times.

    The first of these is Orm. As noted in Chapter 4, his septenary lines have neither obligatory alliteration nor obligatory rhyme: they are blank. The second poet is the anonymous writer who, in 1445, wrote a partial translation of a poem by the classical

Latin poet Claudian (*NIMEV* 1526 | *DIMEV* 2573; Flügel ed. 1905). Circumstantial evidence hints that the poet might be the cosmopolitan friar Osbern Bokenham, but the case is uncertain. This translation's preface appears in orthodox rhyme royal stanzas, and its conclusion uses **septenary** lines in a rhyme royal rhyme scheme. But its core, the main body of the work, is in loose blank septenaries. The original Latin poem obsequiously praises the fourth-century warlord Stilicho. In Englishing it, the anonymous translator probably sought to transmit both the prestige of Classical Latin learning and lessons about princely virtue. Here is part of a passage in which the poem tells Stilicho, in the second person, about all the vices that he doesn't display:

> Thou first defoilest Avarice, the modir of wrecchidnessis,
> That evir in havour is nedy founde, and thristeth more and more,
> Which with chekis right wide sette ope, golde dolve depe seergith;
> With her also thou puttist to shame her loothsom norice, Ambicion,
> Which evir lyeth waite at chambir doorys and at riche mennys gates.

> (First you overcome Avarice, mother of miseries, who is ever found needy in one who has much and thirsts yet more and more, who searches for deep-buried gold with cheeks set open as wide as possible; with her, you also put to shame her loathsome nurse, Ambition, who ever lies in wait at chamber doors and at the gates of rich men. Flügel ed. 1905, 117–121)

Leaving aside this flattery's oiliness, the translator was clearly alert to potential effects created by (among other things) alliteration absent from his source ('dolve depe'), but just as clearly chose not to use regular alliteration or rhyme. Like the sixteenth-century reinventors of blank verse, this fifteenth-century poet seems to have sought a form that would match the lack of ornament in the classical Latin verse being translated. In the sole manuscript in which it survives, the English poem serves as a parallel text to the Latin, presented on facing pages (Edwards 2001, 270–274), and its dense, inward-turning syntax also suggests an attempt to echo the Latin original.

No connection links Orm and the translator of Claudian: they wrote about 250 years apart from each other. Neither the *Ormulum* nor the fifteenth century Claudian translation seem especially suited to modern tastes. However, we should remember that two unrelated poets came up with blank verse in centuries which supposedly lacked this formal idea. This fact punctures literary histories which see Middle English as a dull area not given to invention or change. We must read received literary history gratefully, but without taking its pronouncements for granted. Ordering a set of poems chronologically has useful effects, but always brings in an illusory sense of progress, and diverts attention away from important oddities. A return to the poems themselves often enjoyably complicates things. The case of Middle English blank verse reminds us that, as I said in Chapter 1, poetic form and verse-craft aren't like engineering, and don't improve or accumulate over time.

7
Stanzas

Having considered the choice and ordering of words, the arrangement of phrasing, the metrical marshalling of lines, and adornment with rhyme and alliteration, we can zoom out further to think on poetry's larger-scale patterning. Verse lines can come in one continuous flow, or they can come in short, repeated patterns: stanzas. Continuous verse is **stichic**, verse in stanzas, **stanzaic**.

Stichic verse, whether in alliterative or alternating metres, still has shape: it has line length—horizontal length—and it has total—vertical—length, which is itself an aspect of form. The dominant stichic forms in Middle English are alternating-metre couplets and alliterative verse. Both of these involve a recurring pattern of pairs: two lines in the couplet and two half-lines, a-verse and b-verse, in each alliterative verse line. At least in the surviving evidence, neither Middle English nor Older Scots developed three-line stichic rhyme patterns. Dante's *terza rima*, an interlaced continuous structure rhyming *aba bcb cdc ded efe* and so on, appears once in some experimental English scraps attributed, somewhat unconvincingly, to Chaucer ('Complaint unto His Lady'); *aaa* tercets only, to my knowledge, feature as components within longer and more complex stanza designs. Somewhere between stichic and stanzaic sit a very few poems in *laisses*, distinct runs of lines sharing the same end-rhyme—that is, with **monorhyme**—with no set rule that each *laisse* must have the same number of lines (e.g. NIMEV 4085 | DIMEV 6528 and NIMEV 4162 | DIMEV 6672: †Morris ed. 1872, 89, 92). *Laisses* resemble the more modern idea of the verse paragraph.

Stanzaic verse, meanwhile, offers mid-level formal structures between the small scale of the line and the large scale of the whole poem. Like regular rhyme, the concept of the stanza is largely a Middle English innovation in English verse-craft. Around 1100, the stanza was uncommon. Old English poems are stichic, though shadows of a sense for syntactic sections tied off by refrains appear in *Deor* and the spectacular *Wulf and Eadwacer*, a poem that everyone should read. The idea of the stanza was not uncommon in the British Isles: at this time, Welsh, Irish, and Latin poetry sometimes used stanzas. Yet, at the beginning of the present study's period, the idea of the stanza makes its way only fitfully into the early Middle English written record. A stanza rhymed *aabb* might appear in one of the short early twelfth-century poems attributed to Godric of Finchale:

> Sainte Marie virgine,
> Moder Jesu Cristes Nazarene,
> Onfo, scild, help thin Godric,
> Onfang, bring hehlic with the in Godes ric.

> Sainte Marie, Cristes bur,
> Maidenes clenhad, moderes flur
> Dilie mine sinne, rixe in min mod,
> Bring me to winne with self God.

(Saint Mary, virgin, mother of Jesus Christ the Nazarene, receive, protect, and help your Godric, receive and bring him gloriously with you into God's kingdom. Saint Mary, Christ's bower, purity of virgins, flower of motherhood, wipe out my sins, reign in my heart, bring me to joy with God Himself. *NIMEV* 2988 | *DIMEV* 4701; Jones ed. and trans. 2012, 102–103)

These *aabb* stanzas do not, though, cleanly separate from stichic couplets, two stanzas rhymed *aabb aabb* being functionally the same as four couplets rhymed *aabbccdd*. It is content, syntactic division, and, in three copies, accompanying musical notation that mark separations in this piece, not the rhyme scheme. What I quote as one poem of two stanzas might be two poems (Butterfield 2022, 47), hinting at the messy challenges of editing discussed in Chapter 9.

Stanzas only firmly emerge in the English written record in thirteenth-century poems. Probably the earliest extant sustained story in stanzas, later in the thirteenth century, is *Sir Tristrem (Lupack ed. 1994). Once again, then, the study of earlier poetry shows how something one might take for granted as a natural feature of writing really happened at a particular time in English and might have happened otherwise or at other times. The limited number of surviving early Middle English examples doesn't necessarily show that few were composed: when a cluster of poems in English survives in a multilingual later-thirteenth-century manuscript, Oxford, Bodleian Library, MS Digby 86, it suggests a lively and fruitful tradition, closely linked to French and Latin writings (Fein ed. 2019a).

The wide range of stanza-forms used in the period defies a full accounting here: *DIMEV*, which represents only what survives and has been found, not a full picture of what once existed, records more than eighty known types. Readers must therefore check the introductions of editions for accounts of particular forms, and remember that, as with other aspects of verse form, Middle English stanzas often respond well to close reading techniques used for other periods. This chapter sketches out particular types of stanza and aspects of stanza design significant in Middle English but less familiar today.

Subdivided stanzas

In the fourteenth century, before and beyond the work of Chaucer and Gower, English fostered several traditions of subdivided stanzas. Students and readers encounter one particular example using such stanzas, *Sir Gawain and the Green Knight*, more often than others. Since this poem is more often read, it can be hard to tell what in its stanza design is radical and what isn't. The poem joins several different features in its unique stanza, and these features are not always found together elsewhere. I shall start with *Gawain* and then move back in time to consider its predecessors.

The *Gawain* stanza form begins with a variable number of lines of orthodox alliterative verse, which form its main body. The stanza concludes with what has traditionally been called a 'bob and wheel'. The **bob** is a very short, one-beat line. The 'wheel' is a subsequent rhyming quatrain of alternating three-beat lines permitting double offbeats: that is, a quatrain in a radically different metre, ornamented by rhyme rather than alliteration. Here, for instance, is the end of the startling stanza in which Gawain approaches the Green Chapel for his fateful meeting, hears a weapon being honed for his neck, and steels himself to continue:

> What! hit wharred and whette | as water at a mulne;
> What! hit rusched and ronge, | routhe to here.
> Then 'Bi godde,' quoth Gawan, | 'that gere, as I trowe,
> Is riched at my reverence | me reken to mete
> > Bi rote. [*bob*]
> Let God worke, we lo!
> Hit helpes me not a mote.
> My lif thagh I forgo,
> Drede dotz me no lote.'
>
> (*Gawain*, 2203–2211)

The bob and the following quatrain together create a structure rhyming *ababa*, and given that the number of previous alliterative lines varies, we could say that the whole stanza has a rhyme scheme of *x...xababa*. Since the main body of the stanza lasts for a varying number of lines, it is internally or temporarily stichic, heightening the potential surprise of each bob, which an audience cannot predict as they might if the main body consistently took up the same number of lines. I know of no other Middle English poem which uses internally stichic stanzas in this way. The bob normally joins syntactically to the preceding alliterative line, as here, while its rhyme opens the rhyming sequence which follows. The bob therefore forms a kind of bridge between the stanza's two main components.

Unlike the *Gawain* poet's radical combination of the stichic and the stanzaic, and of alliterative and alternating metres, the bob and the wheel occur in other poets, and don't always occur together. The phrase *bob and wheel* therefore doesn't describe one unified formal entity: there is no set 'bob and wheel stanza' beyond *Gawain*. The phrase also leaves us without a proper word for the stanza's first part, the variable-length block of alliterative lines, and what we cannot name we cannot easily study. I shall retain the word *bob*, but I shall use *frons* to refer to the first part of such subdivided stanzas, and **cauda** to refer to the second part (the two terms originate in Latin words meaning 'front' and 'tail'). Now we're in a position to think through the wider history of subdivided stanzas and consider some techniques for their study.

Subdivided stanzas of various types occur earlier. For instance, they appear in some of the *'Harley lyrics' (Fein ed. 2014–2015). These poems display a plethora of forms, and sometimes elegant sophistication. Consider, for instance, the dense first stanza of this poem of—mock?—repentance:

Weping haveth myn wonges wet	*Weeping has wet my cheeks*
For wikked werk ant wone of wyt!	*work and lack of wit!*
Unblithe Y be til Y ha bet	*Unhappy; have improved*
Bruches broken, ase Bok byt,	*Breaches; as the Book bids*
Of levedis love, that Y ha let,	*ladies'; have blocked*
That lemeth al with luefly lyt.	*[ladies] Who shine all; lovely*
Ofte in song Y have hem set,	*have described them*
That is unsemly—ther hit syt!	*in ugly ways—there it stands!*
Hit syt ant semeth noht,	*it stands and is unseemly*
Ther hit ys seid in song;	*Where*
That Y have of hem wroht,	*What; about them wrought*
Ywis, hit is al wrong!	*Certainly*

(*'Weping haveth myn wonges wet', Fein ed. 2014–2015,
art. 33, 1–12; see Fein 1997, 380)

This is alternating-metre verse (not true of all poems in the manuscript: Cable 2009), with both regular alliteration and regular end rhyme joining lines. The ornamental alliteration and the rhyme run slightly in counterpoint: the rhyme scheme is *ababa-babcdcd*, but the alliteration scheme is *aabbccddddee*. Some **total consonance** also appears in this first stanza: *wet:wyt, bet:byt*, and so on. On this point, though, the poem shows the danger of taking any poem's first stanza alone as a guide for the whole work's form: total consonance only intermittently emerges in the poem, and so isn't basic to its stanza design.

A subdividing metrical shift occurs after the eighth line, when the lines shorten from four beats to three. This shift matches the move away from the *a*- and *b*-rhymes, but comes during the *d*-alliterating section. When a stanza contains a metrical shift of this sort, conventional rhyme notation can use subscript numbers to indicate the numbers of beats in the preceding lines: to describe this stanza, for instance, we can write $ababab_4cdcd_3$, meaning eight lines rhymed *ababab* and in four beats, then four lines rhymed *cdcd* and in three beats.

One other device, **concatenation**, also marks the metrical shift here: an open-class word, *syt*, occurs in both the line before the metrical shift and the line following the shift (8–9). Concatenation of this sort gave poets another way to link up different units in their poems. Alert readers of this poem will spot that the last and first lines of stanzas tend to concatenate too—repetition of *wrong* ties the first stanza to the next (12–13)—and Chapter 8 will revisit the use of this technique between stanzas, rather than lines.

The stanza thus comes in two parts, distinguished from each other both by metre and rhyme: it has a *frons* and a *cauda*, but no bob. With the shift in rhyme and metre comes a shift in thought: the stanza's final lines become more distanced from the past 'song', saying, for example, that the regrettable lies sit 'Ther' rather than here. *Caudae* often do differ from their preceding *frontes* in content as well as form, and the resulting sense of a shift has effects somewhat akin to the contrast between octave and sestet in a Petrarchan sonnet. This tendency to shift offers one route into writing about subdivided *frons–cauda* stanzas: readers can also consider whether the relationship between *frons* and *cauda* varies or stays consistent across a poem's different stanzas.

This subdivided stanza aesthetic enjoyed a long summer of appreciation. Other *frons–cauda* poems include examples in **alternating metres**, such as the **Dispute between Mary and the Cross* (Fein ed. 1998), a poem titled †*Festivals of the Church* by its editor (†Morris ed. 1871, 210–221), and the *plays of the so-called 'Wakefield Master' (*Epp ed. 2017, arts 3, 8, 9, 12, 18). The *frons–cauda* format also appeared in **alliterative-stanzaic** poems, usually in twelve- or thirteen-line stanzas. Examples include *Three Dead Kings (Fein ed. 2014–2015, art. 38), *Somer Soneday* (NIMEV 3838/DIMEV 6125; in Turville-Petre ed. 1989, 140–147), **The Pistil of Swete Susan* (Peck ed. 1991), **The Four Leaves of the Truelove* (Fein ed. 1998 art. 4), **The Awntyrs off Arthur* (Hahn ed. 1995), and Richard Holland's *Buke of the Howlat* (2014). Poets writing alliterative-stanzaic verse in subdivided stanzas didn't switch to alternating metre for the *cauda*, but rather wrote *caudae* in alliterative half-lines, typically three **a-verses** followed by a conclusive **b-verse** to end the stanza:

    With gret questes and quelles,   [xx/xx/x, a-verse]
    Both in frethes and felles.   [xx/xx/x, a-verse]
    All the dure in the delles,   [xx/xx/x, a-verse]
    Thei durken and dare.   [x/xx/x, b-verse]

        (**Awntyrs off Arthure*, Hahn ed. 1995, 49–52)

In having alliterative-verse *caudae* these poems differ from the stanza of *Gawain*, and show how the concept of the *cauda* worked across different metrical families.

I turn now to the bob. Non-specialist resources (e.g. Cuddon 1998, 92–93) often associate the bob with alliterative and alliterative-stanzaic verse. However, both the majority of bobs, and the earliest examples in the surviving evidence, appear in alternating-metre verse (Stanley 1972, 422–425). Some bobs appear in carols (see Chapter 8), and others appear in poems that have no metrical division of *frons* from *cauda*: a bob graces the stanza of *Sir Tristrem, for instance. This romance, probably written in the later thirteenth century, delivers a knockabout version of the story of Tristan and Iseult; I have mentioned it already as probably English's first known stanzaic narrative poem. In the following stanza Tristrem politely explains his origins to the discourteously ignorant King Mark:

The king seyd, 'Where were thou born?	
What hattou, *bel amye*?'	*are you called, fair friend*
Tristrem spac biforn:	*spoke up*
"Sir, in Hermonie.	*Hermonie* (a place-name)
Mi fader me hath forlorn,	*left*
Sir Rohand, sikerly,	*certainly*
The best blower of horn	
And king of venery	*hunting*
For thought.'	*imaginable.*
The lasse gaf Mark forthi,	*Mark didn't care one bit*
For Rohand he no knewe nought.	*did not know.*

(*Lupack ed. 1994, 529–539)

This bob focuses the audience's attention on thought—here, imagination as well as cogitation—not something in which Mark himself much indulges. Note that the two lines in the stanza after the bob stay metrically the same as the rest of the stanza, in three beats, and aren't fully separated by rhyme: this stanza's design is *ababa-bab₃c₁bc₃*. If a *cauda* exists here, its presence is weaker, distinguished not by a lasting metrical shift or by wholly new rhymes, but only by the bob's eruption. Some stanzas in *Tristrem* vary from this pattern and retain the *a*-rhyme after the bob rather than the *b*-rhyme (*ababbabab₃c₁ac₃*, e.g. lines 34–44), but this too ties the lines following the bob more closely to the rest of the stanza than one might expect in a *cauda*. *Sir Tristrem* uses an alternating metre, and its probable time of composition predates both any known alliterative-stanzaic poem, and the flourishing of alliterative poetry in the fourteenth century's second half. The existence of alternating-metre poems with bobs earlier than surviving alliterative-stanzaic poetry suggests that the bob was probably adopted into English verse from Latin and French models, rather than originating in alliterative or alliterative-stanzaic verse-craft. Later in the surviving evidence, the bob then appears in alliterative-stanzaic poems as something which can lead into a metrically distinct *cauda* (*Pistil of Swete Susan*, *Somer Soneday*). Not all alliterative-stanzaic poems in subdivided *frons–cauda* stanzas feature a bob in their stanza, however: *The Awntyrs off Arthure* and *Three Dead Kings* have stanzas subdivided between *frons* and *cauda*, but lack bobs, for instance.

To modern ears, bobs can sound jolting when merely read aloud, but perhaps unfamiliarity causes this effect. Alternatively, Ad Putter has suggested that early readers might have sung or declaimed each bob with something like a normal line's length (2015, 155–157). Normally, in a predictable stanza with a bob, the bob offers emphasis for one idea, but if sustained to a normal line's length in performance, it would also offer time for the audience's minds to rest. Such a resting or pausing quality would fit with the fact that the bob is almost always end-stopped and usually joins syntactically to the preceding lines rather than those which follow.

The Middle English subdivided stanza wasn't a single, agreed stanza template. Rather, poets had a palette of options for the design of subdivided stanzas. This palette included (1) distinctions of metrical length between a *frons* and a *cauda*; (2) division by bob between a *frons* and a *cauda*; and (3) ornamentation through regular rhyme or, in alliterative-stanzaic poems, through regular rhyme and regular alliteration. *Sir Gawain and the Green Knight* stands unique, in the surviving evidence, in choosing to distinguish *frons* and *cauda* not by metrical length but by metrical family—alliterative metre versus alternating metre—and in choosing an internally stichic *frons*, so that the bob would come as a surprise. The *Gawain* stanza seems a radical offshoot, with no matching ancestors or direct descendants known. Other poets, meanwhile, found other combinations that suited their other purposes.

Tail rhyme

The splitting of the stanza into *frons* and *cauda* was not the only way poets could achieve a neat tailing-off effect. **Tail rhyme** offered another option. Like *frons–cauda* stanzas, tail rhyme is a family of formal approaches rather than a single stanza template; like the *frons–cauda* concept, it usually involves a metrical shift in line length. It entered English through the imitation of Latin and French models. Its simplest form is an *aabccb* pattern. Early in the anonymous verse life of **Saint Eustace*, Eustace and his family become refugees:

All that hym lovyd went hym fro,	*abandoned him*
Bot his wyfe and his childer two;	*Except*
Son thei must wende.	*Soon; leave*
Erly or it was any daye,	*before any daylight*
Stylly thei stalkyd away	*Silently; crept*
By a woddys ende.	*wood's edge*
To a water thei gan gone,	
A schype thei found sone anon;	*soon, right away*
Thei went ther-tyll.	*to it*
Into the schype thei went tho,	*then*
His wyfe and his chylder two;	*children*
The water was sterne and ylle.	*alarming; dangerous*

(in **Shuffelton ed. 2008, 118–129)

The 'tail' b-lines are metrically shorter in this $aa_4b_3cc_4b_3$ stanza, but, unlike a *cauda* concentrated at a stanza's end, they disperse across the structure. The passage's language stays simple, and this version of Eustace's story emphasizes event and plot over devotion or meditation. Much of the effect of these lines must be assessed cumulatively, together with the preceding and following stanzas. I'd note, though, the presence of the wood and the water in tail- lines—the water modified by adjectives providing some important tonal colouring (129)—and the fact that the second tail-line quoted, unlike the others, integrates syntactically with the previous line (123).

Tail rhyme meant an approach to rhyme patterns, not a single stanza stencil, and it extended to many designs besides $aa_4b_3cc_4b_3$. Perhaps roughly a third of the surviving Middle English verse romances use some variety of tail rhyme. *Sir Amadace*, for instance, uses $aa_4b_3cc_4b_3dd_4b_3ee_4b_3$ stanzas (Foster ed. 2007), and several dozen poems on this model survive. The base of the stanza could be a triplet rather than a couplet, and the pattern of beats did not need to be 4–3, as in *Sir Perceval of Galles* (in Braswell ed. 1995), which rhymes—readers brace, brace—*aaabcccbdddbeeeb*; just a few poems rhyming $aa_4b_3cc_4b_3dd_4b_3$ have reached us, but they show that this scheme was thinkable too; the Harley poem *'Ne mai no lewed lued libben in londe' (Fein ed. 2014–2015, art. 40) shows that a poet could attach a *cauda* of seven shorter lines in a row to a tail-rhyme *frons*: *aabccbddbeebffgggf*, combining tail rhyme and a subdivided stanza.

Tail-rhyme stanzas usually have syntactic breaks after *b*-rhymes. Stanzas syntactically divided after each *b*-rhyme emphasize the *b*-rhyme lines, and when the stanza has more than two tail lines, readers will hear the *b*-rhyme more often than the other rhyme sounds. In close reading, a poet's choice to run syntax straight through *b*-lines, either locally or systematically, might deserve comment. It is also worth looking out for places where tail- rhyme structure coordinates with other features, such as a stanza in which the tail lines have **masculine rhymes** and all other lines have **feminine rhymes** (*Fein ed. 2014–2015, art. 30, 11–20), or vice versa.

The form was useful for memory and recitation, and probably had strong ties to performance aloud, though not necessarily to composition on the fly. Poets seem, from the surviving evidence, to have often chosen longer tail-rhyme stanzas for romances, and it is in romances that tail rhyme has received its most sophisticated study (Purdie 2008). Yet more than 200 tail-rhyme poems survive (at the least), and the majority are short, less- or non-narrative pieces. These pursue a variety of purposes, such as devotional meditation on the Crucifixion (*Audelay 2009, art. 19), love lament, political satire, and jingoistic rejoicing at victory in battle (*Minot 1996, art. 4). At our period's end, works in tail rhyme were still being copied and read. For example, a witty piece in the Findern Manuscript (*c.*1500) warns of the duplicity and false complaints of men who claim to be in love in four *aaabaaab* stanzas:

Whatso men seyn,	*Whatever*
Love is no peyn	*pain*
To them, serteyn,	*certainly*
But varians;	*But [rather] changeability*
For they constreyn	
Ther hertes to feyn,	*feign*

Ther mowthes to pleyn	*mouths; complain*
Ther displesauns.	*suffering*

(Duncan ed. 2013, ll.39, 1–8)

Though tail rhyme gradually fell out of use in sustained narratives, poets have drawn on it for shorter poems in every century since. Sometimes, though not always, they have done so intentionally to echo early poetry, as in Algernon Charles Swinburne's rewriting of Thomas Malory's Middle English prose into $aaaa_4 b_4 ccc_4 b_3$ stanzas in his *Tale of Balen*.

Both subdivided *frons–cauda* stanzas and tail rhyme received short shrift from Chaucer. His surviving works never use *frons–cauda* stanzas, and he only deployed tail rhyme in his Tale of Sir Thopas, which is a parody. As Sir Thopas goes on, Chaucer heightens the joke by suddenly tossing in a bob to create extra chaos (VII 793 and following). Either through ignorance of the form or deliberate, studied incompetence, one of the Thopas bobs joins syntactically to what follows rather than, as is normal for bobs, what precedes (VII 823). With no surviving commentary from Chaucer, we cannot know his motives. It seems likely, though, that he wished to distance himself from the more provincial and less erudite settings which his urban, urbane, and sometimes outright aristocratic readers might have associated—fairly or not—with tail rhyme. His surviving works also suggest a strong preference for consistent metrical line lengths: in almost all of his poems, he picks a length of either four or five beats, and then sticks to it like glue. Such a preference rules out metrically distinct *caudae*. However, although Chaucer didn't favour subdivided stanzas, he did deploy and shape several other iconic Middle English stanza forms.

Chaucerian stanzas

In Chaucer's work, and for some of the poets following him, we can speak of some specific, set stanza patterns. Literary history particularly associates two stanza forms with Chaucer: **rhyme royal** (sometimes spelled 'rime royal') and the **Monk's Tale stanza**. Both have curious features, and both lived on beyond Chaucer's own career.

Chaucer's first rhyme-royal poem was probably the beautiful *Parliament of Fowls*. Early in the *Parliament*, the speaker stops reading at dusk:

The day gan faylen, and the derke nyght,	*began to end*
That reveth bestes from here besynesse,	*tears beasts; business*
Berafte me my bok for lak of lyght,	*took from me*
And to my bed I gan me for to dresse,	
Fulfyld of thought and busy hevynesse;	*filled by; sombreness*
For bothe I hadde thyng which that I nolde,	*did not want*
And ek I ne hadde that thyng that I wolde.	*also; did not have; wanted*

(85–91)

A rhyme royal stanza is seven lines, rhymed *ababbcc*; some evidence suggests that this number defined the stanza for people at the time (see *James I's *Kingis Quair* in Mooney and Arn eds 2005, line 1378; and Cowen ed. 2015, lines i–ii). The stanza contains both an interlaced quatrain (*abab*) and a pair of couplets (*bbcc*), but the two structures contest control of the fourth line and second *b*-rhyme. Only the *b*-rhyme sounds thrice in the stanza, lending its third appearance, the fifth line, an excessive or unbalanced quality. At the unbalanced fifth line, the stanza drops the interlaced (*ab*) expectations it has given to readers or listeners and slides suddenly into adjacent (*bb*) rhyme. Manuscript evidence suggests that readers in the period noticed this unbalanced quality themselves (Sawyer 2020, 123–8). Seven lines proffer a lot of space to fill with one syntactic unit, and so most rhyme royal stanzas have at least one major syntactic break. This can fall anywhere, but it often comes around the start, middle, or end of the fifth line, just where the rhyme feels least stable, and before the resolution of the closing couplet's new *c*-rhyme. In the stanza just quoted, the main syntactic break comes at the fifth line's end. Like a fighter jet deliberately designed to be unstable for extra manoeuvrability, the rhyme royal stanza has imbalances that make it flexible and endlessly surprising.

Chaucer used rhyme royal for several *Canterbury Tales* and throughout *Troilus and Criseyde*. A small host of other poets picked the stanza up in the following century: various anonymous poets—some of them probably women—plus named poets such as Hoccleve, King James I of Scotland, Lydgate, John Capgrave, John Metham, George Ashby, Robert Henryson, and John Skelton. Later poets could experiment with rhyme royal. For example, the anonymous later Middle English *Storie of Asneth*, a tale distantly originating in midrash, uses the rhyme royal *ababbcc* scheme for its rhymes, but adopts a different metre and much ornamental alliteration (in *Peck ed. 1991). Rhyme royal has had a long afterlife. Shakespeare deployed it in *The Rape of Lucrece*, W. H. Auden used it for comic effect in his *Letter to Lord Byron* (2007, 79–113; see especially lines 141–147); Thom Gunn wrote rhyme royal stanzas, perhaps for their Middle English associations, in 'Merlin in the Cave' (1993, 81–84); and Evie Shockley has used the rhyme scheme in a formally inventive lyric on the times, 'the way we live now ::' (Shockley 2017, 6, 103).

The **Monk's Tale stanza** rhymes *ababbcbc*, and is so called for its most noted use, in Chaucer's Monk's Tale. The Monk delivers a lugubrious series of short retellings of the falls of illustrious men. Here is the ending of his three-stanza story of Holofernes, an Assyrian general who, in the biblical (or apocryphal) Book of Judith, invaded Israel only to find his career and self both suddenly cut short:

> But tak kep of the deth of Oloferne: *take note*
> Amydde his hoost he dronke lay a-nyght,   *at night*
> Withinne his tente, large as is a berne,   *barn*
> And yet, for al his pompe and al his myght,
> Judith, a womman, as he lay upright

Slepynge, his heed of smoot, and from his tente *head off smote*
Ful pryvely she stal from every wight, *secretly; hid; person*
And with his heed unto hir toun she wente. *town*
(*Canterbury Tales*, VII 2567–2574)

The *b*-rhyme rings insistently throughout, giving the whole stanza its coherence. Unlike rhyme royal, this stanza does split into two balanced halves. Like rhyme royal, though, it often delivers a fruitful interplay between its own shape and other aspects of the verse: here, readers might note Judith's arrival exactly at the second half's start, and the eruption of **enjambment** at the ends of the fifth and sixth lines as she goes about her deadly work. The enjambment after the fifth line falls within an adverbial phrase, 'upright / Slepynge', and so strikes particularly hard. The *c*-rhyme bursts in as the last new element in any Monk's Tale stanza, and in this example it pleasingly marries up with the point in the stanza of Holofernes' downfall and Judith's stealthy escape. Many routes can be taken through the *ababbcbc* pattern, and this is just one. Chaucer was the first poet to write Monk's Tale stanzas with five-beat lines (*ababbcbc$_5$*) but the same rhyming pattern appeared in English before Chaucer's career in a four-beat pattern (*ababbcbc$_4$*): an early example mourns Edward III (*NIMEV* 205 | *DIMEV* 366; *Fein ed. 2014–2015, art. 47). The stanza was perhaps roughly half as popular as rhyme royal, but experienced similar sustained use to and beyond the end of the fifteenth century, by the prolific Anonymous, together with writers such as Hoccleve, Lydgate, Charles d'Orleans, Dunbar, and Henryson. It might have possessed moral and devotional associations (Gillespie 2005, 93–95), though these did not limit its possible subjects.

As in other areas of verse form, poets can undertake extra, elective tasks within their general stanzaic obligations. Several poets using Chaucerian stanzas in this period could, when they wished, reduce the number of rhyme sounds in a stanza. George Ashby wrote a stanza rhyming *ababbbb* and then carried the *b*-rhyme on as the *a*-rhyme of the following stanza (*Complaint of a Prisoner in the Fleet*, in *Mooney and Arn eds 2005, 162–171), and John Metham, a poet given to playful variations of stanza shape, has one stanza rhyming *aaaaaabb* in his romance *Amoryus and Cleopes* (ll. 1989–1996). Such moments of variation are detected more easily when one reads the verse aloud, even if only aloud in one's head.

Divisions of alliterative verse

This chapter has so far focused on end-rhymed verse in alternating metre and alliterative-stanzaic forms. Most of the surviving orthodox alliterative verse poems might look purely stichic. However, some, such as *Cleanness, Patience, St Erkenwald*, and *The Siege of Jerusalem*, appear to have been composed to a norm of a hard break in syntax every four lines. These four-line clumps rather defy the word *quatrain*, and perhaps even *stanza*: only syntax creates them. We might expect a true quatrain, by contrast, to have some kind of connective ornamentation, such as a shared alliterating sound. Yet some support for the reality of these four-line units comes from the distribution of topic- and speaker-shifts in these poems, very frequently falling on the first lines of four-line units: design explains this correlation much more efficiently than coincidence can. In the sole surviving copy of *Cleanness* and *Patience*, too, small signs in the left margin appear to mark off some of these units; the manuscript is not an absolute authority, but it does show us authentic evidence of one reader from the time—the scribe—responding to the material. There the four-line clumps sit, inviting us to think about their formal relations. In a similar example, the consecutive alliteration or through-alliteration in the *Alliterative Morte Arthure* (Benson ed. 1994)—alliteration, that is, running on the same sound over multiple consecutive lines—might parcel certain parts of that poem up into different, but related, units. Since ornamentation does connect these groupings in the *Morte Arthure*, they come closer to normal stanzas than purely syntactic four-line blocks do. Little scholarship has moved from observing these patterns in alliterative verse to using them in close reading, and rewards might await adventurous readers who do.

The poet of the alliterative *Wars of Alexander* wrote in four-line units of syntax too, but also went further, grouping these units in yet larger blocks, sometimes called strophes, of twenty-four lines (Duggan and Turville-Petre eds 1989, xxii–xxiv). The *Alexander* strophe works as a regular, predictable chunk; twenty-four lines last long enough that each block feels like a short poem in its own right. The poet was willing to have dialogue end in the middles of the smaller four-line units, but rigidly maintained the divisions between the full twenty-four line blocks. The twenty-four line blocks of the *Wars* often begin with temporal or spatial positioning: *Then, When, Thare, Sone,* and *Now* all often broach new chunks. Perhaps the measured succession of consistent larger units lent more stateliness to what the poet evidently regarded as a grand topic. The regular subdivisions found in some alliterative-verse poems form an intriguing coda to the topic of the stanza: even in some seemingly stichic verse, poets tried out subtle partitions.

8
Grander Designs

Beyond the building of individual stanzas, poets can play with successive different forms. Constants and contrasts from passage to passage of poetry probably mattered even more in Middle English poetry than they do now, given the more linear experience offered by poetry heard aloud. Verse-craft offered poets various techniques for pointing up or pointing out the relations between different stanzas, and also other, subtler ways to play stanzas off against each other.

Refrains, carols, burdens

Among these techniques, the **refrain** might have the most familiarity for readers who know modern English verse. A refrain is a repeated section of text, usually either a phrase or a whole line, typically present at each stanza's end, returning each stanza to the same place. Refrains have persisted in poetry and song right up to the present: Edgar Allen Poe's 'The Raven' takes 'nothing more' and then 'nevermore' as refrains; 'As in the Prison of Grevous Displesaunce' is the refrain in the twenty-seventh ballade in Charles d'Orleans' fifteenth-century collection now known as *Fortunes Stabilnes* (excerpted in *Mooney and Arn eds 2005). The technique appears in many European verse traditions comparable to or influential on Middle English. In the fifteenth century, poets found the final *c*-rhyme of the Monk's Tale stanza particularly well suited to service as a refrain, but the technique was used widely, across many forms, and had no single set of associations.

A special type of refrain appears in a specific verse form of this period, the **carol**. Although some early carols celebrate Christmas, 'carol' didn't at this time have the topical specificity it has today, specific to Christmas. Instead, a particular formal arrangement defines the Middle English carol: it begins with a short single-stanza **burden**, and then proceeds through a series of uniform stanzas, most often quatrains, with the burden repeating after each stanza. The burden resembles the chorus of a present-day pop song, and when people performed carols together, the group perhaps had one singer deliver the stanzas and then joined to sing the burden. Readers familiar with Shakespeare's *As You Like It* will have encountered later surviving forms of the carol and its burden (2.5; 2.7, 175–194; 3.2, 243–244; 4.2; 5.3); Thom Gunn wove a heartbreaking pun on the technical, verse-craft sense of 'burden' into his late poem 'The Gas-Poker' (2017, 184–185, l. 18).

Carols are primarily a fifteenth-century phenomenon in the written record. The small amount of surviving written evidence for the carol before the fifteenth century doesn't necessarily mean that fewer carols circulated: the younger a manuscript of a poem, the higher that manuscript's chances of reaching us today. Many carols were probably composed to be sung rather than recited. Indeed, people probably composed some carols aloud, much as some present-day songwriters generate songs by playing aloud with words and brief sequences of melody. Surviving mentions of carols often link them to dance, raising fascinating practical and theoretical questions (Chaganti 2018). That said, some carols probably emerged through more written, pen-crafted modes of creation. A whole collection of carols in what seems to be a deliberate, crafted, and written sequence appears within the works of John the Blind Audelay (*2009, art. 35).

As an example of a carol having nothing to do with Christmas, consider the opening stanzas of this biting lament on the times, in which I mark the burden with 'B' and the lines of the stanzas proper with 'S':

God be with Trewthe wher he be;	B	*Truth wherever*
I wolde he were in this cuntré!		*wish; country*
A man that shuld of Trewthe telle,	S1	*wishes to*
With grete lordes he may not dwelle;		
In trewe story, as clerkes telle,		*report, as the learned*
Trewthe is put in low degré.		*held in low esteem*
God be with Trewthe wher he be;	B	
I wolde he were in this cuntré!		
In laydys chaumberes cometh he not;	S2	*chambers*
Ther dar Trewthe setten non fot;		*dares; set no foot*
Thow he wolde he may not		*Though; wishes*
Comen among the heye mené.		*high society*
God be with Trewthe wher he be;	B	
I wolde he were in this cuntré!		

(*NIMEV* 72/*DIMEV* 113; Duncan ed. 2013, art. II.96, 1–12)

The sad truth about the lightly personified figure of Truth (5) is that he is excluded from high places (6), and the poem marches bitterly through different places where Truth is not, all pinned to the burden's general insistence on Truth's absence. The poem closes, in further stanzas not quoted here, by mentioning Mary as a source of consolation, but it spends most of its length lamenting the state of the world rather than encouraging devotion. Its stanzas rhyme *aaab*$_4$, with the *b*-rhyme matching the burden, so that the full rhyme sequence is *aaabbb*$_4$ *cccbbb*$_4$, and so forth. This combination of *aaab* stanzas and a *bb* burden crops up very commonly in Middle English carols, though other patterns of rhyme, lineation, and metre appear. While a carol must have a burden to qualify as a carol, no rule prevented carols from, for instance, having a refrain built into each stanza as well. The presence of the burden persists, though, and the burden above all other features defines the carol as a form.

A poem using either a refrain or a burden circles out from and back to a central pole. The repetition might convey steadfastness or confinement, but sometimes the repeated lines play differently as different stanzas recontextualize them. It is usually useful to ask how refrain or burden lands differently in the context of each different stanza. Repetition creates expectations which can be met or, especially at a poem's end, refused.

Fixed forms

In later Middle English, the French-derived **fixed forms** offered another way to muster and link stanzas in a recognizable pattern. Just as we today maintain an idea of the sonnet as one form which nevertheless admits much variation among sub-types, the fixed forms could vary somewhat within themselves. I write 'fixed forms' as an Anglicization of *formes fixes*, the modern name for a set of French verse templates that influenced poets right across the wide ambit of French influence in north-western Europe (Strakhova 2022, 24–35).

Of these forms, only the *ballade* achieved truly sustained English use (Cohen 1915, 222–299). (As well as a defined form, in Middle English itself *ballade* was sometimes used simply to mean a stanza of any kind. Using this sense in present-day writing causes confusion, and I shall avoid it.) The English *ballade* most prototypically consisted of three **rhyme royal** or **Monk's Tale stanzas**, each ending with an internal one- or two-line refrain, and carrying **through-rhyme**, that is, all stanzas using not only the same rhyme scheme but also the same rhyme *sounds*. If we add capitalization to rhyme scheme notation to show a refrain, typical *ballade* rhyme schemes are *ababbcC ababbcC ababbcC*, *ababbcbC ababbcbC ababbcbC*, or *ababbcBC ababbcBC ababbcBC*. Part of the pleasure in this approach to ordering stanzas lies in clever responses to tight self-imposed rules. Refrains and through-rhyme test a poet's ingenuity, and their solutions can reveal much about a poem's priorities.

Surviving English *ballades* date from the late fourteenth century and the fifteenth century. 'To Rosemounde', a short poem attributed to Chaucer and containing a famously fishy simile, consists of three through-rhymed Monk's Tale stanzas with a refrain line, *ababbcbC ababbcbC ababbcbC*; in the three-*ballade* sequence—or triple *ballade*—'Fortune', also attributed to Chaucer, two speakers each get one *ballade*, and then the third contains dialogue from both, giving Fortune the last word. To take a couple of fifteenth-century examples, Lydgate's longer *Flour of Courtesye* ends with an orthodox *ballade* (in MacCracken ed. 1911–1934, lines 246–270), and Charles d'Orleans' fifteenth-century Ballade 118, *'O fy, Fortune! Fy thi dissayt and skorne!' delivers three Monk's Tale stanzas (in *Mooney and Arn eds 2005).

Charles d'Orleans cuts a fascinating figure in fifteenth-century English poetry (Perry and Arn eds 2020). French Duke of Orleans, he found himself captured by the English at the 1415 Battle of Agincourt and spent a quarter-century in relatively comfortable English captivity. Unusually, he learned and wrote in English as well as French; as one of the earliest nameable exophonic writers working in English, he counts as a long-range predecessor of, say, Elif Shafak or Joseph Conrad. Charles probably wrote the body of English work now known as *Fortunes Stabilnes* (Charles d'Orleans 1994; a modern editor applied the title), which has a claim to be English's first long lyric cycle. *Fortunes Stabilnes* is at once a running chain of verse detailing, in an elusive and allegorized fashion, a story of joy and sorrow in love, and an anthology of many individually handsome poems. The sequence includes runs of *ballades*, and displays a range of forms possible within the nominally 'fixed' idea of the *ballade* (Strakhov 2020, 68–81), including the *'Double Ballade' of six Monk's Tale stanzas all sharing the same refrain in their eighth lines, and therefore the same *c*-rhyme in every stanza (in *Mooney and Arn eds 2005).

Fourteenth-century French *ballades* sometimes ended with an **envoy** (also *envoi*, *lenvoy*), a kind of dangling pendant-poem, usually one stanza in a different, shorter form, often addressing a patron. The envoy travelled into English, where its forms and roles shifted in ways that helpfully trouble the apparent fixity of fixed forms (Engler 1990, 62–76; Nuttall 2018). John Gower used envoys in his French *Cinkante Ballades*, and envoys appear in various short English pieces linked to his acquaintance Chaucer: the *Complaint of Venus*, 'Fortune', 'Truth', 'Lack of Steadfastness', and the 'Complaint of Chaucer to His Purse'. Already an uncertainty lurks around the envoy in the poetry attributed to Chaucer, for two of these short poems, the 'Envoy to Bukton' and the 'Envoy to Scogan', not only bear 'Envoy' as the name for the whole work, but also come with a short dangling envoy-to-the-envoy at the end. In the fifteenth century, the English envoy grew: poets wrote sustained multi-stanzaic pieces to dangle from much longer works, as well as shorter chasers to follow short poems. Hoccleve, for instance, includes a three-stanza envoy to his *Regiment* (1999, 5440–5464). In Lydgate's mighty *Fall of Princes*, the envoys become extended discussions of his poem, patron, and verse-craft (Nuttall 2018, 41–43), embellished with showy form. At the end of the *Fall*, he includes a handful of different short poems; manuscript copies overtly label two of these as envoys, and one of those two envoys runs on for more than 200 lines (1924–1927, IX.3303–3540). Given that Lydgate had just finished one of English's longest poems, then or now, perhaps he deserved his victory lap.

The two other main French-derived fixed forms are the *virelai* and the roundel. A few English poets used the word *virelai*, but no instance of the actual French *virelai* form survives in early English (Nuttall 2016). In English, the word *virelai* probably only meant a looser idea of sophisticated poetry. The **roundel** has more significance. English roundels developed from one among a range of French templates for cyclical poems, themselves originating in cyclical dancing songs. These templates went by various French names, hazily used in the period, such as *rondeau*, *rondel*, *roundel*, and *chanson*. I shall stick to 'roundel' for the English. The roundel relies on the recurrence of a refrain, as the *ballade* does, but it has a more interwoven structure (I adapt the following account from Fallows 1992, 123–124; and Nuttall 2020, 87). It has two and only two rhyme sounds and is thoroughly through-rhymed. The musical form underpinning the concept consists of two units which are repeated according to the following pattern

> I+II
> 1+I
> 1+2
> I+II

in which

1. a Roman numeral ('I', 'II') indicates the repetition of a unit of both the same words *and* the same music, and
2. an Arabic numeral ('1', '2') indicates the same music with *different* words.

The English roundel could be, but did not have to be, set to music. Whether or not music was directly involved, though, the roundel usually retains the same structuring principle, with identical words and rhyme in Roman-numeral positions and identical rhyme but different words in Arabic-numeral positions. The roundel's first stanza is read as two units of rhyme, which are then repeated according to the pattern. A roundel which begins *abba*, for instance, has as its two units *ab* and *ba*, and unspools as:

> I + II   1+I   1+2   I + II
> ABBA abAB abba ABBA

A roundel which begins *aabba* has as its two units *abb* and *ba*, and becomes:

> I + II   1+I   1+2   I + II
> AABBA aabAAB aabba AABBA

To complicate matters further, many scribes copied only short prompts for repeated lines, and even omitted the last stanza, which would be made up wholly of refrain material. In some cases, such scribes might have anticipated readers who recognized the form, and who conceived of the roundel through its heard expression (see Chapter 11) rather than as something sitting in a book. In other cases, manuscript evidence hints that some scribes lacked familiarity with the roundel or its French ancestors, showing the idea's relatively narrow distribution in England (Nuttall 2020, 89–90).

Thomas Hoccleve and John Lydgate both wrote a few roundels, and one anonymous triplet of roundels, 'Merciles Beauté', has been attributed, without comfortable certainty, to Chaucer. The quintessential Middle English roundelist, though, was the Frenchman Charles d'Orleans. One section of *Fortunes Stabilnes* consists of roundels, the largest sustained run of them in early English; some of these have equivalents in Charles's French poetry, which invite comparison. Here is one of his English roundels:

I:*A*	Not oft Y prayse, but blame, as in substaunce,	
I:*B*	All the welthe of lovis paynful blis,	*wealth*
II:*B*	For every joy with woo en-meyntid is	*in-minted*
II:*A*	Of gret foysoun of frawde and false semblaunce.	*plenty; pretence*
1:*a*	The wele and woo of hit dothe rolle and daunce	
1:*b*	As shippe in see for tempest that veris	*sea; veers*
I:*A*	Not oft Y *prayse, but blame, as in substaunce,*	
I:*B*	Al the welth *of lovis paynful blis.*	
1:*a*	This is the cause Y make such resemblaunce:	*comparison*
1:*b*	For as the shippe for-possid is this and this,	*tossed about*
2:*b*	Right so of love the hertis arne, ywis,	*Just so; are*
2:*a*	As now in wele and now in gret penaunce.	*wellness*
I:*A*	Not oft Y *prayse, but blame, as in substaunce,*	
I:*B*	Al the welth *of lovis paynful blis.*	
II:*B*	*For every joy with woo en-meyntid is*	
II:*A*	*Of gret foysoun of frawde and false semblaunce.*	

(Charles d'Orleans 1994, 281; art. R49)

The scribe left the italicized parts out of the manuscript (London, British Library, MS Harley 682, folio 84 verso). This roundel stays conventional in its matter—love is stormy!—but then fixed-form poetry worked with and through conventions, rather than avoiding them. The poem takes unusual routes in its manner. Its two governing images come from active, worldly affairs, and coinage, in particular, might seem rather unromantic. Charles invokes the debasement of coinage, a widespread European practice at the time, in which a government reduced the real amount of silver or gold in its coins. Debasement happened more slowly in fifteenth-century England than in (say) France, Scotland, or the Low Countries, but the problem was known and understood in England as elsewhere. Other poets had used coinage as a fruitful image (*Canterbury Tales*, I 3255–3256; Nolan 2007; Turner 2019, 246–256), and the storm-tossed ship might be a similar stock comparison. Oddly, though, the third stanza overtly explains the imagery: 'This is the cause', Charles writes, 'Y make such resemblaunce'. Most verse doesn't pause to think aloud over its own similes, as Charles does here. Is this poem about image-making, or image-minting, as well as love? At the head and tail of the poem, 'prayse' and 'penaunce' invite a background sense of the extended metaphor of the religion of love, something at issue in, for instance, *Troilus and Criseyde*. Yet, in the light of the coinage simile, the ship-simile begins to sound less conventionally romantic and more practical and mercantile.

Like many of Charles's English poems, this roundel has a French equivalent (Charles d'Orleans 1923-1927, art. C.49, p. 233), and whenever related poems exist in two languages, a comparison proves fruitful. The French equivalent lacks the concrete imagery of the English roundel: 'en-meyntid' has no French counterpart, obscuring the coinage metaphor, and instead of the ship, the French text makes generalized mention of the sea's dangers ('les perilz de mer', 6). The third stanza of the French version uses a wholly different image, a metaphor of lovers' hearts being excised and embalmed (9–12). The two poems diverge more and more as they go on, and it rather looks like Charles began his English translation of the French poem with the same two initial AB lines, and then wandered off on a new route in his second language.

From the limited pattern of survivals, the English roundel probably remained, more so than the *ballade*, a somewhat niche idea. The roundel offers an interesting cultural-historical nexus for study thanks to its French ties, though, and Charles's roundels make up a key part of a vital early English lyric sequence. The roundel is also, in itself, a satisfying form. A good roundel achieves a playful, complete, worked pattern, a similar effect to that of the refrain in looser forms: the intense re-thinking of repeated words.

Poets didn't have to adopt existing fixed forms and could spin-up intricate designs of their own. We might take as an example one elaborate love-poem attributed to either Elizabeth Woodville (c.1437 to 1492), the queen whose rise from middling rank to marry King Edward IV—in a secret wedding—hit English politics like a bomb, or her eldest daughter, Elizabeth of York (1466 to 1503), wife of King Henry VII. Scholarship hasn't worked out which 'Queen Elizabeth' the piece's attribution means (Boffey 1993, 171-172). However—and in contrast to the portion of anonymous poems written by women—Middle English verse overtly assigned to a named woman is rare, so the attribution matters despite its ambiguity. The poem has six stanzas (in Barratt ed. 2010, 294-296; *NIMEV* 2179 | *DIMEV* 3506). The first stanza rhymes *ababbaa*, with its first line repeating as its last line, what notation with capitalization for repetition might call *AbabbaA*. The second stanza takes the first stanza's second line as *its* first and last line, and again rhymes *AbabbaA*; the third stanza takes the first stanza's third line as its first and last line; and so the work goes on, each new stanza enveloped by a subsequent line taken from the first stanza, gradually prising open and exploring every one of the first stanza's parts. Its editor suggests that poem adapts the sestina (Barratt ed. 2010, 294), a continental form. But the sestina form follows a different formal path: it lacks rhyme within stanzas, and it repeats line-endings between stanzas, not whole lines. Perhaps the form of the Elizabeth poem is the poet's own design.

Concatenation

Besides the relatively strict demands of refrains, carol burdens, and the fixed forms, poets also had suppler ways to make stanzas interact. I noted a technique called **concatenation** in the design of some subdivided stanzas (Chapter 7). The same technique—sometimes called, less precisely, stanza-linking or, more forbiddingly, *concatenatio*—could appear at the boundaries between stanzas, or at the boundaries between their subsidiary units. For example, the first stanza of **Sir Perceval of Galles* ends with the line 'Whoso *redis ryghte*' (16), and the next stanza's first line runs 'Who that *righte* can *rede*' (17, my emphasis in both cases). The following stanzas make it clear that the repetition here is no coincidence, for the closing and opening lines of stanzas routinely pair up across stanza breaks:

>With robes in folde. // He gaffe hym *robes in folde* (32–33)
>Wolde he none forsake. // *Wolde he none forsake* (48–49)
>And lygges in the felde. // There he *lygges in the felde* (64–65)
>And blythe was his bryde. // And thofe the *bryde blythe* be (80–81)

Any poem might repeat words as a one-off, local event, but concatenation, this consistent linking of lines through recurring open-class words, raises repetition to the status of a regular part of the stanzaic pattern.

Concatenation had no discernible restriction to particular genres or modes: it appears in short poems and longer narratives, and in different metrical systems. A contrast with the refrain helpfully shows how concatenation works. In a poem with an insistent refrain, the refrain forms a kind of centre from which stanzas depart and to which they return, all sharing a uniform feature. Stanza by stanza, the refrain takes on new resonances from its new surroundings, but it nevertheless pulls the poem back to a common point. Since refrains usually occur at the end of each stanza, without tying to the beginning of the next, they offer an experience of return or orbit rather than continuity. Concatenation, by contrast, ties each stanza to the next without hammering on one idea continuously. It chains content together without imposing one uniform, persistent summation, and it constrains the first lines of stanzas as well as their last lines.

A poet could use concatenation within stanzas, too. Often such internal linkages link sub-units within the stanza. In *Three Dead Kings, for instance, the final halfline of each *frons* forms the first line of the following *cauda*. Here, in the *frons–cauda* transition of the eighth stanza, one of the ghostly kings points out the grave clothes in which he was buried:

>Lo, here the wrase of the wede | that I was in wondon!
>Herein was I wondon, iwys,
>In word wan that me worthelokyst was.
>
>(See here the band of the shroud in which I was wrapped! I was wrapped in this, yes, when I was most esteemed in the world. *Audelay 2009, 99–101)

The earlier Harley poem *'Wepyng haveth myn wonges wet', quoted in part in Chapter 7, deploys similar concatenation across the units of its subdivided stanza (*Fein ed. 2014–2015, art. 33).

As with any other feature of verse, after spotting concatenation's presence, one must ask what it does and why audiences enjoyed it. Concatenation tends to repurpose, expand on, or otherwise alter the lexis which repeats. It could be quite rigid: a set, predictable type of concatenation appears in *'Calays men, now mai ye care', a nationalistic commemoration of the 1346–1347 siege of Calais attributed to the hazy figure of Laurence Minot (*1996, art. 8). In this poem, the rhyme-word of each stanza's last line repeats as the first open-class word of the next stanza's first line. Concatenation could work more flexibly, though, and it gets a full workout in the alliterative-stanzaic *Awntyrs off Arthure (Hahn ed. 1995). The poet can repeat just one open-class word:

> An anlas of stele. // In *stele* he was stuffed, that stourne uppon stede
> (390–391)

Equally, though, nearly the whole final line can repeat:

> And dayntés on des. // With riche *dayntés on des* thi diotes ar dight...'
> (182–183)

Sometimes the repeated elements reverse in order:

> That prodly was pight. // *Pight* was it *prodly* with purpour and palle
> (442–443)

The poet also sometimes altered the grammar across the concatenation, as at the end of the poem's seventh stanza (91–92). The poem involves a revenant ghost that appears to warn Arthur's queen, Guinevere. Here, the first speech of the ghost ends with the last *cauda* line 'I gloppen and I grete!' ('I grieve and weep', 91), and the first line of the next stanza's *frons* begins with narration, which says 'Then gloppenet and grete Gaynour the gay' ('Then Guinevere the gay grieved and wept', 92). The tense and person of these verbs change across the concatenation, linking Guinevere and the ghost even as they underline a perspectival shift. The link fits the plot well: soon afterwards, we learn that the ghost is Guinevere's mother (160). The verbs (*gloppenet*, *grete*) alliterate with the conventional tag or epithet applied to Gaynour, *gay*, but although their sounds align, they rather undercut the epithet. In Middle English *gay* could mean 'joyful', but it could also mean 'bright' or 'noble', and its use here perhaps invites the audience to wonder whether Guinevere remains *gay* when she weeps—are we meant to find a contrast in a bright-bedecked queen weeping, or a pathos in the nobility of someone who weeps with the ghost, or an irony, given that the ghost brings a grim warning for those who shine brightly with nobility and wealth?

The *Awntyrs* was composed in **alliterative-stanzaic** verse, with regular alliteration and end rhyme. Sometimes concatenation makes the rhyme word of a stanza's final line recur as the rhyme word of the next stanza's first line, so that the c-rhyme of the preceding stanza becomes the a-rhyme of the next (e.g. 598–599); in a particular coup, at least one instance of this trick also delivers gentle **punning rhyme** (507–508;

see Chapter 6), playing off the 'grene', the field on which Gawain jousts, and the 'grene' of his green clothing.

In a phenomenon analogous to concatenation, and often—though not always—found together with it, poems could become fully circular. This happens in the *Awntyrs*: the poem's last lines ('In the tyme of Arthore / This anter betide', 714–715) tie right back to the very first ('In the tyme of Arthur an aunter bytydde', 1). Patience Agbabi has used both concatenation and a circular end-to-start link of this sort to organize 'Joined-Up Writing', a modern sonnet sequence reimagining Chaucer's Man of Law's Tale (2014, 21–27). Agbabi's use of concatenation, a non-Chaucerian system, with English sonnets, a post-Chaucerian phenomenon, creates a neat formal dislocation appropriate to the themes of journey, distance, and e(n)strangement which pulse through both the original tale and her poem. *Sir Gawain and the Green Knight* lacks universal, systematic stanza concatenation, but the poet used some local and particular concatenation, together with narrative repetition (Weiskott 2021b), and it ties its last stanza to its first via repeated words.

Concatenation's most famous Middle English use occurs in *Pearl*, where, unusually, concatenation behaves more like a refrain, tying multiple stanzas together. Concatenation works atypically in *Pearl*: it is an example worth knowing, but not the model for concatenation elsewhere. Each five-stanza section of *Pearl* concatenates on the same element, and the first line of each section concatenates with the dominant element of the previous section's last line; the first line of the poem concatenates with the very last line of the poem. The individual sections return again and again to the same idea, like poems cycling back to refrains, but at the transitions between sections these larger units join together as stanzas do in other concatenating poems. There is one break in the chain in *Pearl*, between lines 720–721. Some have argued that this example stems from a knowing poetic choice to create just one point of worldly imperfection in the structure (Casling and Scattergood 1974, 87–89); a similar case has been made for intent in apparent error in the poem's fortieth stanza, which comes in underlength and seems to lack a line where one would expect line 472 (Carlson 1991). Then again, these moments might be scribal slip-ups. As general Middle English traditions of concatenation have a modern echo in Agbabi's work, the particular combination of refrain and concatenation in *Pearl* has a powerful descendant in Douglas Oliver's *The Infant and the Pearl* (1990, 1–36). Oliver's poem offers a searching personal and political vision of the UK in the 1980s, and is written throughout in an adapted, concatenating form of the *Pearl* stanza.

Run-on stanzas

Many stanzaic poems lack any regular formal links between stanzas. Yet stanza-to-stanza relations in these poems still deserve thought. Like the line and the couplet, the stanza divides language into even blocks with a regularity not natural to language. Like the line and the couplet, therefore (Chapter 3), the stanza creates chances to track a poet's syntactic dealing-out of speech into artificial structures. Many Middle English stanzaic poems close either every stanza or almost every stanza with a hard syntactic break, of the sort editors today mark with a full stop. More so than the couplet, and far more so than the line, a stanza defaults to breaking syntax at its end. Significance therefore attaches to a poet's choice to run syntax on over the end of a stanza. Such running-on of sense can occur even with an end-stopped line. Here is a simple example from *Troilus and Criseyde*. Troilus has habitually mocked lovers (I.183–205), drawing the ire of the God of Love. But when Troilus' eye falls on Criseyde in the temple of Pallas Athena, he finds himself stricken with love (I.271–315). Returning home, he tries to avoid revealing his passion, outwardly keeping up his previous jests at lovers' expense:

> He straight anon unto his palais turneth,
> Right with hir look thurgh-shoten and thurgh-darted—
> Al feineth he in lust that he sojorneth;
> And al his cheere and speeche also he borneth,
> And ay of Loves servants every while,
> Himself to wrye, at hem he gan to smile,
>
> And saide, 'Lord, so ye live alle in lest,
> Ye loveres! For the conningeste of you
> That serven most ententifliche and best,
> Him tit as often harm therof as prow'.
>
> (At once he returns straight to his palace, shot right through and pierced by her look—although he pretends that he dwells in happiness; he also burnishes all of his appearance and speech, and—to cloak himself—ever, all the time, at Love's servants he was smiling, // and said, 'Good Lord, how all you lovers live in joy! For the most clever among you, who serves best and most attentively, he receives from it harm as often as gain'. I.324–333)

A natural pause occurs after 'smile', at the stanza's end, and this line (329) is end-stopped rather than enjambed. Nevertheless, the sense runs on into the following stanza, for the subject of 'saide' is the 'he' of the preceding line, and one's ears might prick up on hearing this.

What can be said of any given example of sense running across a stanza division depends on the local context. At its simplest this one might just invite readers to listen up, to pay special attention to Troilus' double-layered speech, in which he pretends to sustain his jokes at lovers' expense, but also—in mentioning the 'harm' that might come by love—quietly lets himself begin to find words for his new and devastating lovesickness. The technique can develop more force when used in a repeated pattern. In the second book of *Troilus and Criseyde*, a pattern emerges in which sense running on between stanzas coincides with Criseyde considering the problem presented by Troilus, first in the abstract (II.602–603, II.658–659) and then prompted by the concrete sight of him in person (II.1267–1268).

A poet can both enjamb and run over a stanza break at once:

> Nas nevere yet seyn thyng to ben preysed derre, *Never was never yet seen*
> Nor under cloude blak so bright a sterre
>
> As was Criseyde, as folk seyde everichone *every one*
> That hir behelden. *Who beheld her*
> (I.174–177)

At the very most only the smallest pause occurs after 'sterre', and the force of the promised comparison pulls right across the stanza break. Such fully enjambed stanza breaks occur only rarely in Chaucer's work. This one lets the description of Criseyde's matchless beauty run on, just before that beauty devastates Troilus.

Some poets exercised less restraint on sense running across stanza-breaks than Chaucer did. As with other aspects of verse form, a stanza system which looks the same at a glance can vary in the details of its use between poets. For instance, *The Kingis Quair* of James I of Scotland, the anonymous poem *The Floure and the Leafe*, the anonymous *Assembly of Ladies*, and George Ashby's *Complaint of a Prisoner in the Fleet* all use rhyme royal stanzas, just like *Troilus and Criseyde*, but all four shunt syntax on across stanza breaks noticeably more often than Chaucer did. Syntax travels across about two-fifths of the stanza transitions in *The Floure and the Leafe*, for example, sometimes halting very shortly thereafter:

> and if that it you please
> To go with me, I shall do you the ease
>
> In all the pleasure that I can or may.
> (*Pearsall ed. 1990, 391–393)

These poems were written after Chaucer's death, but they do not deal syntax out more loosely across stanzaic structures simply because they were composed later: Skelton's *Bowge of Court*, written at the turn of the sixteenth century and therefore later still, begins with some rhyme royal stanzas which run into each other but then rigorously separates stanzas for most of its length. Rather, these poems pursue a looser mapping of syntax to stanzas as an aesthetic choice. What looks like one uniform system varies meaningfully from poet to poet, and indeed from poem to poem.

Form changes

Poems can deploy very large-scale shapes or shifts in form, shuttling between different stanza systems, or switching between stichic and stanzaic verse. Sometimes early poets achieved diagrammatic designs. *The Bird with Four Feathers*, a mid-length work of penitential sorrow, shuffles between stanzas of four different sizes, possibly creating the shape of a core with two wings, each bearing two feathers, in its 241 lines (*Fein ed. 1998); *The Dispute between Mary and the Cross plays similarly with a cruciform shape achieved through the varying distribution of dialogue (*Fein ed. 1998). These works offer bigger, earlier, and more abstract counterparts to later shaped poetry, such as George Herbert's famous 'Easter Wings'.

Poets sometimes thought about very large-scale design trickery, despite the challenges of working in handwriting, with no digital ability to zoom out and search across a long poem's whole structure. The *Pearl* Poet takes the prize for the most intense obsession with form in the period. The four poems usually attributed to this poet display an overt interest in symbolic numbers (e.g. *Pearl* 985–1080, *Gawain* 619–665). Unsurprisingly, therefore, critics have generally detected intentional design behind the facts that *Pearl* lasts for 101 twelve-line stanzas in a total of 1212 lines, and that *Gawain* too runs to 101 stanzas. While the *Pearl* Poet was unusually obsessive, other poets showed similar interests: *Troilus and Criseyde* tells the story of Troilus' rise to happiness and his descent back into sadness—'Fro wo to wele, and after out of joye' (I.4)—and the exact middle line of the poem, line 4120 of 8239 in total, delivers Troilus' remark that Love, as a personified deity, has 'bistowed' him 'in so heigh a place' (III.1271): the pinnacle of his happiness, before he travels 'out of joye'. Meanwhile, John Clerk, maker of the alliterative †*Destruction of Troy* (1869–1874), never mentions himself. We only know he wrote it because he named himself acrostically in the first letters of the books into which he split the poem, knowing that in the transmission of the poem scribes and decorators would highlight each of these first letters (Turville-Petre 1988). Many attempts to find acrostic, encoded names in literature become both crankish and irrelevant—witness the labour spent hunting illusory ciphers and cryptograms in Shakespeare—but in this case Clerk's name is plainly there, showing a resourceful capacity to think at the very largest scale of form.

Poets could also alter form across whole sections, and thinking carefully about such changes can helpfully propel a reading. John Lydgate's *Testament*, for instance, has five sections, and while the first, third, and fifth are in Monk's Tale stanzas, the second and fourth are in rhyme royal (1911–1934, vol. 1, 329–362). In the *Canterbury Tales*, Chaucer enacts very large-scale switches between stichic verse and several types of stanza, plus prose in the Tale of Melibee and the Parson's Tale, all folded into a kind of super-poem. The basic idea of formal switching was hardly limited to Chaucer's work, however. Most versions of the anonymous romance *Sir Bevis of Hampton* shift to couplets from **tail rhyme** after around 500 lines, possibly to ease the challenge of translating a new type of verse unit in the Anglo-Norman work from which the poet was writing (*Herzman, Drake, and Salisbury eds 1997). John Metham, an eccentric poet in every respect, wrote *Amoryus and Cleopes* (1999), a romance which orbits a rhyme royal norm, but shape-shifts through varied rhyme schemes, plus eight- and six-line stanzas. At one point, when his heroine is instructing the hero in outlandish dragon lore, Metham creates an elaborate chiastic ABBCCCBBA structure using varied stanza lengths across nine stanzas:

A: One eight-line stanza (1241–1248)
BB: Two seven-line stanzas (1249–1262)
CCC: Three six-line stanzas (1263–1280)
BB: Two seven-line stanzas (1281–1294)
A: One eight-line stanza (1295–1302)

The passage delivers many playful ideas about dragons and creates a particular highlight in a poem that stays interested in the pleasure of artifice throughout.

Changes of form also offer one way to approach some verse saints' lives, such as those by the fifteenth-century friar Osbern Bokenham. Saints' lives—or hagiographies (*hagio-* means 'holy', *-graphy*, 'writing')—form an important, widespread genre of early prose and poetry that can be harder to grasp today. As narratives, they don't usually aim for inventive storytelling. But they have varied purposes, styles, and contexts, and they offered one culturally central body of work with which ordinary people could think through matters of life and death, vice and virtue, gender and space, power and force. Bokenham does not austerely address his *life of St Anne to a universal audience (in *Reames ed. 2003). Instead, it has a personal connection: he says that he wrote it for 'my frende Denston Kateryne' (66: Katherine Clopton Denston), who had a young daughter named Anne, after the saint (696–697).

Bokenham adopts a challenging rhyme scheme for his stanzas in the St Anne prologue, a chiastic *ababbcbccbcbbaba* pattern that dances between interlaced and adjacent rhyme. In this stretching rhyme scheme, Bokenham ironically claims incompetence in verse-craft, name-checking other poets: Chaucer, Gower, and his contemporary Lydgate. This manoeuvre of Bokenham's is a familiar reflex, denying skill with false modesty in stanzas that display care and wit. In another of his prologues (Bokenham 1938, p. 111, 4035–4066), he eloquently imagines Pallas Athena, a mythological Greek goddess associated with wisdom, shooing him away when he seeks instruction, saying that Chaucer, Gower, and Lydgate have already gathered up all the available flowers of eloquence. Bokenham, like Lydgate, can see that a line, of a sort, does separate saints' lives from more secular poetry—secular poetry that might play with Greek goddesses—but, again like Lydgate, he reacts by trampling wittily back and forth over that line, making sure that readers can see his footprints.

To sustain a *ababbcbccbcbbaba* pattern over six stanzas, as Bokenham does in his life of Anne, is an achievement. For the main body of the legend he shifts, perhaps with some relief, into normal *ababbcc* rhyme royal stanzas. We can read the force and associations of the forms involved: from elegant but, if anything, over-elaborate structures in the prologue to the standard workhorse of fifteenth-century stanzaic narrative, rhyme royal, for the main poem. We can also, however, note the force of the switch in form itself: Bokenham likes to do this, often shifting forms when he finishes a prologue, but using different formal combinations in different stories. To an audience hearing a poem aloud (see Chapter 11), the form switch helped signal the entry into the main narrative and might have prompted refreshed attention.

Major switches in form strike with special force when heard aloud, and Middle English drama frequently displays some formal variation both within plays and between plays within play collections. Variation between plays within collections might sometimes, of course, simply result from multiple authorship, though one can still ask how an audience might have experienced it. Both the York plays (*Davidson ed. 2011) and the Towneley plays (*Epp ed. 2017) show types of variation in stanza form both within and between plays. The allegorical *Castle of Perseverance, meanwhile, primarily uses thirteen-line subdivided *frons–cauda* stanzas. However, several of the personified vices who try to destroy the play's hero announce their intentions in tail-rhyme stanzas of short two-beat lines:

And I, Folye,	*Folly*
Schal hyen hym hye	*lift; high*
Tyl sum enmye	*enemy*
Hym ovyrgoo.	*overthrow*
In worldys wyt	*worldly knowledge*
That in Foly syt,	*he who sits in Folly*
I thynke yyt	*mean yet*
Hys sowle to sloo.	*slay*

(*Klausner ed. 2010, 639–646)

The play contains many other moments of formal variation, both in rhyme scheme and line length, sometimes with an intricacy that might escape an audience, perhaps mostly registering the poet's enthusiasm (Henry 1997).

Cursor Mundi, one of the great Northern Middle English poems of instruction, shifts between stichic and stanzaic verse and, unusually, contains a remark from the poet justifying the choice. Most of the poem, a universal history of the world, is written in four-beat lines rhymed in couplets (aa_4), but the poem shifts to septenary lines in **monorhymed** quatrains ($aaaa_7$) to narrate Jesus' execution. The poet comments that a 'langer bastun' ('longer stanza') is needed for 'that ranscon [*redemption*] / That richer es than erth and heven' (†Morris ed. 1874–1893, 14923, 14915–14916): the text delivers graver matters in a more patterned manner, and appears to display overt interest in imitative form. Though the gargantuan *Cursor* sometimes winds up written off as a mundane teaching work, its poet stayed alert to form and showed a willingness to experiment.

Later still in the work, some copies of the *Cursor* also contain various examples of another form change which can create fruitful contrast between stanzas in Middle English verse: **inset lyrics**, short poems embedded in larger poems (for instance, in *Cursor*, NIMEV 780 | DIMEV 1285; NIMEV 1885 | DIMEV 3092; NIMEV 3208 | DIMEV 5020). A lyric can come within a larger poem in any period, of course, but poets writing in Middle English and Older Scots had some specific models which inset poetry could invoke. Sermons offered one such model: substantial evidence suggests that some preachers wove short poems both sacred and secular into their exhortations (Wenzel 1986). French verse also hosted a tradition of *complaintes*, love laments lodged in longer, more narrative works. Being both neat units for consideration in themselves and opportunities for comparison to the surrounding text, inset lyrics often offer great scope for close reading. They found their way into longer poems through active insertions by the original poets, but also through addition by other people during transmission, as possibly in *Cursor Mundi*'s case.

Some particularly fine modulations of form, including an inset complaint, occur in the magnificent *Orpheus and Eurydice* of the fifteenth-century Scots poet Robert Henryson (in *Henryson 2010). As I noted in Chapter 3, the Greco-Roman myth of Orpheus was widely available to readers in Ovid, Virgil and, most importantly for Henryson, Boethius. Henryson's *Orpheus* is a learned and elegant poem, transmitting the story embellished with adventurous additions, such as Orpheus journeying into the heavens, where the harmony of the celestial spheres enhances his music. Henryson wrote most of this poem in rhyme royal stanzas, normally closed, but with syntax running between them at crucial moments (e.g. 98–99, 112–113). He included as an inset lyric a mourning complaint from Orpheus after Eurydice's death, in stanzas inventively rhymed *aabaabbcbc* (134–184), with a refrain.

In looking at this short poem, as in any instance of a formal shift in stanzaic verse, a reader might usefully begin by asking when the shift becomes apparent to a listening audience. Henryson ends the last rhyme royal stanza before the complaint and shifts into the complaint proper like this:

Half out of mynd he maid no tary moir	*[he: Orpheus]; tarry more*
Bot tuk his harp and to the wod cowth go	*wood did*
Wrinkand his handis, walkand to and fro	*Wringing; walking*
Quhill he mycht stand, syne sat doun on a stone	*while; then*
And till his harp thusgait he maid his mone,	*to; like this; moan*
'O dulfull herp with mony dully string	*doleful*
Turne all thy mirth and musik in murning	*to mourning*
And seis of all thy sutell sangis sweit'.	*cease; subtle songs*
(*2010, 129–136)	

In this case, the shift in rhyme scheme makes itself felt almost at once, as the adjacent (*aa*) opening couplet of the complaint stanza form (134–135) would refuse to deliver the interlaced (*abab*) rhyme an audience expects at the beginning of a new rhyme royal stanza. As the work begins purporting to deliver some of the legendary song of Orpheus, it audibly alters its framework. Although I have called this an inset lyric, this passage contains a surprising amount of narration: Henryson fits in the traditional image of the natural world responding to Orpheus' music (144–152) and has the narratorial voice deliver the last refrain element (183). The merging of complaint and narration lets the poet compliment himself by uniting his narration with the legendary music of Orpheus. The complaint is not the only formal transformation in Henryson's poem. The 'moralitas' that follows the story proper (415–633) transmits an intellectual, allegorical interpretation of the story and becomes **stichic**, proceeding in couplets. Perhaps Henryson deployed couplets here to allow for longer, more drawn-out blocks of rationalization in a less demanding rhyme scheme. Perhaps, too, the couplets sharpen the contrast between the story and its learned moralization, a contrast often taken as part of the challenge the poem presents to readers. Certainly the formal shifts in this poem matter, and they also exemplify the mutability, invention, and delight in contrast possible in fifteenth-century writing.

Chaucer breaks from the surrounding rhyme pattern in a piece rhyming *aabbaaccdccd* in his *Book of the Duchess* (475–486; see Butterfield 1991). He also translated a Petrarch sonnet as a short internal lyric within *Troilus and Criseyde*, though in that case he stuck to his surrounding verse form and rendered it in three rhyme-royal stanzas, and thus twenty-one lines rather than the sonnet's fourteen (I.400–420). John Metham, inveterate varier of stanza forms, put a complaint lyric into *Amoryus and Cleopes* (1999, 436–458). It differs from rhyme royal, rhyming *ababcdcdefefgg*. This rhyme scheme has local effects of its own. Integrated into a rhyme-royal romance, however, it acts like the shift of form in Henryson's *Orpheus and Eurydice*, creating a denial or delay of the couplet that would signal progress in the stanza. Trained by the surrounding rhyme royal, an audience will expect to hear such a couplet five lines into a stanza and will begin to notice its absence at the fifth line of Metham's lyric. This delay of adjacent rhyme, born from tension with the surrounding formal context, puts more weight on the poem's concluding couplet statement when that statement finally arrives, more weight than the lyric could achieve alone: in this case the relationship between inset piece and surrounding text adds to the effect.

As readers might have noticed, this poem's *ababcdcdefefgg* rhyme scheme matches that of the later 'English' or 'Shakespearean' sonnet (on the name, see Guy-Bray 2022). Metham almost certainly did not knowingly write his inset work as a sonnet and did not, as far as we know, influence any later sonneteers (Sawyer 2021a, 193–210). Indeed, Middle English very occasionally used the word *sonnet*, with a broader meaning of pleasant song (see *Cleanness*, 1516), an etymology that Patience Agbabi uses to close a series of reflections on verse history in sonnet lineation (2008, 46). Yet Metham's inset lyric remains the English sonnet rhyme scheme's first known appearance, and as such it represents verse-form outside tradition. In understanding it, we must choose between form and history; I chose form (Sawyer 2021a, 219–224), because—or perhaps and therefore—I am a literary critic. As Chaucer, Henryson, and Metham show, Scottish and English poets were trying new things everywhere, in strange, obscure works such as *Amoryus and Cleopes* as much as in the famous formal playground of the *Canterbury Tales*.

9
Manuscripts, Texts, Editions

> The double sorwe of Troilus to tellen,   *sorrow*
> That was the king Priamus sone of Troye, *Priam's*
> In loving how his aventures fellen   *happened*
> Fro wo to wele, and after out of joye,   *woe to bliss*
> My purpose is er that I parte fro ye.   *ere: before*
>
> (Chaucer, *Troilus and Criseyde*, I.1–5)

The opening lines of *Troilus and Criseyde* have justly drawn praise. They lay out the whole poem's elegant double structure of sorrow, joy, and sorrow once more. Sixteen substantial manuscript copies of the poem survive. Let's consider how the poem begins in one of these manuscripts—not a manuscript on which any editions of the poem are based. In the following transcription, italics represent expansions of scribal abbreviations, and bold text represents sharp differences from the previous quotation.

> ᵗ he **doleful** sorow of Troilus to tellen
>   That was the Kyng *pri*am*us* sone of Troye
> In louyng how hys auentures fellen
> Fro wo to wele and after **on to** joie
> My purpos is or that **I passe** fro ye
>
> (Oxford, Bodleian Library, MS Rawlinson poet. 163, folio 1 recto, lines 1–5; see Figure 1)

The manuscript—again, only one of sixteen different substantial copies—differs from the print in any edition of the poem in both appearance and text.

Comparing the *Norton Chaucer* against the manuscript, we might first note the manuscript text's upbeat misinterpretation of the poem's overall plot, in which Troilus' sorrow is not 'double' but 'doleful', and he goes 'on to' joy rather than out of it. The manuscript's text almost certainly fails to transmit what Chaucer wrote in these lines: we cannot absolutely rule out the possibility that he wrote about a 'doleful' sorrow, but the 'double' alternative fits far better with the poem's story. Scribes were conscientious workers, but they also had to work hard, and one can see how on finding, in the manuscript from which they were copying, a word before *sorrow* beginning *do-* and featuring an *-l-* later, a scribe might misread *doleful*, not *double*. 'Double sorrow' is a strange, engaging phrase, and an odd thing to say outside of a specific narrative context such as the story of Troilus; 'doleful sorrow' is a natural combination, into which

How to Read Middle English Poetry. Daniel Sawyer, Oxford University Press. © Daniel Sawyer (2024).
DOI: 10.1093/oso/ 9780198895237.003.0010

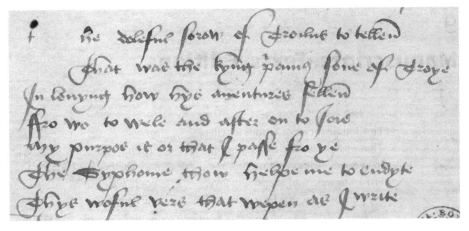

Figure 1 Opening lines of *Troilus and Criseyde* in Oxford, Bodleian Library, MS Rawlinson poet. 163, folio 1 recto. Reproduced by kind permission of the Bodleian Libraries, University of Oxford, under Creative Commons licence CC-BY-NC 4.0 (<https://creativecommons.org/licenses/by-nc/4.0>).

a scribe might easily stumble. In an edition which aims to present a text closer to the work as Chaucer produced it, an editor can justifiably prefer 'double' to 'doleful'. We shouldn't forget the variation, though: some readers encountered this manuscript as their only copy of the poem, and so the variation in the text is part of the history of Chaucer's reception.

In appearance, meanwhile, the manuscript uses some abbreviations, including two in 'priamus', represented by italics in my transcription above. The scribe capitalizes less consistently than modern English conventions require, writing 'priamus', not 'Priamus'. At the opening of the poem, the manuscript has a space left for a large initial *T* which was never filled in, leaving us to read the very small *t* which the scribe left as a hint for a potential future decorator. Such gaps for initials that never appeared occur often in manuscripts in this period.

Both appearance and text traditionally feature in close reading: critics attend, or ought to attend, to what the poem says, and it would be a brave reader indeed who neglected to think about the layout of (say) a concrete poem. Both aspects, presentation and text, also stand rooted in this poem's transmission via a hand-copied book, a manuscript. But manuscripts vary among themselves, differing in presentation and text, and very few Middle English poems survive in manuscripts created by the original poet in person. When a reader names a poem by (say) Percy Bysshe Shelley, they don't normally imagine an array of diverging manuscripts. The manuscript circumstances of Middle English might, therefore, seem a problem for close reading: aren't unitary, fixed texts with settled appearances and layouts necessary for literary criticism? Couldn't the complexities and uncertainties created by manuscripts of early poetry prevent the study of its form? Could these conditions—usually no authorial copies, no printing, and a high degree of variation in text and layout—make earlier

Scots and English poetry categorically different to, for example, the writings of Elizabeth Bishop or Samuel Beckett?

This chapter's answer is 'No'. Rather, the complications of manuscript transmission add interest to early poetry, and open up scope for more close reading, not less. Indeed, verse from this period more clearly raises problems which continue in subtler forms right up to the present: manuscripts and editions of earlier poetry can train us to detect and enjoy similar challenges in more recent work. The rich world of manuscripts containing Middle English stretches far further than I can cover in one chapter, and readers can enjoy fuller introductions in useful books by Jessica Brantley (2022); Kathryn Kerby-Fulton, Maidie Hilmo, and Linda Olson (2012); and Ralph Hanna (2013). The work of editing, too, has fascinations and even beauties, rarely overtly discussed—though Stephen A. Barney did write an engaging and detailed account of his work as one editor of *Troilus and Criseyde* (1993). This chapter offers ways to find the pleasure and interest of manuscript complications and of the details of editions, rather than experiencing these things as threats. Literary criticism, editing, and the study of manuscripts can all inform each other, rather than sitting at odds.

Changing pages

Here are the opening lines of a short poem as presented in a modern edition:

> ¶ Bytuene Mersh ant Averil   *and April*
> When spray biginneth to springe,   *shoot/twig*
> The lutel foul hath hire wyl   *little bird*
> On hyre lud to synge.   *in her language*
>   (*Fein ed. 2014–15, art. 29, 1–4)

In the surviving manuscript copy these lines look something like this:

> ¶ Bytuene mersh 7 aueril. When spray biginneþ to sp^{ri}nge
> Þe lutel foul haþ hire wyl / on hyre lud to synge
>   (London, British Library, MS Harley 2253, folio 63 verso, 7–8)

Readers can play spot-the-difference here, and they can also consult a facsimile of this manuscript page online (at the time of writing: <http://www.bl.uk/manuscripts/Viewer.aspx?ref=harley_ms_2253_f063v>). Changes made in the present-day edition include the replacement of some letters (see Appendix section 2), the replacement of punctuation with other punctuation marks in new places, the expansion of the abbreviation I have represented using '7' with the word meant ('ant', *and*), and relineation. This poem provides another example of the phenomenon I noted in the case of *Sir Ferumbras* in Chapter 4: verse which can be understood either as septenary couplets (aa_7) with internal rhyme just before the metrical caesura in each line, or as $a_4b_3a_4b_3$

quatrains. Even poetry's layout in modern editions comes in part from the work of editors.

For a more extreme example, consider the Towneley Plays, which dramatize parts of the Bible. At one point, they portray King Herod, a character in the story of Jesus' birth. The Towneley Plays depict him as a bombastic tyrant, chewing the scenery. A herald, serving as a terrified warm-up act, announces the king's arrival directly to the audience in verse that uses some regular alliteration, but not alliterative metre. Here is a brief sample, in the play's thirteen-line subdivided stanza:

He is the worthyest of all	*He*: Herod
Barnes that ar borne;	*People who are*
Fre men ar his thrall,	*free; are; slaves*
Full teynfully torne.	*painfully*
Begyn he to brall,	*[Should] he begin to brawl*
Many man cach skorne;	*[will] catch harm*
Obey must we all,	
Or els be ye lorne	*otherwise; lost*
Att onys.	*once*
Downe dyng of youre knees	*fall to*
All that hym seys;	*see*
Dysplesyd he beys,	
And brykyn many bonys.	*breaking*

(Stevens and Cawley eds 1994, Play 16, 79–91)

It is thirteen lines, at least, in one edition, that produced by Martin Stevens and A. C. Cawley; note, recalling Chapter 7, the **bob** in the ninth line and the following *cauda*. Another edition, though, prints something different:

He is the worthyest of alle barnes that are borne,
Free men ar his thralle full teynfully torne,
Begyn he to bralle many men cache skorne,
Obey must we alle or els be ye lorne
    Att onys.
Downe dyng of youre knees,
Alle that hym seys,
Dysplesyd he beys,
    And brykyn many bonys.

(†Raine ed. 1836, page 141)

This is James Raine's edition from the first half of the nineteenth century. Does this stanza rhyme *ababababcdddc*, or does it have internal rhyme in longer lines end-rhyming *aaaabcccb*? Does one of these editions misrepresent what the manuscript says? Really, both editions must differently misrepresent the manuscript: any edition sets out to make the work more accessible, which inevitably means differing from the manuscript or manuscripts that preserve the poetry. Such misrepresentation is one of the goals of editing, and a service to modern readers. Neither edition, then, can ever be the source manuscript. But one of the two must stick more faithfully to the manuscript in its layout. Raine's nine-line layout reproduces the manuscript layout more closely. Stevens and Cawley argue cogently in their introduction, though, that this stanza-form was conceived of as thirteen lines and was only copied in nine lines by the scribe to save space. They note, among other things, that the very first time the scribe copied out one of these stanzas, he lineated it in thirteen rather than nine lines (ed. 1994, xviii–xxxi). If these stanzas were heard as thirteen units rather than nine, then there is a case for laying them out as such, whatever the manuscript page does. Here, again, the sound of poetry demands attention: these visual re-presentations might lie beyond the boundaries of what the original poets would have imagined, but then in many cases poets probably primarily imagined their poems as *heard*, aural things. The manuscript is important, but it does not provide a final ruling on how the work should be received.

Every edition creates an argument about its text, not a simple transmission of the available evidence. Every edition intervenes in its materials. Every edition therefore invites careful reading for its own sake. But editions create arguments to help us, and although editorial capitalization, punctuation, and layout cannot be read closely, and can sometimes be questioned (Horobin and Smith 2002, 19–20), they can still help indirectly, for they represent an expert's best judgement of the way a work might be organized and perceived.

Resonant images

Some manuscripts relate text and image or contain image-poems. These images challenge representation in print editions, since reproducing a manuscript image in print raises sets of practical and copyright problems. On the plus side, images in manuscripts can ground fruitful interpretative work. When grand English literary manuscripts became a little more common, in the fifteenth century, they bore work by professional illuminators. These illuminators found themselves having to work out how to represent the nascent concept of the authoritative English poet, with fascinating results (Drimmer 2019). Many other manuscripts containing Middle English were more humble productions, without lavish decoration, but even more mundane-seeming books sometimes make poetry diagrammatic or—as in the case of the poems of the *Pearl* manuscript (Hilmo 2017; Hilmo 2018)—accompany it with illustrations. Humbler manuscript book production tied image to text more closely than printing would: one person could move fluidly between copying text and drawing or decorating, with fewer of the hassles involved in putting images through a printing press. One relatively humble copy of *Piers Plowman*, for instance, contains a cycle of marginal images, probably the work of the scribe (Oxford, Bodleian Library, MS Douce 104; Shepherd and Harshbarger 2020), and these marginal images seem to engage in sophisticated allusion and intellectual play responding to the poem.

Beyond the interaction of text with marginal image, sometimes Middle English poetry actively melds with images. Consider, for example, the image-poem pictured in Figure 2. Jesus appears bloodied, with nails visible in his hands and feet, and surrounded by symbols of his torture before the crucifixion. Beneath his outstretched arms there is a drawing of a charter, a legal document. The drawing contains text laid out in prose lineation, as it would be in a real charter, but the text is a poem. It is a poem spoken by Jesus and borrowing, in places, the Latin formulas of a legal charter. Transcribed, with the abbreviations expanded and line-divisions imposed, its opening lines read:

Sciant presentes et futuri.	*Know, those present and to be*
Wete now al that ar here	*Know*; are
And after sal be, lefe and dere,	*cherished and dear*
That I, Ihesus of Nazareth,	*Jesus*
For luf of man has sufferd deth	*love*
Opon the cros with woundes fyfe,	*five*
While I was man and Erth on lyfe.	*alive*
Dedi et concessi.	*I have given and granted*
I hafe gyfen and made a graunt	
To al that askes it, repentaunt…	

(London, British Library MS Additional 37049, folio 23 recto)

The image of the poem presented as a charter sports a drawing of a large seal, of the sort a real charter would have, at its base. This copy of the 'Short Charter of Christ' has drawn scholarly attention for its fusion of image and text, and the poem in general (*NIMEV* 4184 | *DIMEV* 6769) attracts readers for, among other things, the analogy that it draws between the imagined parchment skin of the charter and the skin of Jesus. Such a combined image-poem presents us with a limit case for the relation between manuscript and verse, and for that matter for the relationship between belief and poetry. To study it in this manuscript is to push into art history and archaeology, to think about how readers might have handled and looked upon this page and about the images and the poem-charter as one entity; Jessica Brantley uses this manuscript to offer a broader introduction to literary illustration in the period (2022, 276–296).

Should editors print this poem as conventional verse, separated from its visual presentation, given that the image seems such an integral part of its effect? Perhaps not. Then again, readers today cannot recover exactly the fifteenth-century experience of seeing this poem-image: to us it unavoidably looks old, distant. No tool, not even photography, can fully convey the lost historical experience of an object transmitting Middle English poetry, whether that object is a manuscript book, a church wall, or a jug (Wakelin 2018, 10–11, 174–178). Furthermore, the poem appears elsewhere in other layouts, without images: one of these other copies is set to music (British Library, MS Additional 5465, folios 118 verso to 122 recto), suggesting that people didn't always contemplate the verse visually. Manuscript appearance offers

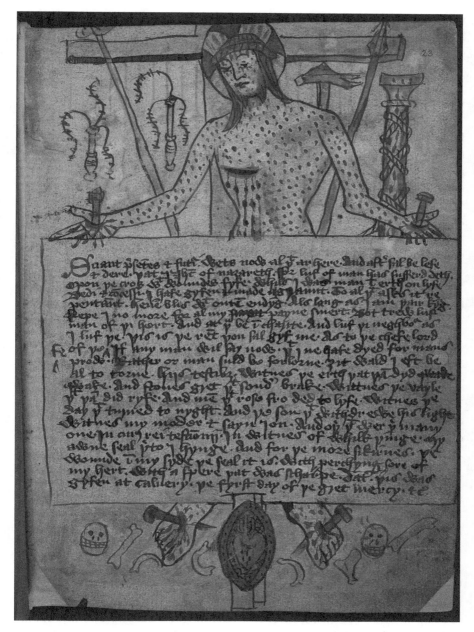

Figure 2 Poetry presented as a charter held out by Jesus from the cross. © The British Library Board; London, British Library, MS Additional 37049, folio 23 recto.

vital evidence about interpretation, but it cannot give final, conclusive judgements. If we keep that in mind, though, examples such as this one offer ripe material for the study of image and word together.

Clashing words

Editors of Middle English poetry do not—cannot—restrict themselves only to matters of layout, punctuation, capitalization, and accompanying images. As the example of Troilus' 'doleful sorrow' that I noted earlier shows, the surviving manuscripts don't offer settled texts. Another noted Chaucerian example is the opening of the Wife of Bath's Prologue in the *Canterbury Tales*: most editions give her first word as 'Experience', though some manuscripts have 'Experiment'. Many such scribal tweaks, unintentional or otherwise, lurk in the critical apparatuses of scholarly editions.

A more developed example from *Orfeo can bring out more of the issues at play. When Orfeo reaches the fairy castle to which his wife Heurodys has been stolen away, the poem compares the castle, in Orfeo's perception, to 'Paradis', heaven:

> Bi al thing him think that it is
> The proude court of Paradis.
> (Laskaya and Salisbury eds 1995, 375–376)

This comparison has drawn critical attention, for two reasons: first, besides the overt comparison, other details echo common descriptions of heaven from the time; second, the poem invokes Paradise exactly one other time, very early on:

> In al the warld was no man bore   *no one living*
> That ones Orfeo sat bifore—   *once*
> And he might of his harping here—   *hear*
> Bot he schuld thenche that he were   *think*
> In on of the joies of Paradis.   *One*
> (33–37)

Understandably, the poem's interpreters have latched on to these two parallel mentions (e.g. Lerer 1985, 102; Weber 2011; Byrne 2016, 26–27). But do those opening lines of *Orfeo* exist at all? Alert readers might already have noticed another TEAMS edition of the poem, edited by George Shuffelton (*2008), and a cursory comparison of opening lines at once shows that these are not exactly the same text:

We redeth oft and findeth y-write,	Mery tyme is in Aperelle,
And this clerkes wele it wite,	That mekyll schewys of manys wylle.
Layes that ben in harping	In feldys and medewys flowrys spryng;
Ben y-founde of ferli thing.	In grovys and wodys foules syng.
(Laskaya and Salisbury eds, 1–4)	(Shuffelton ed., 1–4)

Lines from the two editions differ even when they seem to have some relationship to each other:

Himself he lerned forto harp,	Hymselve he lernyd for to herpe
And leyd theron his wittes scharp;	And leyd theron hys wytte so scherpe.
He lerned so ther nothing was	He lernyd so wele, withouten les,
A better harpour in no plas.	So gode herper never non was.
(29–32)	(31–34)

What's going on?

The two editions are based on two different manuscripts, offering two different texts. Considerable time separates the two: the Laskaya–Salisbury edition uses a manuscript copied at some point around 1340, the 'Auchinleck Manuscript', while the Shuffelton edition uses a manuscript copied around 1500, Bodleian Library, MS Ashmole 61; 160 years separate 1340 from 1500, and that's no little time—we tend today to think of the nineteenth century as old, after all. Can we not simply take the older manuscript, Auchinleck, precisely because it is earlier? This instinct is understandable, but not safe. Both manuscripts contain errors, and the later manuscript is not descended from the earlier. More generations of copying can lie behind an earlier manuscript than lie behind a later one—if, that is, we can rule out the further complication of memorial transmission, which in *Orfeo*'s case we cannot (Purdie 2018). Only comparative thought can give a sense of what the text of each manuscript is like, and where or how each manuscript might be better.

Yet we cannot say, without laying out our goals, what 'better' means: do we want a text of the poem as close as reasonably possible to what the poet wrote, or do we want a text representing the type of copy likely seen by more readers in the period? These two things differ, and different manuscripts might be better for different purposes. Knowledge of what *Orfeo* looked like to some readers around 1500 can serve literary criticism as well as knowledge of what *Orfeo* looked like to readers several generations earlier: Shuffelton's edition based on a younger manuscript therefore helps scholars interested in English literary culture at the turn of the sixteenth century more than the Laskaya–Salibsury edition can. The desires with which we approach a work determine which edition serves us best.

Look closer, though, and the situation becomes stickier still. Laskaya and Salisbury use the Auchinleck Manuscript for their edition. But at those opening lines in which I earlier picked out the word 'Paradis', here is what the Auchinleck Manuscript itself says:

That is, a leaf is missing from the manuscript here, and so it lacks these lines entirely! Readers can check this for themselves in a digital reproduction of the manuscript (<https://auchinleck.nls.uk>); the missing leaf is **folio** ('leaf') 299, and the manuscript's surviving copy of the poem starts at line 39 of the Laskaya–Salisbury edition, at the beginning of the next leaf, folio 300.

Laskaya and Salisbury follow the general approach of A. J. Bliss, who concocted a solution to this problem in the middle of the last century (1953; 1966 ed.). To edit a work, editors must first find where all the available evidence lurks. Three copies of *Orfeo* survive:

A   Edinburgh, National Library of Scotland, MS Advocates' 19.2.1; the Auchinleck Manuscript; around 1340; used in *Laskaya and Salisbury eds
H   London, British Library, MS Harley 3810; around 1400
B   Oxford, Bodleian Library, MS Ashmole 61; around 1500; used in *Shuffelton ed.

H and B probably have a common ancestor manuscript, now lost; that is, they were probably both copied from copies taken from copies (descending through an unknown number of generations) which eventually trace back to the same earlier manuscript. The common ancestor of H and B probably did not itself descend from A. H or B might, therefore, be able on occasion to offer independent evidence about the poem where A fails, even though they were copied later.

With these blocks of evidence in hand, what to do about the missing opening in A? Editors can choose to omit the lines absent from A entirely: Laura Ashe does so in an anthology for a general readership (2015 ed., 317). There is nothing wrong with this. However, the lines missing from the opening of A are roughly the number that would have occupied one column of the missing leaf, if that leaf bore a large decorated initial letter of the sort that adorned the openings of other works in this manuscript. It's not unreasonable, therefore, for an editor to imagine that those lines did once exist in A, and then to supply text of those lines from H and/or B as a kind of stand-in at the start of an edition based on A. Just such an editorial hypothesis underpins the lines printed at the start of the poem in the Laskaya and Salisbury edition. These lines require some care from readers, but they are also a sensible probabilistic solution to the textual problem.

I don't suggest that in the opening lines of their editions Bliss, Laskaya, and Salisbury erred, or engaged in a cover-up. They deserve our gratitude for their hard work making it possible for us to read the poem. Rather, I am showing how any edition is an argument about likelihoods, and how an editor's usual task—making a work available and accessible for present-day readers—requires such argument. All editions intervene in their evidence: even printing a raw, 'diplomatic' transcription of a manuscript shifts the text into print and argues implicitly for the value of such rawness; even digitally hosting a photographic reproduction of a manuscript alters the reading experience, and, unlike an edition, argues implicitly—perhaps misleadingly—for the new experience's authenticity: no one in the Middle English period, after all, ever read a manuscript through a screen.

The lines in the poem's opening about Orfeo's harping, with their mention of Paradise, seem potentially important, but at this point, we might wonder whether they count as part of the poem, given that A doesn't have them. The two surviving copies of those lines, in H and B, do themselves significantly differ:

> [*damage*] the world was never man born
> That onus Orpheo sat byforn   *once; before*
> And he myght of his harpyng her   *If; hear*
> He schulde thinke that he wer
> In one of the joys of Paradys
> Suche joy and melody in his harpyng is
>
>   (H 41–46)

> In all thys werld was no man bore
> That had Kyng Orfeo ben before   *had [he been]*
> And he myght hys herpe here   *If; hear*
> Bot he wold wene that it were   *would believe*
> A blyssydfull note of Paradys   *blissful*
> Suche melody therin is   *therein*
>
>   (B 35–40)

Careful readers will see the gaps between thinking that Orfeo's harping *is* blissful *music from* Paradise (B) and thinking *oneself in* one of the *joys of* Paradise (H). Such disagreements between manuscripts can set up fruitful close readings: a student could think their way to interesting work by pursuing differences between the texts of these manuscripts and their possible contexts. If we want to discuss the poem as one entity, though, we have a problem: A is absent, while H and B differ.

Editors can argue sensibly that the first mention of Paradise in the poem once existed on the now-missing leaf at the poem's start in A, yet our only firm evidence for it hails from H and B. Bearing this problem in mind, we might turn to the other reference to Paradise: when Orfeo enters fairy land, 'Bi al thing him think that it is / The proude court of Paradis' (Laskaya and Salisbury eds 1995, 375–376). I am sorry to report that this second mention of Paradise only appears in A (Bliss ed. 1966, 32–33,

A ll. 375–376; compare H ll. 360–361, B ll. 369–370). No single copy of *Orfeo* provably contains both mentions, then: the first 'Paradis' appears in H and B, but not any surviving part of A, while the second 'Paradis' appears in A, but not in H or B. The prospects for anyone trying to link the poem's two mentions of 'Paradis' might seem grim.

Yet we need not give up the enticing link between these two mentions of Paradise in the poem. On this point, literary sensitivity and close reading help editors: textual complexity and literary-critical appreciation aren't enemies. It is not, looking with eyes attuned to verse-craft, the concept of Paradise alone which repeats. It is the concept and the rhyme: *Paradis:is* (Laskaya and Salisbury eds 1995, 37–38), then *is:Paradis* (375–376). If meaningfully repeated rhyme pairings are a general feature of *Orfeo*, then both mentions of Paradise are more likely to be original to the poem, for they cohere not only with each other but also with the poet's practice elsewhere, in more secure parts of the text. We can check this by asking whether the poet was alert to rhyme in general, and then looking in particular for meaningfully repeated rhyme pairings which appear in both A and at least one of the other two copies.

The poem as it survives certainly suggests some thoughtful craft in rhyme: for instance, the poem indulges in **through-rhyme**, four contiguous lines rhymed on the same sound, exactly twice, both times at points of high drama (325–328, 453–456); in the second of these examples, the through-rhymed lines exactly delineate a crucial speech by Orfeo himself. *Orfeo* is also one of the few English poems before Chaucer to feature **rhyme-breaking** (327–328, 471–472, 529–530; see Chapter 3). These techniques remain consistent in all cases across A and at least one of H and B, strengthening the chance that they go back to the poet. *Orfeo* does display an interest in crafting rhyme in general.

What about repeated rhyme pairings in particular? Some other repetitions of rhyme pairs, more textually secure than the first *is:Paradis* rhyme, suggest the crafty use of this technique, too. *Steward*, for example, only occurs at the end of a line twice, and both times it is rhymed with *afterward*, a word neatly tied to the steward's role in the plot as twice inheritor of the kingdom from Orfeo (205–206, also in B; 595–596, also in H and B). *Priis* occurs only twice as a rhyme word, in both cases rhymed with *Heurodis*, and in this case the rhyming pair repeats in close proximity (51–52, also in H and B; 63–64, also in H and B). Both pairs, *steward:afterward* and *priis:Heurodis*, also reverse in their second appearances, as the pair of *is* and *Paradis* does, or does if we admit it into the text. Similarly, *liif* and *wiif* only appear as end rhymes when they rhyme with each other, on four separate occasions, in an insistent repetition which seems closely bound up with the plot (177–178, 335–336, 405–406, 485–486). Again, these pairings remain consistent across A, H, and B. To close-read just one manuscript text of *Orfeo* would be perfectly legitimate, but these consistencies remind us that there is, despite the variation, one crafted poem identifiable as *Orfeo*.

No doubt convenience and habit affected these rhymes. It suited the poet that *afterward* and *steward* rhyme, given that the steward twice rules after Orfeo. Given that Orfeo must often mention his *wiif*, *liif* helpfully matched. Like all poets working with regular end rhyme, the *Orfeo*-poet surely had a habitual mental stock of handy rhyme pairs, the mnemonic precursor to a present-day rhyming dictionary. However, in studying regular verse, convenience and craft cannot fully separate. Repeated rhyme pairs helped the poet, but they also make up part of the poem's crafty elegance: the *liif:wiif* rhyme might well come from habit, but it seems to me that it also lets texture enhance theme. In any case, the poet certainly used pairs of rhymes repeated and sometimes reversed. This fact in turn makes it more likely that A did once contain the first *is:Paradis* rhyme and that the poet originally wrote both rhymes. The poem probably did contain both references to Paradise, and probably did contain both instances of this rhymed pair.

Has this argument merely circled about, questioning the Paradise references only to restore them? No, because we now know rather more about *Orfeo*: we have spotted the poet's use of repeated rhyme pairings, and learned that the mentions of Paradise, if they are original to the poem, repeat not just an idea, but also a rhyme. What's more, we have clarified the choices open to someone wishing to write criticism about the poem. Critics can think on one or more of the surviving copies in their specific times and manuscript contexts. For students, Shuffelton's edition provides a good way to explore a poem in manuscript context, because it edits the whole manuscript that I have been calling B, MS Ashmole 61, so readers can see how *Orfeo* might have been read alongside the works surrounding it. Those other works in B include the copy of the *Northern Passion* mentioned in Chapter 3, and a different copy of the 'Short Charter of Christ' discussed in the present chapter. Critics can also, though, think on *Orfeo* as an entity in time in and of itself, trying to read the most-probably most-original parts by examining editions and asking which parts are most textually secure. Work taking either route will bear fruit, and many poems in early English and Scots can similarly be studied either through thinking about more-authorial texts or through texts representing what later readers encountered. Both approaches shed light.

Textual trouble, then and now

Orfeo presents a tough but relatively simple version of a routine editorial situation. Disagreement between manuscripts stands as the normal background to *any* Middle English or Older Scots work surviving in more than one copy. In Chapters 4 and 6 I have quoted from Susanna Fein's edition of *The Owl and the Nightingale* (*2022), which bases itself on Oxford, Jesus College, MS 29 (II); one other copy of the poem survives, in London, British Library Cotton MS Caligula A.ix, represented in a good modern edition edited by Neil Cartlidge (2003). Tantalizingly, both manuscripts seem to have been copied from the same earlier manuscript, which is now lost. Despite this shared parent, the two surviving copies differ instructively in their spellings and sometimes in the substance of what they say. Both copies contain unique problems that drive Fein and Cartlidge to intervene in their texts.

Even when just one copy survives, that copy routinely displays what an editor seeking a plausible text would call errors. *Sir Gawain*, for instance, survives in only one manuscript, which contains mistakes. The edition I have quoted in this book sometimes intervenes to change what that manuscript says. The editors, Ad Putter and Myra Stokes, set out to present a clear, readable text that they can argue might sit closer to what the poet first wrote; that is not the only legitimate goal of editing, but it is one legitimate goal.

At points Putter and Stokes intervene in—emend—things we can all agree are slip-ups: when at line 95 the scribe in the manuscript has written 'of of', an easy error to make then as now, they print one 'of'. Where the manuscript reads 'Chymbled ou*er* hir blake chyn w*ith* mylk quyte vayles' (London, British Library, MS Cotton Nero A.X/2, folio 107 verso), the editors print 'Chymbled over her blake chyn with **chalk**-white vayles' (958); 'mylk' doesn't alliterate properly with 'Chymbled' and 'chyn', and many editors have agreed that in changing the text here they probably correct an error that occurred during the poem's transmission. At points, the editors are more adventurous. Any editor would agree that something has gone wrong when the manuscript reads 'And ay þe lady let lyk ahym loued mych' (MS Cotton Nero A.X/2, folio 112 recto), because the line doesn't deliver sensible Middle English; not all editors have intervened as extensively as Putter and Stokes do by printing 'And aye the lady let **as ho** liked him and loved **him swythe**' (1281). But they explain their reasoning (eds 2014, 714), which draws on among other things the metre—readers might recall from Chapter 5 that a **b-verse** shouldn't end with a **lift** such as 'mych'—and other, somewhat more textually conservative editions are available (e.g. Andrew and Waldron eds 2007).

Sometimes the evidence available to editors itself comes from well after a work's likely composition, even after the end of the long time that some awkwardly call the Middle Ages. **The Squire of Low Degree* seems to be a later fifteenth-century romance, but survives only in sixteenth- and seventeenth-century printed copies (Kooper ed. 2005). William Caxton, the first businessman to print books in English, put out two editions of the *Canterbury Tales*, seemingly from two different manuscripts; those manuscripts are now lost; consequently, Caxton's two printings of the *Tales* must be treated as two extra witnesses to the work. The great Scots poet William Dunbar, writing at the end of and just after our period, is perhaps most famous for his *'Lament for the Makars', or '*Timor mortis conturbat me*'; the earliest extant text of this poem is a print copy, printed within Dunbar's lifetime though probably without his oversight. This printed copy also ends, uniquely, with a paratextual comment after the final stanza: 'Quod Dunbar quhen he wes sek' ('...Dunbar said when he was sick'). Such an ending comment reinforces and cycles back to the poem's opening:

I that in heill wes and gladnes	*health was*
Am trublit now with gret seiknes	*troubled; sickness*
And feblit with infermité:	*enfeebled; infirmity*
Timor mortis conturbat me.	*The fear of death perturbs me.*

(*Dunbar 2004, 1–4)

The closing comment in the early printed copy affects how readers might receive the poem, but it appears only in this early printed copy, and an editor must choose either to include it, or to relegate it to the notes. For many other Dunbar works, editors must rely on much later manuscripts, and so he presents a case in which shreds of earlier *printed* evidence precede fuller but later *manuscript* evidence.

The most famous editorial challenge in Middle English poetry is *Piers Plowman*, which survives in a complex array of manuscript witnesses with debated relationships. The edition that I have been quoting, A. V. C. Schmidt's 1995 Everyman second edition, bears on its title page the words 'A Critical Edition of the B-Text'. The phrase 'B-Text' suggests that other texts might be kicking around, and so scholarship thinks. Researchers refer as well to other versions: the A text, C text, and in some cases Z text. The student writing on *Piers* often benefits from thinking across the versions: comparative attention to the C text (in, e.g., Langland 2014) can hone an argument hitherto attending to the B text, which is the version most commonly read (see discussion in Calabrese 2016, 17–22). It must be argument: just like the mere identification of features of verse-form, the mere identification of differences only gets one so far. But the comparison still opens up more field for that argument.

We can and should, though, dig deeper. The versions of *Piers Plowman* are a modern idea, developed by the greatest nineteenth-century researcher in early English, W. W. Skeat, as a way to explain the manuscript evidence. Fourteenth- and fifteenth-century readers didn't experience versions with labels, and some surviving manuscripts refuse to come in neat versioned packages. One copy, for instance, folds lines and passages from the other versions into the B text, and transmits new, fresh-invented lines as well (San Marino, Henry E. Huntington Library, MS HM 114; see Brantley 2022, 245–259). To its owners and readers, this manuscript probably was *Piers Plowman*; they had no editions or manuscript catalogues to tell them that they happened to have met a most unusual copy. We might note, too, that to talk of versions lettered A-B-C imposes a particular view of their order of composition. What's more, the name William Langland, so comforting in its normal, authorial appearance—plausible first and second parts, no archaic *of* as in, say, Robert Mannyng of Brunne—nowhere appears in *Piers*. The name comes from notes by later readers scribbled inside the covers of three manuscripts, together with the line '"I have lyved in londe," quod I, "my name is Longe Wille"' (B.XV.152), which might—might!—give us a riddling 'Wille Longelonde'. And although critics often assume that the poem's protagonist has the resonant, potentially allegorical name *Will*, Helen Cooper has observed that only lines in the C text really undergird this idea (Cooper 2023). As

Michael Calabrese says, starting a book chapter titled 'Life of the Poet', 'No one knows who wrote *Piers Plowman*, and if someone called William Langland did so, no one knows anything certain about him' (2016, 1).

Piers Plowman is, then, potentially a poem written by a vanishing textual cipher and presented in versions either identified or invented 500 years later. Potentially: the versioning of *Piers* was an attempt to interpret the evidence, that is, an argument. It might yet remain the argument that best fits the evidence. William Langland might cut a rather empty figure, but we have more snippets of evidence for his authorship than for anyone else's. To stop thinking about these problems simply because their solutions are uncertain would be lazy. Rather, we should remember that these are matters of argument, and that an edition's argument about *Piers Plowman* begins on its cover, when it declares a version and an author.

At least *Piers* enjoys rough agreement that there is an existing literary work, *Piers Plowman*, that one might edit. What of looser collections that mutated as time passed and as scribes copied manuscripts? The changing set of saints' lives now called the *South English Legendary* supplies a good example. More than sixty extant manuscripts contain material associated with the *Legendary*, and that number shows its long-lasting, widespread influence and significance. But the members of that club of sixty range from substantial, full or near-complete copies, through miscellanies including a few or just one of the tales, to short, damaged fragments (Görlach 1974, viii–ix). Different manuscripts include changing sets of saints, because different saints interested different people; each part of England had its own local figures to fit in among the well-known names venerated to some degree everywhere. The cluster of saints' lives that make up the *Legendary* probably represent the work of several different poets.

The TEAMS METS series of editions contains two lives of St Frideswide (in *Reames ed. 2003, 23–50): their present-day anthology describes them confidently and in some sense rightly as the Shorter and Longer *South English Legendary* lives of the saint. Yet the Shorter life survives in only two manuscripts, the Longer in only six. These small numbers make sense, since Frideswide was not a widespread saint. She received veneration primarily in a region centred on Oxford, where she had lived. But these small numbers within the *South English Legendary*'s large manuscript tradition mean that Frideswide's story did not feature in most audiences' experiences of the *Legendary*. That fact shows how the collection travelled through time and through different manuscripts as a hospitable, changeable clump of poems that could receive new members. Equally, readers could pluck out individual stories within the *Legendary* for copying alone, or for copying into books alongside other religious writings in varied anthologies.

Such compiled, collective works that mutated as they travelled hold importance in and of themselves, but also as models and influences. One of Chaucer's models for the *Canterbury Tales* was the Italian prose *Decameron* of Giovanni Boccaccio. But Chaucer's *Tales* range more widely across different speakers, social classes, and textual forms than the *Decameron*, which sticks universally to prose stories told by the well-to-do. The *Canterbury Tales* is a single-author literary work lightly masquerading as a multi-author anthology of the sort that might fold in a poem from the *South English Legendary*—and, of course, the *Tales* include both a saint's life, the Second Nun's Tale, and poems that approach the genre, such as the Man of Law's Tale and the Clerk's Tale.

The *Tales* also absorbed, in twenty-five surviving manuscripts, the distinctly un-saintly *Tale of Gamelyn*, an outlaw story probably not by Chaucer (Knight and Ohlgren eds 1997). *Gamelyn* entered manuscripts of the *Tales* to stand as the Cook's second tale, filling in a felt gap after he breaks off his first (I 4422). Today editors tend to print it separately, but to many readers in the fifteenth century *Gamelyn* could have seemed as Chaucerian as the Knight's Tale. Later, *Gamelyn* entered broader literary tradition via sixteenth-century adaptations, and Shakespeare's *As You Like It* descends from the poem. Chaucer's *Parliament of Fowls* offers a curious modern parallel. In many editions, including the *Norton Chaucer* (680–693), this poem ends with a short **inset lyric** sung by the birds. However, Ralph Hanna has noted that this inset work doesn't seem to fit with bird singers—its words refer to the birds in the third person—and that the earliest evidence for it emerges more than a half-century after the poem's likely composition (1995, 185–190). Whether or not Chaucer wrote the inset material, he probably didn't mean for it to appear in the *Parliament* at this point. Like *Gamelyn*, this short poem has hitched a ride in the Chaucer tradition, this time during modern editing. I could multiply to the point of tedium examples of such textual difficulty.

Nevertheless, as this chapter has laid out, research does have tools for making sensible proposals about what poets wrote, even when the surviving manuscripts disagree, or are inadequate, or differ in their visual presentation. Since we have tools, we should use them. Close reading and editing enjoy strong ties. Peering into the messy world of manuscript evidence forever changes the way one reads editions, but the change can be positive, opening up new, subtler readings. Editors are guided by their literary-critical judgements so that, for example, a sense for a poet's use of repeated rhymes can bolster a textual-critical argument. To compare the different surviving texts of a poem carefully is to read it closely.

Readers should feel freed to read early poems closely, but they should read editions closely too. For any poem, readers can at least check what the edition's introduction says about how the editor crafted the text as presented. Check whether the edition provides a glossary and a set of explanatory notes, and use these aids if they are available. Ask where the editors get their text, and what they think they've done to it. Have the editors standardized the spelling, for instance? Have they altered the text at points on metrical grounds? Ask, too, what they think the purpose and audience of their edition is; editions are time-bound texts themselves, and the older the edition the more cultural difference to be found in it. Ideas of the Middle Ages were harnessed to propel contemporary cultural obsessions in the nineteenth century, just as they are today, and editions from that period often offer an eyebrow-raising window on their own time of creation even as they make yet-older works available. Sections of textual notes, records of variants in different manuscripts, and editors' introductions can all reveal much, and an enterprising critic can wring incisive ideas out of such materials. The field needs future editors, and some books guide those interested in editing for its own sake (Kelemen 2009; Gillespie and Hudson eds 2013; Hanna 2015). For everyone else, a little familiarity with the architecture of editions goes a long way.

In the longest historical perspective, the instability of early poetry isn't unusual. A critical, thoughtful attitude to editions helps in work on literature from any period, because all works make a journey to reach readers, even more recent ones that seem more stable. A publisher's logistical demands, for instance, required Virginia Woolf to remove two and a half pages from her novel *To the Lighthouse* shortly before printing: the small difference in length saved a noticeable production expense (Shillingsburg 2017, 66–82). This cut was an authorial choice, but it was not a choice driven by literary craft. Should the text which Woolf cut appear in the novel? Moreover, the two first editions of the novel printed in the UK and in the USA also differ in a number of small but potentially significant ways, because Woolf simultaneously proofread and then returned two distinct physical drafts to her two distinct UK and US publishers (Shillingsburg 2017, 70). Both first editions of the novel originate with Woolf; which one is *To the Lighthouse*? Few copies of the novel clearly signal these questions.

Similarly, I mentioned Percy Bysshe Shelley at this chapter's start, as an instance of a canonical poet whose works tend to be presented as clean, finished, iconic lyrics. Really, though, his poems offer their own textual problems. In its first published form, *Mont Blanc*, for instance, begins 'The everlasting universe of things / Flows through the mind' (Shelley and Shelley 1817, 175). However, in an **autograph** fair copy which turned up in 1976, the first lines run 'In day the eternal universe of things / Flows through the mind' (London, British Library, Loan MS 70/8, folio 4 recto). The two versions differ meaningfully right through the poem, and both texts originate with Shelley himself. Examples of textual trouble involving other modern writers abound (Kelemen 2009, 387–508, 554–566). And manuscript rediscoveries happen for Middle English poetry too: a large new set of stories by Osbern Bokenham came to light in 2004, for example, and is being published volume by volume at the time of writing (Bokenham 2020–2022).

All works, at all times, make a journey to reach readers. Knowledge of the journey often sharpens literary criticism. On this point, early writings are not categorically different. Their editions simply talk more openly about their evidence's difficulty and the complexity of their problems. An alertness to editorial issues in early verse has value for its own sake, but it can also prime us to ask the same fruitful questions of modern works that might seem more secure. The ideal critical reader of literature from any time looks at once and with pleasure through an edition to the literary work, and at the same edition as one particular set of arguments about the evidence.

10
Poetry of Many Tongues

> Pité, prouesse, humblesse, honour roial.   *Mercy, power, humility; royal*

When I first met these words, the beginning of the dedicatory poems in John Gower's *Cinkante Balades* (2011, 1), I thought they were English. The following lines dispel the illusion: 'Se sont en vous, mon liege seignour, mis / Du providence q'est celestial' ('belong to you, my liege lord, sent by Providence, that is heavenly', 2–3). This is French. The illusion's possibility reveals something, though. I erred when I first read this because the line delivers five open-class words which were all borrowed into English from French, and so could be from either language.

It is fitting that this happened to me in Gower's later fourteenth-century poetry, because literary history remembers him as the last English poet to write major works in all three of French, Latin, and English, England's most common written languages in these centuries: respectively, the *Mirour de l'Omme*, *Vox Clamantis*, and *Confessio Amantis*. By this chapter, readers will have grasped some of the impact of other languages on Middle English and Older Scots, but the multilingual situation of the British Isles in this period deserves attention as a topic in its own right. In reading early literature, we work with categories laid down in the nineteenth century, when unitary, increasingly monolingual European nation-states served as the default boxes into which researchers sorted works. Earlier writings, however, usually came forth in cultural groupings either above or below the level of the nation. Early poems had local, regional ties created by the great variation in English from place to place and by the person-to-person movement of manuscripts; such works also had very far-reaching ties: think of the influence on Chaucer of French and Italian poetry and indeed, at some remove, Arabic science; or the legend of the Christian saints Barlaam and Josaphat (in poems such as *NIMEV* 39 | *DIMEV* 54), which descends, though changed beyond recognition, from stories about Siddhartha Gautama, the Buddha. Writing's tendency towards the sub-national and the supra-national created many overlapping multi-language contexts. Middle English poems are often directly multilingual, and England's multilingual situation offers crucial context for them. The topic comes closely bound up with one of the qualities which make Middle English so valuable today: its relatively low status in its own time. This chapter sketches out multilinguistic contexts for Older Scots and Middle English, and then explores some implications through specific examples.

Languages and literacy

English, normally learned as a first language, was the most widely spoken tongue within England, and as this book's period progressed Scots grew more widespread in lowland Scotland. In England, legislation regularized the use of English in legal proceedings in the middle of the fourteenth century, and in the fifteenth century more documents and records began to use English. These changes later in our period hardly meant, though, that English swept out other languages.

If anything, English was something of an othered tongue even in England. Middle English lacked standardization and—as far as the surviving evidence can suggest—no one bothered to write any substantial commentary on its grammar, its vocabulary or its verse-craft. The seeming lack of serious writing about English in this period contrasts both with Latin, and with other European vernaculars such as Icelandic, Welsh, and Provençal (Machan 1994, 149–150). Literate people sometimes said of English during the Middle English period what English-speakers would go on to say centuries later about some other languages: that it was ungrammatical, disorganized, and illogical. This historical reversal shows how such judgements about the inherent qualities of languages often stem not from linguistic observation, but from power.

Latin served as western and northern Europe's intellectual and international language: it was the language of the church, of science, of theology, and of literary criticism. Latin's ubiquity meant someone could write in Galway, on Ireland's west coast, and potentially find readers in Porvoo (in what is now Finland), Prague (now in the Czech Republic), or Porto (Portugal). The common form of the Bible in Western Europe, the Vulgate, was a Latin translation of the original Hebrew and Greek texts. The late fourteenth century did bring forth a sophisticated translation of the Vulgate into Middle English, the Wycliffite Bible, which became the most widely circulated English work before print (Solopova ed. 2017). However, the Latin Vulgate remained the normative and prototypical Bible, with even more copies in circulation—many, many more. Poets in England still wrote in Latin: in the fourteenth century Gower did, and Ralph Strode, Chaucer's 'philosophical Strode' (*Troilus and Criseyde*, V.1857), probably did too, though the relevant work hasn't survived. In the thirteenth century, Thomas of Hales, the likely author of the Middle English poem *Love Rune* (Fein ed. 1998, art. 1), probably didn't regard himself as an English poet: he was a Franciscan friar who gathered saints' lives in Latin and wrote sermons in French alongside English verse-making. In religious and scholarly contexts, Latin persisted as a spoken language too. In some ways, Latin occupied a social place like that of tongues such as French, Spanish, and English today in regions where they rarely serve as first languages but see use as languages of exchange; Latin held this place for similar reasons, for it too was an empire's residue.

However, unlike Spanish, French, and English today, Latin was no longer a first language. First-language Latin had branched off into the various 'Romance' tongues, such as present-day Romanian, Spanish, Italian, and French, and all of these had changed enough that their speakers learned Latin as a distinct second language.

Though Latin continued to be heard aloud, it had become closely identified with the very idea of writing itself, partly thanks to its role as the language of the Vulgate, but also because it was baked into formal education. Learning to read and write usually meant learning to read and write in Latin, with literacy in any other languages coming as a handy by-product. (Poetry itself had a pragmatic role in basic literacy as a memory aid, and so education and verse went hand-in-hand: Cannon 2016.) Because education meant Latin education, most people writing down Middle English poetry probably, given that they could write at all, had at least a partial grasp of a written language other than English. One might say that readers and poets often had Latin as a first written language.

The thought of education invites a brief account of literacy. The literacy rate was low by present-day standards, but steadily increased across this book's period. As Michael Clanchy showed in a classic study (2013), during the twelfth and thirteenth centuries writing grew more and more important to society, and by 1300 writing already affected almost everyone, at all social levels; anyone illiterate could have found someone to read documents for them if necessary. Although reading and writing come together today, they are separate skills, and some readers in this period did not write. Any family with lettered parents or servants could offer some education within the home (Orme 2006, 60–61; Clanchy 2018), and training in reading and composition was available for boys in schools (Orme 2006). Schooling lay within the reach of the most prosperous sections of the rural peasantry and was probably more accessible in cities. Those who were male, smart, and lucky could find in education a narrow but real route by which they could rise, often to university study, followed by ecclesiastical or bureaucratic careers.

John Lydgate, pillar of fifteenth-century English poetry, seems to have been such a riser. He emerged from obscure and rural circumstances in the small village of Lidgate, propelled upwards because people judged—rightly—that his talents might prove useful: in a surviving letter, the Prince of Wales, the future Henry V, encourages Lydgate's superiors to keep Lydgate at university, and he went on to write poetry for earls, dukes, and Henry VI, as well as for members of the gentry and for institutions. The others born with him in Lidgate likely lived rather less comfortable lives. To highlight a career like Lydgate's is not to suggest that, even if only for men, society in Great Britain in these centuries was meritocratic or egalitarian. Rather, as in most other places and times, power could co-opt skill found in low places, and risers found hierarchies less rigid in practice than in theory; one of the universal images of the period is the Wheel of Fortune, alternately raising people up and casting them down.

Books cost more to produce than they do today, but many were still relatively affordable, and an enthusiast could spend their own labour time copying a desired work personally. Increasingly over the centuries covered here, reading and writing ceased to be elite skills. They were certainly not, as people today sometimes imagine, skills restricted to churchmen, or indeed to men: probably the earliest surviving Valentine's message in English was written by a woman named Margery Brews, in 1477. We should remember, too, that reading and writing are two skills: some people could read but not write. Whether fully literate in our terms or not, people could write by dictation or read by listening to someone else reading aloud. In *Troilus and Criseyde*, Chaucer depicts Criseyde listening, together with other women, to 'a maiden' who reads for them (II.78–112). Although in today's terms someone else does the act of reading, Criseyde says that 'we rede', collectively (II.100), and she spots and reads the red-ink headings in their book (II.103–105). These lines offer an idealized image, but they still puncture present-day assumptions that reading must or should be a solo pursuit, and show how people could have been social readers (Coleman 1996). I shall say more on early poetry heard aloud in Chapter 11.

French had a strong presence in England as a language of power, because of the conquest of the country in 1066 by the French-speaking Normans. Over time, Norman French in England diverged further from the varieties of French spoken in France, becoming a type which scholars now call 'Anglo-Norman', 'Anglo-French', 'Insular French', or 'the French of England' (Wogan-Browne ed. 2009; Busby 2023, 105–106). The distinction between Norman and English people slowly faded out, but Anglo-Norman lasted long as an elite and administrative tongue; sometimes administrative work that shifted from Latin to the vernacular shifted to the vernacular of Anglo-Norman, not to English. It is hard to overstate the impact of French on the English language, and especially its vocabulary. French generated much of the variety in lexis discussed in Chapter 2. By the later fourteenth century even aristocrats tended to have English as a first language, but French remained as a standard second tongue among many of the educated.

As the French of England diverged from the French of Northern France and of Paris, the continental types became a separate, more prestigious influence. The English crown owned some parts of what is now France, and England spent many spells of the thirteenth, fourteenth, and fifteenth centuries at war with the nascent French state; the conflict might have stoked jingoism (e.g. *Minot 1996), but it also brought the English into closer contact with France's varieties of French, as, variably, soldiers, diplomats, occupiers, administrators, captives in France, and the hosts of captives in England (Butterfield 2009; Bellis 2016; Strakhov 2022). The Norman Conquest of 1066 didn't directly affect Scotland, but Scots language and literature received strong influences from continental French through simple proximity, through trade and travel, and through frequent alliances joining France and Scotland against England. France was a larger country, and French had a transnational role as a language of cultural exchange in north-western Europe, as Latin did as a language for universities and the church.

Besides linguistic influence, the prestige of France's literature and perhaps the prospect of a more international audience also encouraged English poets to write in French. In the thirteenth and especially the twelfth century, much English writing was writing in French when it wasn't writing in Latin. The strength and earliness of this English work in French makes it possible to argue, as Laura Ashe does, that 'the earliest French literature was written in England' (ed. 2015, xv). In the fourteenth century, English writers continued to write in French. Gower did, as I have noted, and so, probably, did John Montagu (*c.*1350 to *c.*1400), a figure moving in the same circles as Chaucer, though placed higher in society and more caught up in the messy politics of later fourteenth-century England. Montagu's poetry doesn't survive, but in its day it won praise from the French writer Christine de Pizan, whom he befriended (Turner 2023, 109). Some fourteenth-century French poems survive annotated with a mysterious 'Ch', and likely written in England (*Wimsatt ed. 2009). Chaucer probably didn't compose these, but the idea is tantalizing. In the fifteenth century, well after the heyday of Anglo-Norman, active English composition in French dwindled, but French poetry remained a widespread source of words and formal models. Some English mentions of French in this century suggest associations with sophistication and beauty. Those associations have stuck around, as the menus found in a certain kind of restaurant in England today can attest.

Since French was a medium of cultural transmission across borders, poets writing in English also often drew on French sources, even when adapting works not originally written in French. Lydgate used Laurent de Premierfait's French translation of Giovanni Boccaccio's Latin *De casibus virorum illustrium* to write his own English *Fall of Princes*, and says so in his opening stanza:

> He that whilom dede his dilligence   *He: i.e. Laurent*
> The book of Bochas in Frensh to translate   *Boccaccio*
> Out of Latyn, he callid was Laurence;
> The tyme trewli remembrid and the date,
> The yere whan Kyng John thoruh his mortal fate   *John II of France*
> Was prisoner brouht to this regioun,   *to England*
> Whan he first gan on this translacioun.   *he: Laurent*
> (1924–1927, 1–7)

Lydgate uses the English victory over a French army at the battle of Poitiers, at which King John II of France was captured, to date Laurent's translation to 1356 (4–6): his stanza simultaneously registers French's prestige and international reach, the memory of a victory over France, and an example of the kind of princely fall which his own poem takes as its subject. He fits the concept of translation in twice, in different parts of speech but as a rhyme word both times (2, 7). In Middle English, as its *MED* entry shows, *translacioun* retained some of its etymological sense of movement, and writers used it to describe shifts in might and knowledge between regions, shifts of the sort in which Lydgate might have seen himself participating. As it happens, the battle of Poitiers involved two firmly multilingual armies: the French forces included Germans and Scots, while the English side contained substantial groups of Gascons and Welshmen.

Pretty much everyone who spoke English or Scots therefore had some contact with other languages. Even at the bottom of the social ladder, the least educated, unluckiest people would have encountered church Latin, probably shreds of French from their social superiors, and, depending on geography, other vernaculars of the British Isles such as Welsh, Gaelic, Cornish, or Irish. In the middle and higher parts of society, some multilingualism was normal and necessary for trade (Hsy 2013) and administration. The scribe who assembled the Harley Manuscript (*Fein ed. 2014–2015) in the fourteenth century, for instance, comfortably assimilated works in Latin, French, and English, and we can assume the same for some in his audience. Multilingualism has been normal in many places for most of human history, and those populations who are monolingual today—usually because they speak, as their first languages, tongues with regional prestige, such as Standard Mandarin Chinese or English—seem, in historical or global perspective, rather odd. Few speakers learned English as a second language. People rarely translated English works into other languages, and when they did, they normally used English materials for convenience rather than for cultural cachet (Byrne 2020). English had less prestige than French and Latin, and writing in English was in some ways less normal. Such conditions left Middle English verse more precarious and experimental and make it at once a shaky foundation for any idea of a glorious national tradition, and a body of work all the more fascinating for its unfixed, uncentred qualities.

The British Isles heard plenty of languages other than Latin, French, Scots, and English. Visitors and immigrants from elsewhere brought many tongues to the archipelago, and some, such as Dutch and Flemish, added to Middle English's vocabulary. Until the 1290 Edict of Expulsion, Jewish communities in England kept up written Hebrew, and just a few of their Hebrew poems survive (e.g. Roth 2020). One set of living languages had sounded consistently in the British Isles longer than English: Cornish in Cornwall, Welsh in Wales, Manx on the Isle of Man, Irish in Ireland, and Gaelic in many parts of Scotland.

Ireland, to consider just one of these contexts, had its own complex linguistic situation. The Norman rulers of England had subjugated parts of Ireland in the later twelfth century, and these parts of the country were administrated from Dublin. An Irish variety of English, Hiberno-English, had developed around that city, but English rule also meant the administrative use of English French, while in ecclesiastical and educational contexts Latin was used throughout Ireland much as it was throughout England and other nearby parts of Europe. Irish itself, meanwhile, continued in wide use. Verse existed in all of these languages. Ireland in these centuries was not a harmonious place, with disputes within and across different linguistic and cultural communities. But it was also not a place of total division. The fourteenth century saw attempts from the island's nominal overlords to separate out post-Norman or English groups by legislating for their language and customs, notably in the 1366 Statutes of Kilkenny. These attempts failed, though, and the fact that rulers made them in the first place shows that the lines dividing categories of people had become hazier in practice than they might have been in theory. Exactly how research should file verse written in English in Ireland at this time is a question for a different kind of book. The surviving material is, though, historically and formally fruitful (Turville-Petre ed. 2015; Kerby-Fulton 2020), and includes such fascinating items as the earliest known morality play in English, *Pride of Life* (Klausner ed. 2008).

Readers of Middle English and early Scots writings should keep these complex surrounding contexts in mind, and always remember that these works emerged when English had close contact with many other tongues, some of them more standardized and more prestigious than itself.

Mixing speech

Given this background, the trilingual career of John Gower comes as no surprise; if there was an adventurous language choice in Gower's career, perhaps it was the decision to compose *Confessio Amantis*, a substantial poem for an elevated audience, in English. The multilingual background also helps to explain Gower's decision to scatter *Confessio Amantis* with chunks of Latin, both blocks of Latin verse in the poem itself and Latin marginal commentary. For at least some readers, the Latin passages would have been not difficult barriers, but rather engaging changes of pace; for all readers, meanwhile, the Latin would have conveyed Gower's learning and claimed some level of authority.

Sustained English verse with interspersed blocks of Latin was a normal mode for poetry at the time. The most well-witnessed English poem of the period, the *Prik of Conscience*, proceeds in just this manner: Latin quotations of authorities, followed by translations and elaborations in Middle English verse (*Morey ed. 2012). In surviving manuscripts, where the Latin sections often come highlighted by red ink, underlining, or script changes, pages of the two poems even resemble each other visually. Religious instructional poems such as the *Prik of Conscience* might have furnished Gower with one model for his ostensibly confessional work. Yet the two also differ in the relationship they create between Latin and English. The *Prik of Conscience* always carefully translates its Latin material: its poet thought at least portions of its audience would lack knowledge of authoritative Latin works and the ability to translate heard Latin. This expectation fits with—and helps to explain—the very wide audience that the poem achieved. *Confessio Amantis*, by contrast, usually expects its audience to keep up with Latin without help, and sometimes seems to play Latin and English off against each other. Despite the time's prevailing multilingualism, not every multilingual work expects full facility in all its tongues. It's worth asking what language skills a poem does or doesn't expect in its audience.

Take a seemingly simple use of Latin early in the *Prik of Conscience*. During a discussion of life's unhappiness, the poem remarks that babies cry as soon as they enter the world and then, in a digression typical of its baggy, inclusive manner, pauses to tell the audience about those cries. Any baby will cry, and

By that crye mon may knowe thon	then
Whether hit be monn or wemon.	it; man or woman
When hit is borne hit cryeth wa:	woe
Yif hit be mon hit cryeth 'a',	If
That is the fyrst letter of the name	
Of oure formoure fadur Adame;	forefather
And if the childe a woman be	
When hit is borne then seyth hit 'e',	it says
The fyrste lettre that is of Eve	
That bygon us fyrst to greve.	to grieve us
Therfore were maad on this maner	
Thes versus that ben writen here:	verses
Dicentes E vel A quotquot nascuntur ab Eva;	
A dat Adam genitor E dedit Eua mater.	
[All are born of 'Eva', saying 'E' or 'A'	
Adam the father gives 'A', Eve the mother gave 'E'.]	
'Al tho', he seyth, 'that comen of Eve	those
That ben alle men as we byleve,	
When they be borne, what so they be	
Thei shul seyn, outher "a" or "e".'	

(*Morey ed. 2012, I.106–123)

Setting aside for a moment this idea's implausibility, consider the use of Latin. The poet adapted the quotation, along with much else in this passage, from *De miseria condicionis humane* (*On the Miserable State of Humanity*), a work written in the twelfth century and well known at this time. Chaucer used *De miseria* as a source for parts of the Man of Law's Tale, and claimed to have translated it, though no copy of such a translation survives (*Legend of Good Women*, G Prologue 414–415). Note too, though, how the poem translates the Latin quotation twice, both before and after it occurs: again, unlike Gower's *Confessio Amantis*, this work wants to ensure comprehension by readers without Latin. Note also how this is an intensely lettered set of ideas: in describing *e* as 'The fyrste lettre that is of Eve', these lines expect all of their audience, literate or not, to exercise some sense of what a letter is and how a letter works (on which see Scase 2022). Similar expectations appear in the carol *'M and A and R and I' (*Saupe ed. 1997, art. 45; *NIMEV* 1650 | *DIMEV* 2771). As a carol, this might have started life being sung aloud, but it nevertheless determinedly frames its Marian devotion through the idea of Mary's written name:

M and A, R and I.	
Tho wern letteris of Mary	
Of hom al our joye sprong.	whom; sprang

(2–4)

Other tongues did not always arrive in English poetry in neat units, as the Latin does in *Confessio Amantis* and the *Prik of Conscience*. Plenty of surviving poems mix multiple languages together, often in syntactically linked ways; we call such verse **macaronic**. We might fruitfully order such poems by the intimacy of their mingling of tongues. A poem can, after all, fold in multiple languages distributed across distinct parts, as in carols with Latin **burdens** (Chapter 8). The first stanza of one carol with a Latin burden runs as follows:

> When Cryst was born of Mary fre
> In Bedlem, in that fayre cité   *Bethelehem*
> Angelles songen with myrth and gle,   *sang; glee*
> 'In excelsis gloria'   *Glory in the highest*
> Christo paremus cantica: *Let's ready songs for Christ*
> 'In excelsis gloria.'
>   (Duncan ed. 2013, art. II.58, 3–7; *NIMEV* 2932 | *DIMEV* 6283)

The Latin sits partly integrated in the same syntactic unit as the English, but the shift in language matches the shift into the carol's burden, enhancing the burden's capstone impact; in other forms, poets could achieve similar effects with refrains (Duncan ed. 2013, arts II.63, II.73). The burden or refrain in such multilingual verse can integrate into the English syntax, but separations in verse form still distinguish languages.

Verse form and performance could weave languages closer together. One of the somewhat mysterious fifteenth-century *N-Town Plays—so-called for letter *N* in their manuscript, a place-holder standing in for any settlement's name—portrays and expands on a biblical passage, Luke 1: 39–56, in which Mary visits her relative Elizabeth (*Sugano ed. 2007, art. 13). In the Bible, Mary sings a song of joy that became a regular feature of Christian liturgy, the Magnificat; in the play, Mary delivers the Vulgate's Latin version of the Magnificat in paired lines, which Elizabeth matches with rhyming English translations to form quatrains:

> MARIA: *Esurientes implevit bonis,*
>   *Et divites dimisit inanes.*
> ELIZABETH: Alle the pore and the nedy he fulfyllyth with his goodys,
>   And the ryche, he fellyth to voydnes.
> ('He wholly fills the poor and needy with his goods, and He knocks down the rich to emptiness.' *Sugano ed. 2007, 106–9)

In these lines the Latin and English parts stay syntactically separated, since the English translates the Latin, but the two elements join in the rhymes, which only work across languages.

Poets could make even more granular shifts between tongues, operating at the line level. Various examples of this survive (e.g. *Audelay 2009, art. W35.15); perhaps one of the most charming is a trilingual love piece in which each stanza takes this form:

> *Icest est ma volunte,*   *This is my wish*
> That I mighte be with thee
> *Ludendo;*   *Playing*
> *Vostre amour en moun qoer*   *Your love in my heart*
> Brenneth hote as doth the fyr   *Burns hot; fire*
> *Cressendo.*   *Springing up.*
>   (Duncan ed. 2013, II.12, 37–42; *NIMEV* 16 | *DIMEV* 19)

This poem consists of *aabccb* **tail-rhyme** stanzas, organized so that each half of a stanza contains a couplet made up of one French line and one English line, followed by a single-word tail-rhymed Latin line. The three languages integrate more closely here than in my earlier examples: the grammatical subject of the verb 'Brenneth', for instance, is 'Vostre amour' at the previous line's start—it is 'your love' that 'burns'—and both of the Latin lines modify elements in the preceding English. These lines show one advantage of macaronic verse: surprising links. *Heart* and *fire*—or *herte* and *fyr*—don't rhyme in English, and nor do *coeur* and *feu* in French, but this poet can, just about, aurally link the two concepts by writing in both languages: *qoer:fyr*. The number of languages deployed in this poem—three—was not a hard limit. Somewhere in the west of the German-speaking part of Europe, someone known only to us as Brother (or Bruder) Hans wrote quadrilingual poetry in praise of Mary around the turn of the fifteenth century, cycling in his elaborate prologue through lines of German, Latin, French, and English (1963). Brother Hans was exceptional: almost no second-language speakers of English in the European mainland bothered to try writing poetry in the obscure insular tongue, and the oddity of Hans's choice comes through in the ways that the scribes copying his work tend to mangle the English lines. His rare example does, though, show how far multilingual writing could go.

 At the turn of the sixteenth century, similar line-by-line separations appear at points in John Skelton's *Phyllyp Sparowe*, a fizzingly energetic poem which sometimes comically repurposes fragments from Bible passages and church services for the dead in order to mourn a pet bird:

> *Si iniquita es*   *[Psalm 130:3]*
> Alas, I was evyll at ease!   *distressed*
> *De profundis clamavi,*   *[Psalm 130:1]*
> Whan I sawe my sparowe dye!
>   (Skelton 2015, art. 7, 143–146)

Here Skelton neatly rhymes Latin and English together, including, in the first of these two couplets, something close to a bilingual **punning rhyme**, *es:ease*. Yet he lays out the rhyme in counterpoint to the syntax, and the syntax separates the two languages. Skelton expects the audience to join the two English lines together, apart from the Latin: the fourth line quoted provides a subordinate clause modifying the 'was' of the second line quoted.

The most macaronic poems of all mix tongues within lines. Thus one late poem's startling description of dying:

> *Corpus migrat* and my sowle, *The body departs; soul*
> *Respicit demon* in his rowle, *The demon checks; roll (i.e. list)*
> *Desiderat ipse* to have his tolle. *He wants; toll*
> (Duncan ed. 2013, art. II.88, 13–15)

This poem maintains a left–right distinction, putting Latin at each line's start, but otherwise fully mingles the two languages.

Each example so far has come from a short poem, but one of the most notable macaronic English poems from the period is *Piers Plowman*. Often Langland folds Latin into his poem in units of one or a few lines. Early on, the personification of Holy Church memorably uses Latin in this marked-off way while rebuking the poem's speaker, Will, for his limited Latinity:

> 'Thow doted daffe!' quod she, 'dulle are thi wittes. *silly fool*
> To litel Latyn thow lernedest, leode, in thi youthe: *too little; fellow*
> "*Heu michi quod sterilem duxi vitam iuvenilem!*"
> [Ah, what a fruitless life I led in my youth! (a proverb)]
> (Langland 1995, I.140–142, trans. Schmidt)

Many of us wish we had learned more Latin, or any Latin, in our youths; today knowledge of other languages, living or dead, is often restricted on the basis of wealth, and on this specific point we do little better than earlier societies, perhaps sometimes worse. It might be comforting to see Langland touching on a related anxiety, and it's certainly worth remembering that the experience of multilingual life and multilingual reading within this period was sometimes one of misunderstanding and frustration rather than playful fluency. In any case, this single-line quotation of a proverb exemplifies Langland's delivery of Latin in distinct units.

However he wanted his audience to judge Will's abilities, Langland himself could fluently use English and Latin together in even more precise ways. He frequently works shorter Latin phrases into otherwise English lines, fully fitting them into syntax and alliteration. At the start of Passus X of the B text, Dame Study rebukes Wit for teaching Will:

> [She] seide, '*Noli mittere*, man, margery perles   *Do not cast*
> Among hogges that han hawes at wille'.   *swine; have hawthorn-berries*
>   (Langland 1995, X.9–10)

Study invokes the Bible here, recalling one instruction of Jesus among those grouped together in the Gospel according to Matthew: 'Do not give what is holy to dogs, and do not throw your pearls before swine' or, as Langland would have known it in the Latin Vulgate translation, 'nolite dare sanctum canibus neque mittatis margaritas vestras ante porcos' (Matthew 7: 6). In the verse line, 'margery' serves as an alliterating but otherwise rather redundant word, best taken as an intensifying adjective: 'margery perles' means something like *pearly pearls* (*MED*). However, we can clarify why 'margery' appears when we look at the actual Latin text Langland would have had in mind and see that it includes the word *margaritas*: Langland used 'margery' partly to summon up the relevant Bible passage in his audiences' heads. Study elaborates slightly on the biblical text in the second line quoted, for Jesus doesn't mention haws, hawthorn berries, proverbial in Middle English as a low-value food (Whiting and Whiting 1968, entries H189–193); to have something *at wille* means to have something as desired, when one likes, but the phrase might also pun on the possible name of *Piers Plowman*'s point of view, Will, who is—in Study's view—the hog on whom Wit wastes words.

As in the short phrase '*Noli mittere*', Langland's Latin often calls on a longer quotation or even passage, from the Bible or another significant work, in readers' minds. *Mittere* slides neatly into the surrounding alliterative structure, and this intimate integration of Latin into English verse-craft is also typical of Langland. On occasion, he even imposes English word-endings on Latin words: when he writes 'thorugh *Beatus virr*es teaching', the Latin phrase *Beatus vir* takes on the Middle English possessive word-ending -*es* (X.318). *Beatus vir*, 'Blessed [is] the man', is the first phrase of the first Psalm in the Latin Vulgate translation of the Bible, so again here Langland is calling on a much larger and very well-known passage. Not without cause has it been suggested that for those lucky enough to have full literacy at this time, what seem to us distinct languages might have been experienced as one unified terrain (Hanna 2019).

How, then, to deal with the many-tongued nature of many poems, in practical terms? Readers shouldn't feel overawed. The eye should not skip past multilingual material: use the notes or the glossing in a decent edition to understand such passages. Consider whether the verse expects exact comprehension or, like the *Prik of Conscience*, self-glosses its ventures into other tongues. Consider, too, whether other games are being played, as when Chauntecleer mistranslates the proverbial phrase 'Mulier est hominis confusio' in Chaucer's Nun's Priest's Tale (*Canterbury Tales*, VII 3163–3166).

The use of several tongues often ties into verse-craft. How does the verse manage its different languages: in discrete blocks, in lines, or within lines? Do different languages relate syntactically to each other, or sit in separate units? Does the poet use shifts between languages as another type of division, to be coordinated with or placed in counterpoint to divisions between lines, rhymes, and stanzas? Or does the poet weave tongues together as though they are one? Does the poet use separate languages to marry up ideas which do not match in their English sounds? What might these choices suggest about theme, tone, or character? The main thing is to treat the presence of multiple languages not as a threat, but rather something ripe for thought.

Like languages themselves, multilingualism has highly porous borders. Research has increasingly turned to many-tongued works, but we might also ask whether the *mono*lingual Middle English poem is a trustworthy idea itself. Many Middle English works contain subtler uses of other languages. The women in *The Assembly of Ladies wear laconic French mottoes sewn into their clothes (e.g. Pearsall ed. 1990, 308, 364, 489, 583), for instance. Or, at a more basic level, consider all the smaller shreds of French and Latin which served as normal words, so that a character can exclaim 'Depardieux' (*Canterbury Tales*, II 39; *Troilus and Criseyde*, II.1058) or 'Deus!' (*Havelok the Dane, Herzman, Drake, and Salisbury eds 1997, 1313). When, after all, does a word become English? *Depardieux* probably served as a normal oath for many English speakers, much as *adieu* almost certainly seemed a normal word; editors do not normally apply the italics used to mark foreign words to *adieu* in Middle English, yet *depardieux* often is italicized, and this is determined by what readers find familiar today, not by past unfamiliarity.

Then there are the words which never took off or were probably borrowed by just one writer. In one part of *Pearl, for example, the poet uses the noun *(a)dubbement*, borrowed from French, to mean decoration or adornment, **concatenating** stanzas on it (72, 84, 85, 96, 108, 109, 120, 121). As far as the *MED* knows, this word only appears in *Pearl* among all surviving Middle English writings. A normal Middle English vocabulary probably lacked this noun. Perhaps the poet hoped people might work it out laterally from their knowledge of French, and from one of the more niche senses of the related verb *dubben*, which appears once to sustain the concatenation (97). One might reasonably wonder, therefore, just how English a word *adubbement* really was. That is an empty question, but the emptiness itself offers a lesson: we can't neatly judge the Englishness of *adubbement*, because all Middle English writing stretched out into other tongues. The line '*Respicit demon* in his rowle', quoted earlier, offers another good example: modern editors tend to italicize *demon* here, but, as the *MED* shows, this was a word in English as well as in Latin. (We still have it.) As one among the many tasks involved in editing this poem, a scholar might find themselves trying to work out whether *demon* counts as a foreign-language word which therefore needs italics. Yet it's not clear that this question is even appropriate to the material.

The study of any Middle English verse thus engages with many tongues even when the poetry in question doesn't openly contain words which seem foreign now. We cannot say the same for all English writing today. Middle English offers us a chance to study English literature in this opposite situation, contextualizing and undercutting English's present-day ubiquity and seeming inevitability. Once again, the literary unimportance of Middle English in its own time lends it importance now.

Tongues in tension

It would be easy to end the topic here, on a note of playful exchange between languages. We might also learn, though, by pushing at multilingualism's limits and strains. Scholarship sometimes risks flattening out the particularities—linguistic, poetic, ideological, and so forth—of different writings: English books often looked different to French books at this time, for instance, and were decorated differently, registering discernible differences in tradition. Charles d'Orleans learned English and had a remarkable transnational poetic career, but his French and English works do, reasonably enough, differ in their form, content, and political thrust (e.g. Renevey 2018, 205–207). We risk forgetting, too, that while English verse received profound influences from other languages and places, it exercised very little influence in return. Readers of macaronic Middle English verse did need English: the trilingual love poem quoted above, for instance, requires competence in English, despite delivering two-thirds of its lines in French and Latin. Such poems showed the fluid ability to meld languages, but they showed that fluidity to a narrow, English-speaking audience; they were exclusive in ways in which poetry in more widespread languages was not.

In closing, I shall let a Welsh poet complicate the picture further. In the middle of the fifteenth century, Tudur Penllyn wrote, among numerous poems wholly in Welsh, one in Welsh and English:

> 'Dydd daed, Saesnes guyffes, gain,
> yr wyf i'th garu, riain.'
>
> *'What saist, mon?'* ebe honno,
> *'For truthe, harde Welsman I tro.'*
>
> ('Good day to you, fine handy Englishwoman; I really fancy you, girl.'
> 'What do you say, man?' she said, 'Truly, I think you're a Welshman.'
> in Johnston ed. 1998, page 70, 1–4, trans. Johnston)

As this poem continues, in alternating pairs of Welsh lines and English lines, Penllyn makes advances on the English girl, but both remain mutually non-comprehending; the final words are 'Io ddyn, ai caniadu'dd wyd / I Dudur ai nad ydwyd?' ('Oh girl, are you letting Tudur do it, or are you not?', 33–34, trans. Johnston). The poem is an example of a *pastourelle*, a transnational genre about an encounter and dialogue between a man and a woman, involving sex as either possibility or actuality. For an English example different in tone, see *'In a fryht as Y con fare fremede' (Fein ed. 2014–2015, art. 35). The *pastourelle* sometimes had a woman of lower status displaying real or feigned non-comprehension of the courtly romantic lexis used by a man. Penllyn's poem, though, has both of its speakers fail to understand one another's languages. *Pastourelles* typically make an aesthetic object of male sexual aggression, and so they make for challenging reading, but also salutary material for thinking about a history for behaviours that survive today (Baechle, Harris, and Strakhov eds 2022): we delude ourselves if we think we can file such aggression as something that we have escaped, or for that matter if we think that everyone in the fifteenth century judged it acceptable.

Note how the poem's bilingual power dynamics defy modern expectations. Today, we might assume that all macaronic writing reveals fruitful interchange. This poem focuses instead on fractious separation. The poem draws humour from the fact that Penllyn-the-poet clearly grasped some English that Tudur-the-persona doesn't comprehend within the poem. The poem also draws energy from a language hierarchy. Fifteenth-century Wales was subjugated by the English state and subject to English settlement, but here Welsh is the tongue of the male aggressor, and also the framing, narrating tongue of the poem: the separation of languages into distinct pairs of lines breaks only once, in the third line's fully macaronic integration of the framing narratorial 'ebe honno' ('she said'). What's more, although roughly half the poem might use English words, it sticks throughout to Welsh verse-craft: Penllyn writes in *cynghanedd*, the general term for a range of Welsh forms which demand strict arrangements of alliteration, rhyme, and line-internal consonance. It matters that the English lines conform to Penllyn's Welsh verse-craft. Just as humour resides in the gap in English fluency between Penllyn the poet and his persona, another layer of the poem emerges from the imagined girl's combination of an ignorance of Welsh and a fluent grasp of Welsh verse form. Thus the italicization of the English in modern editions of this poem: here, though the poem has two languages, English definitely appears as the foreign one.

English saw use in parts of Wales, among English immigrants and bilingual inhabitants. In fifteenth-century Wales it was beginning to become a language of power and documentation. Yet the complexly linked sets of sexual, ethnic, poetic, and linguistic power dynamics at play in this poem challenge an assumption that English had straightforward power in Wales (see Hopwood 2021). These power dynamics also caution us against seeing macaronic verse as inherently bringing about a meeting of minds or cultures. Penllyn's poem is unimpeachably macaronic, but it still, nevertheless, enacts a stalwartly monolingual attitude. In the early 1470s, another fifteenth-century Welsh poet, Ieuan ap Hywel Swrdwal, played across tongues in a different way, writing a poem in English while still following the tenets of Welsh verse-craft (in Garlick and Mathias eds 1984, 45–48).

Fourteenth- and fifteenth-century contexts for poetry defy easy answers. Neither the verse nor the history will hand literary critics simple, comforting shibboleths, or blunt crowbars with which to lever works open. All Middle English verse at least tacitly draws on several tongues, and each openly multilingual case demands close study for its own details, on its own merits.

11
Verse Takes Breath

When present-day audiences think of verse, they often imagine it being read—and made—in contemplative silence, by a single reader with a written text. This vision is hardly typical even now. In the early twenty-first century, most engagement with verse happens when people listen to music. Some of the most popular textual verse today, verse circulated online, might be read silently and alone, but people nevertheless read it alone together, via online platforms built around sharing rather than simple top-down transmission. What we might call the university student model of verse reading, in a lonely garret—perhaps plagued by noise from next door in a hall of residence—or in an institutional library—perhaps enlivened by chatter from its new café—stands quite distant from normal verse experiences even today.

Such a model lies even further from the practices applied to earlier poems. In this book's period, people read verse aloud together for entertainment (Coleman 1996); poetry could be read aloud over or after a meal; poems were read to households as moral instruction; preachers integrated short poems into sermons (Wenzel 1986); groups sang songs and danced together. Many romances sound both more sensible and more fun when read aloud, and some might even have been sung (Putter 2018). People delivered some poems and songs from memory; in all eras, poetry has the strange quality, strange compared to (say) painting, photography, film, embroidery, architecture, sculpture, or cookery, that to call a poem to mind is to call the very poem itself to mind, as something that one can then pass to others. This is to say nothing of poetry which was written down but communally visible, as in a version of Lydgate's *Dance of Death* displayed on the walls of old St Paul's Cathedral in London, in the now mostly lost world of verse graffiti (Wakelin 2018, 34–37), or in verses at the doors of the cells of Carthusian monks. All of these might have prompted reading aloud, especially if encountered by a group with varied literacy levels.

Much early verse was written, or written down, to be read aloud, or at least with the expectation that most people who encountered it would hear it more than they saw it. We must fold the idea of poetry aloud into our grasp of how poems worked. Thinking on the spoken, heard aspects of early poems might, too, sharpen a sense for the spoken in modern writing, whether in canonical works often met as dry text on the page—the content of *The Waste Land* cries out to be spoken, and its working title, a phrase from Dickens, was *He Do the Police in Different Voices*—or in the vast worlds of contemporary music and spoken-word poetry.

Speech and song

A number of genres and modes simply become much more explicable if put in the context of hearing. Consider, for instance, the popularity of debates in verse: many Middle English poems contain debates or are wholly taken up by debate, from canonical works such as Chaucer's *Parliament of Fowls* and Nun's Priest's Tale, through known titles such as **The Owl and the Nightingale*, to less famous items such as **Wynnere and Wastoure* (Ginsberg ed. 1992) and John Clanvowe's **Boke of Cupide* (Symons ed. 2004). One of my favourites is Lydgate's *Debate of the Horse, Goose, and Sheep* (1911–1934, vol. 2, art. 23), in which the three animals debate which is most useful. The ram, sheep's advocate, points to wool, but also argues that the use of sheepskin for book parchment gives it the best claim. Even this remark on the material survival of texts comes couched in elegant rhetoric that benefits from being heard: from sheepskin, says the ram, 'is made good parchemyn, / To write on bookes in quaiers [*quires, gatherings of pages*] many fold', rising at once via rhyme to wealth and mythology by invoking the legendary Golden Fleece in the next line, 'The Ram of Colcos bar [*bore*] a flees of gold' (367–369). To read one of these debates aloud brings out much more of the comedy or vitriol at play.

Some conversational poems even end in questions perhaps designed to set further discussion going in a social setting. The Scottish poet William Dunbar, for instance, spends his **Tretis of the Twa Mariit Wemen and the Wedo* ventriloquizing the marital views of three imagined women, and then asks an assumed male audience, 'Ye auditoris most honorable, that eris [*ears*] has gevin / Oneto [*unto*] this uncouth aventur', which of the three they would rather marry if they had to choose (*2004, 527–528). Such prompts for discussion can sound stilted and artificial today, but it might help to imagine people leaving a cinema: they discuss the strengths and flaws of what they just saw, and the passive watching experience becomes a manifold, branching set of small exchanges and debates. Poems of this sort, perhaps designed to spark and fit into a following discussion, make it hard to say where the boundaries of the poem or the work fall. Or perhaps such poems bring to the surface some problems in bounding the concept of the work which always lurk around any writing, in any time: isn't every poem in part built socially and communally, by the things people say to one another about it?

More vitriolic than mere debates are the flytings which survive from late in this book's period. Flytings emerge from oral practices of competitive insult, with many analogues around the world and across time. They are literary and aestheticized, and those we have often come from court circles, but they stay pretty coarse and mean nevertheless. Dunbar, flyting Walter Kennedy—a fellow-poet with whom he seems, from other works, to have been on good terms—will go to almost any lengths to insult, lengths which challenge a translator: 'skyttand skarth, thow hes the hurle behind' ('beshitted monster, you've got diarrhoea in rear'), he says, 'ma wormis hes thow beschittin / Nor thair is gers on grund or leif on lind' ('you've shat out more worms than there're blades of grass on the ground or leaves on trees'; *The Flyting of Dunbar and Kennedy*, in *Dunbar 2004, 194–195). Kennedy replies with many more scatological insults of his own later in the same poem, which probably dates from around 1500. It's easy to imagine the poets mock-seriously spitting these words at each other in person. Indeed, this imagined context might have shaped the effect of these works when read by others, outside their original space of competitive social insult. Flytings lived on in writing and, presumably, speech, well into the sixteenth century.

The idea of hearing should also loom large in the study of verse prayer. Anyone unused to reading prayer poems must remember that, whatever we make of them today, they were likely uttered aloud in sincerity. The same is true of the prayers woven into more secular works: when Chaucer began the very final stanza of *Troilus and Criseyde* with 'Thow oon, and two, and thre, eterne on lyve, / That regnest ay in thre, and two, and oon' (V.1863–1864)—an address to God conceived of as the Trinity—his audience would on one level have heard this as something aimed at one particular real listener, however many other levels of convention, habit, and craft coexisted with that prayerful element (Murton 2020, 122–126).

Heard reception places greater weight on verse form as a sign of genre and mode. Without review magazines, advertising campaigns, social media, or publishers' blurbs, literature had fewer tools with which to shape expectations. Seemingly mundane details such as the publishing house and the cover design, or the hosting website, can condition the way we approach poetry now; in (say) the thirteenth century, often all a narrative or contemplative work had at its disposal for this task was the form and sound of its opening lines. This fact might help to explain why so many Middle English romances kick off with a kind of imagined performance setting:

> Lystyns, lordynges, and ye schall here
> Off ansytores, that before us were,
> > Bothe herdy and wyght.
> > > (*Sir Cleges*, in Laskaya and Salisbury eds 1995, 1–3)

Mekyll and littill, olde and yynge,	*young*
Herkyns all to my talkynge	*Hearken*
Of whaym I will yow kythe.	*tell*
[...]	
For full sothe sawis I will yow synge,	*true speech*
Off whaym the worde full wyde gan sprynge,	*Of one of whom*
And ye will a stownde me lythe.	*If; listen to; a while*

(*Octavian*, in Hudson ed. 2006, 1–3, 7–9)

Few, if any, such beginnings prove real off-the-cuff composition, but they seem suited to reading a work aloud for an audience. Regardless of how actual readers used these romances, beginning in this manner constructs the idea of a performance setting, and that idea might have signalled mode and genre.

Thinking about verse aloud opens up helpful questions about readers' relationships with poetry. In extended verse heard by a group of listeners, the audience cannot flick backwards and forwards within passages as a private reader can. Such a linear experience of hearing poetry emphasizes additive, cumulative effects over the brilliant single lapidary line. While my readings in this book have sometimes focused on small details, necessary to convey particular techniques, I have tried to avoid cycling backwards within poems, turning instead to accumulation and linear contrast. Compared to modern writing, later Middle English verse tends, with the exception of very short, pithy proverbs, to rely less on lone well-turned phrases, and more on effects of delay or piling-up, working across several lines in both cases. On the large scale, readers seem often to have taken less linear routes through Middle English poems—the surviving evidence suggests a lot of reading out of order—but on the small scale they probably experienced verse in more linear ways than we do.

Middle English poems frequently contain passages in which readers today must remember this heard quality, and in which readers would do well, moreover, to try reading the work aloud themselves. A celebrated example of both delay and accumulation appears in the first description of the Green Knight in *Sir Gawain and the Green Knight*. The poet says that the Knight is tall, large, rather giant-like though definitely still a man, well-formed and handsome (136–146), filling out the end of the *frons* and the **bob** of the relevant stanza with these details. Clearly the visitor impresses, but so far he could be filed with other knights who walk into courts in other romances. 'For wonder of his hue men hade' begins the *cauda* (147), whetting listeners' curiosity to know why people wondered at the sight of the knight. (This is a pun: Putter and Stokes eds 2014, 268, n. to 147.) The audience must listen until the *cauda*'s end for the surprise: he is 'overal enker grene' (150). This delay works better aloud, even today. Note, too, that the poem wasn't called *Sir Gawain and the Green Knight* in its own time, and the modern title unhelpfully gives the game away. Indeed, though the poem uses the phrase 'the Green Knight', it isn't how the Knight introduces himself. The poem reads a little differently if one keeps in mind the name he gives himself, 'the Knight of the Grene Chapel' (454). While that stanza carefully says nothing about the Green Knight's colour until its last word, the next stanza can't stop saying 'grene'. Now the poet deploys the piling-on, the accumulation, that so suits heard verse (151, 157, 167, 172), in order to hammer home how the Knight is funny in both senses of the word funny: what kind of visitor has a green horse (175)?

Anyone hearing a poem won't see any visual markings of different speakers, and at this time punctuation had no agreed system for marking speech anyway. These facts explain the explicit marking of dialogue in verse. Dialogue comes with overt signalling phrases such as *she seyde* and *answered I*. Terms of address let direct speech plot out the power relations between speakers, allowing a listening audience to track changes of speaker: the socially superior lady met in *The Floure and the Leafe* calls the narrator 'My faire doughter' partly because this says something about their relative positions, and about how women in general relate to each other in the poem's world, but also simply to help listeners follow who is talking (*Pearsall ed. 1990, 467, 547). Poets did not overtly build scaffolding around their dialogue out of clumsiness, but because they often expected their audiences to hear their verse.

Similar practical thought buttresses the subject restatement starting the *longer life of St Frideswide found in some *South English Legendary* mansucripts:

> Seynte Fredeswide was her of Engelonde.
> At Oxenford heo was ibore, as ic understonde.
> Aboute seve hondred yer and sevene and twenti right
> After that God was an Erthe in Is moder alight,
> This holi womman was ibore: Seynte Fredeswide.

(Saint Frideswide was here in England. She was born in Oxford, as far as I know. About 727 years after God came down to Earth in His mother [i.e. after the Incarnation of Jesus], this holy woman was born: Saint Frideswide. *Reames ed. 2003, 1–5)

One must make sure the audience know that they are about to hear Frideswide's story. But, as often, the pragmatism doesn't easily separate out from craft: many clauses in these lines could join syntactically forwards *or* backwards, in ways inevitably obscured by my attempt to add modern punctuation. The poet also achieves a kind of topical chiasmus: Frideswide (1), Frideswide's birth (2), Jesus' birth (3–4), Frideswide's birth (5), Frideswide (5). This writing wants to ensure that listeners get what's going on, and it works best aloud.

A sense of the heard and social context of the poetry also comes through in the frequent asides that pepper the longer life of Frideswide, as they pepper some other parts of the *Legendary*. When the devil tempts Frideswide, an aside speaks to listeners in the second person: 'Ne hure ye hou queynteliche the screwe it couthe bifynde?' ('Don't you hear how cunningly the rogue could devise?', 41). When Frideswide rebuffs temptation and the devil departs 'with wel sori bere / And with strong stench' ('with a very sad face and a foul smell', 51–52), an aside leads the audience in fervently wishing the devil to hell (53–54). And when Frideswide overcomes embarrassment to kiss a man who suffers from leprosy and thereby miraculously heal him, an aside asserts that she acted without sin, even though the kiss seemingly stepped beyond the rules governing her life as a woman in a religious order (154).

Close reading might do various things with these asides: besides looking at the detail of each one, observing their frequency through a saint's life—do asides crop up more thickly in particular parts, or evenly?—might also yield interesting findings. In a modern literary-critical reflex, we might reach for the idea of a characterful narrator. But this idea might not fit every early poem (Spearing 2005), and nor does it fit the likely use of this account of St Frideswide: these lines do not craft a narratorial persona, but rather open themselves to inhabitation by whoever reads the poem aloud. The poem expects readers who can draw out the feeling and comedy of the story, which displays a certain delight in seeing the high brought low. The devil inspires the King of England with lust for Frideswide, but the King's attempts to capture her bring such disaster upon him that 'ne dar no kyng in Oxenford yut to this dai come' ('to this day, no king dares to come to Oxford', 108); when divine power temporarily deprives the king's envoys of their sight, saving Frideswide from kidnapping, 'Hi nolde tho habbe icome ther, vor al hor prute wede' ('they wished they hadn't visited, despite their proud attire', 72).

The probable reception of much verse aloud might also help us think through moments of formal variation and experimentation. The intricate poem *Anelida and Arcite*, usually attributed to Chaucer, engages in a number of shifts in formal design of a sort uncharacteristic in much of the rest of Chaucer's work. There is, for instance, an inset complaint lyric marked out by shifts in both metre and rhyme (256–271). Here the verse moves from the surrounding five-beat lines to four-beat lines with five-beat tail lines for two stanzas, with mirrored through-rhyme, $aaa_4b_5aaa_4b_5 bbb_4a_5bbb_4a_5$. Even more extraordinarily, the following stanza (272–280) consists of nine five-beat lines with a different stanza structure hidden inside them (listen for the rhymes!):

> My swete foo, why do ye so, for shame?
> And thenke ye that furthered be your name
> To love a newe, and ben untrewe? Nay!
> And putte yow in sclaunder now and blame,
> And do to me adversité and grame,
> That love yow most—God, wel thou wost—alway?
> Yet come ayein, and yet be pleyn som day,
> And than shal this, that now is mys, be game,
> And al foryive, while that I lyve may.
>
> (272–280)

As heard verse, marked off by an audience's experience of rhyme, this might break down into an aa_2b_1 template:

> My swete foo,
> Why do ye so,
>   For shame?
> And thenke ye
> That furthered be
>   Your name
> To love a newe,
> And ben untrewe?
>   Nay!
>
> (272–274)

A little later, the poem does the same thing again (317–341). I don't rearrange these lines in print here to offer a definitive ruling on their true structure. These stanzas surely seek to pull taut the ties between several structures: one- and two-beat units, one- and four-beat units, and the five-beat units which form the norm of the surrounding poetry. But an approach to this part of *Anelida and Arcite* must root itself in how the poem sounds, and a reader who actively listens to these lines stands a better chance of grasping what they do.

Hearing's role in the reception of verse moves all verse closer to song. Chapter 9 noted Chaucer's depiction of Criseyde and company reading aloud in her household in *Troilus and Criseyde*, but later in the same book she also hears one of her nieces sing a song for a group of listeners (II.813–884), a song apparently composed by 'the goodlieste maide / Of greet estat in al the town of Troye' (880–881). Like the earlier moment of reading, this scene must present an idealized picture but, again like the earlier reading, it also shows us how the later fourteenth century could imagine social literature, this time as sung words.

Thought about music can add to a reading, and might be an essential part of the context to many short pieces of verse. Accompanying music survives with only a tiny proportion of Middle English short verse compositions (Butterfield 2022, 37), but this small group of cases provides much to discuss, and hints at what we might be missing in other poems. The song 'Sumer is icumen in' is one of the most well-known, widely anthologized, and even sometimes parodied pieces from the period. It is a round for several voices: when heard, rather than met as inert printed words, it creates a cyclical experience with distinct vocal strata. Scholars have explored how its Middle English words might relate to its melody, and to the alternative set of Latin words on a different topic supplied in the one known copy (London, British Library, MS Harley 978, folio 11 verso). Further fruitful questions open up when a work survives in several copies, set to music in some instances and not in others, as in the charter-poem also mentioned in Chapter 9: might some readers of a copy without music have associated poetry to tunes with which they had heard it paired elsewhere? For that matter, how many short poems which lack music in their surviving copies in fact had well-known musical connections in their own time? Where we only have text, we can only read, but we can at least bear absent music, or the absence of music, in mind. Research into early song needs, ideally, to bring together musicology, manuscript studies, and literary criticism, and remembering these extra aspects helps in reading and studying works of this sort for the first time.

Hearing's role in the reception of verse also moves all verse closer to drama. Every poem from this period sits somewhere closer than later verse to live, spoken back-and-forth. Even lone readers with their eyes on the page probably felt poetry in a more auditory way than many modern readers. This fact helps to explain why *Piers Plowman*, for instance, often reads as a highly dramatic work, powered by dialogue, resembling at points a closet drama full of dispute and interjection. Similarly, the pilgrims of the *Canterbury Tales* argue loudly with one another, frame whole tales as replies in conversation (e.g. I 3120–3135, I 3913–3920, III 1278–1297, III 1665–1671), and on occasion interrupt (e.g. VII 919). The pilgrims hear another kind of speech, preaching, in the nihilistic, bleakly funny Pardoner's Tale and the serious, sincere Parson's Tale. Then again, as anyone who's heard a skilled preacher knows, the distance between sermons and drama can be surprisingly short.

Drama

What of actual drama? To begin with, consider two fairly short, fairly early works related by theme. One, surviving as *Interludium de clerico et puella* ('The Interlude of the Clerk and the Girl'), appears to be only part of a once-longer piece, either true drama or at least something to be read with dramatic expression (*Lundeen 2009), perhaps by multiple readers. *Interludium* here seems to mean a short, staged, comic entertainment: in *Sir Gawain*, Arthur compares the Green Knight's eruption into the court to 'enterludes' (472). It concerns the efforts of a lecherous clerk to persuade a woman to sleep with him. This might seem insubstantial, but it offers an interesting study in technique. The initial lines, for instance, offer back-and-forth dialogue with matching rhymes:

CLERICUS	'Damishel, reste wel!'	
PUELLA	'Sir, welcum, by Saynt Michel!'	
CLERICUS	'Wer es ty sire, wer es ty dame?'	
PUELLA	'By Gode, es nother her at hame.'	

(*Salisbury ed. 2002, 1–4)

Shared rhymes of this sort would later appear in other contexts: the technique would find use in biblical drama, and still later, after Middle English, in flourishes such as the sonnet Romeo and Juliet construct together at their first meeting (1.5, 104–116). The same point of craft occurs in the rather more complete but tonally similar *Dame Sirith* (e.g. Salisbury ed. 2002, 85–90). *Dame Sirith* occupies similar narrative space to that of the *Interludium*: the inept Wilekin gets help from Dame Sirith to coerce Margery into adultery. Sirith herself, resourceful and unscrupulous, dominates the action, and the poet can neatly split a stanza across a rhyme to let her deliver a put-down. Her trickery, on which the plot turns, involves feeding her dog mustard and pepper, for reasons not immediately obvious to Wilekin:

WILEKIN	'Wat! Nou const thou no god?	*Can you do no good?*
	Me thinketh that thou art wod:	*mad*
	Gevest thou the welpe mustard?'	*whelp*
SIRITH	'Be stille, boinard!	*Silence, idiot!*
	I shal mit this ilke gin	*with; same trick*
	Gar hire love to ben al thin.'	*Make*

(*Salisbury ed. 2002, 285–290)

Unmarked transitions between speakers in the surviving copy, which in modern print require an editor to step in (e.g. 138–139, 278–279), might be copying errors, but possibly they show that this was a true play, with these transitions comprehensible to an audience because they could see people acting. At the work's end, Sirith turns and addresses the audience directly:

And wose is onwis,	*whoever; unskilled*
And for non pris	*price/payment*
Ne con geten his levemon,	*cannot get; beloved*
I shal, for mi mede,	*wages*
Garen him to spede,	*help; succeed*
For ful wel I con.	*can/know*

(*Salisbury ed. 2002, 445–450)

Direct metatheatrical address to the audience is a familiar technique in modern drama, and here is an early example.

Grander-scale religious drama survives from a little later than *Dame Sirith*. I take as an example the fall of Adam and Eve in the *York 'cycle' of plays (Davidson ed. 2011). So as to model the reading process, I'll show my working in more detail than I would writing pure literary criticism, outside a teaching context. The Fall play runs to a mere 176 lines, but the York drama as a whole needs a little scene-setting (for more, see Twycross 2008; Beadle 2008). Together, the York plays cover some parts of the Bible, and some para-biblical traditions which seemed especially important to the plays' organizers; since the plays were arranged chronologically and include the Bible's beginning and end, they encompass all of time. The plays were performed together on a particular religious feast day in summer, Corpus Christi ('the Body of Christ': the feast celebrates the Eucharist). The plays were not organized by local church authorities. Rather, York's various craft guilds collaborated to put the plays on, each guild producing a particular play, collectively creating a giant civic operation.

The nature of the plays' performance is extraordinary, and important. The guilds mounted the set for each play on a mobile wagon, and arranged a route through the city with twelve to sixteen fixed performance stations. The first play in the chronological sequence would happen at the first station, then roll to the next station and be performed again there, and so on to the third station; while the first play happened at the second station, the second play appeared at the first station. This system of performance echoes my remarks about the linear experience of Middle English verse above: on the small scale the plays were linear, for in live performance the audience couldn't linger over one especially resonant line; on a larger scale, this was nonlinear, as motivated audience members could revisit the same play multiple times, shuttling back and forth in biblical chronology as they shuttled back and forth on the wagon route. Indeed, given the length of the full cycle, occupying a long summer's day, the result probably felt 'like a party one could drop into and out of at will' (Twycross 2008, 34).

The staging on wagons within an urban space probably helped actors to involve the audience: stage directions and lines in the York plays and elsewhere suggest that actors could dismount from the stage, and some early English plays seem to have some characters emerge from or through the audience. The earliest evidence for the performance of the York plays dates to 1377, and their last recorded performance was in 1569: anachronistically speaking, they had (so to speak) a remarkably long run, albeit one punctuated by the intermittent use in some years of other plays, now lost, on the Creed or the Paternoster. The texts we have of the York cycle are not some set-in-stone fair copy used throughout performance history, but rather one lucky later-fifteenth-century snapshot.

Although it always used verse, early English drama took other forms besides sets of biblical plays on mobile stages: plays could be performed in open, communal spaces with temporary platforms, in large buildings, or on a smaller scale within a household. In a sense public religious plays do, though, represent the most successful tradition of English drama ever, a tradition which could take over the business of an entire urban community. At this time, Great Britain lacked permanent theatres. Indeed, as the quotations in the entry in the *MED* for *theatere* show, English writers only used the word for the theatres of Greek and Roman antiquity. They knew of these through written accounts, and they sometimes had to explain the idea for their readers. In the sixteenth century, English public drama would dwindle, and plays would privatize, becoming more the business of ticketing groups of players and fixed, permanent playhouses. The stage has never since recovered the same reach. For a time in the fourteenth and fifteenth centuries, drama had been a truly mass affair.

To the play of the Fall, then. This play might lack the stateliness and rich texture of *Paradise Lost*. But it has an engaging directness, and a series of accumulating resonances for the listening audience. In broad outline, the Fall play follows its ultimate biblical source (Genesis 3.1–19): the serpent persuades Eve to eat the forbidden fruit, which is not specifically an apple in either the Bible or in the play; Eve persuades Adam to eat the fruit; both realize their nakedness and cover themselves with fig leaves; God curses the serpent and announces the banishment of Adam and Eve. Their departure gets a whole play, the next, to itself. Readers who check Genesis will note, however, that the serpent in the biblical account is simply the serpent, not Satan; the thought that Satan took on the serpent's form had become, by the fifteenth century, entirely traditional, but it is an accretion. This accretion lets the play start with a bit of suturing: Satan's soliloquy, in which, following up the preceding play depicting the fall of the angels, he announces his distaste for humanity driven by envy at the future Incarnation, when Jesus will take on human form ('For woo my witte es in a were', 1–22).

The York plays use stanzas, but the exact forms vary from play to play. Satan's opening soliloquy runs for two full stanzas and a further two-and-a-half lines. This initial consistency helps to establish the stanzaic pattern in the audience's minds, repeating it twice before introducing the complications of dialogue between speakers. The stanza form lasts eleven lines, rhyming *ababcbcdcdc*. The fifth line has just two beats, however, and the stanza also closes with a four-line **cauda** distinguished by metre, making the shape $abab_4c_2bc_4dcdc_3$.

Once Satan has put this form into the audience's heads, he enters a rapid dialogue with Eve, a dialogue which sometimes uses specific chunks of the stanza form: the *cauda* can make a set-piece speech on its own (30–33) and the short two-beat line can start an emphatic rejoinder (60) or a fateful decision (104). After Satan's opening speech, someone speaks a complete stanza only once, when Eve delivers her case to Adam (89–99); we can, I think, take this set-piece stanza as an especially marked and pressured moment in the play. Eve's stanza does not achieve this by standing alone, but through the audible contrast of its unitary structure against the earlier rapid exchanges of dialogue.

Eve's set-piece speech contains two clusters of **enjambment** (93–95, 96–98), the first broken mid-line by a **rhetorical caesura** which firmly places syntactic structure in tension with metrical structure (94). (Readers will recall that the punctuation in this text is an editorial judgement, and it is up to us to decide whether it is right; I agree with most of the editor's punctuation here.) These clusters of enjambment strengthen in Eve's dialogue a feature hitherto more characteristic of Satan's language—up until now, his lines have run on about twice as often as Eve's—but they also catch something of the quality of hurried speech, pressured and pressurizing. Unlike Milton's Eve, the York Eve frames the choice primarily as something she and Adam achieve together, in the first-person plural (92–98, 103).

This play also offers something of a masterclass in the use of cumulative alliteration outside the tradition of alliterative metre. The poet used alternating rather than alliterative metre, but as the play continues it deploys certain key repeated terms to build up associations with particular alliterations. Now, the idea here is not that certain sounds have special natural associations: most arguments for onomatopoeia leave me sceptical. Rather, the play gradually and craftily ties certain tones and ideas, via words which it must in any case repeat, to certain alliterating consonants.

Consider the consonant sound represented by *t*. Certain words, words in which this sound begins the primary stressed syllable, belong in a play about the Fall: *betraye*, for instance, and *tree*, together with *traste* ('trust'), *taste*, and *trouthe*. As I mentioned in Chapter 2, *trouthe* in Middle English has the sense of present-day *truth*, but also a wider range of meanings tied to loyalty, trust, and oaths, as in the now-archaic word *troth*, which survives in *betrothal*. The poetry begins to link alliteration on *t* with danger in its audience's minds only gently, when Satan states in his opening speech that

My travayle were wele sette	*My work would be well spent*
Myght I hym so betraye,	hym: *God*
His likyng for to lette.	*delight; stop/end*

(19–21)

Eve first mentions the *tree* in a line which alliterates but seems innocuous, as innocuous as her conversation with the serpent seems to her. We can eat the fruit of any tree, she says, 'Save a tree outt is tane' ('Apart from one tree which is excluded', 33). The poem layers on a note of caution in the next *t*-alliterating line, when Eve asks a crucial question: 'Why what kynne thyng art though / That telles this tale to me?' (52–53); the telling of tales is not necessarily evil, but it is also not necessarily good. In response, of course, Satan simply lies, and about twenty lines later he adopts a wounded tone and repeats some of the same wording to complain:

> Yhe, why trowes thou noght me?　*don't you believe*
> I wolde be no-kynnes wayes　　*in no way*
> Telle noght but trouthe to thee.
>
> 　　　　　　　　　　(75–77)

Adam's own first use of *t*- and *tr*-alliteration resists the general drift—God, he says, has told them 'To tente the tree', to watch over or attend to it (86)—but his second marks the play's second catastrophe: 'I schalle it taste at thy techyng', he says, immediately before the stage direction noting that he eats (105). When Eve and Adam assess the damage done, they return to the sound to blame their tempters:

> EVE　'The worme to wite wele worthy were,　*deserves blame*
> 　　　With tales untrewe he me betrayed.'
> ADAM　'Allas that I lete at thy lare　　　　*heeded; advice*
> 　　　Or trowed the trufuls that thou me saide.'　*trusted; foolishness*
> 　　　　　　　　　　(122–125)

The play achieves a similar development in *b*-alliteration, which I locate but leave readers to trace for themselves (80–82, 102, 116–119, 127).

I have pursued this example at some length and in greater detail than I would expect in a journal article for specialists, or even perhaps in a student essay. I hope, though, that it shows how these effects accumulate as the play continues, and also how readers—or better, listeners, an audience—might trace them. Singly, each of these instances seems minor: an argument that any of these alliterations alone does much would overreach. Taken together, though, taken as elements which pile up while the linear, heard experience of the play goes on, they grow into a strong network of associations.

In practice, a real argument would not stop here. Readers interested by the Eve of the York Cycle might wish to compare the figure of Noah's wife (indicated simply as 'Uxor', 'Wife') in the ninth play, the Flood, who has provoked critical interest (e.g. Tolmie 2002). Other themes which seem at issue in this play and connected to the matter of other York plays are bodies, human and—thinking of Satan—animal, and true tale-telling: the whole play cycle invests, naturally, in the idea of the true report and of events transmitted in some sense as they happened, even as everyone involved also knew that they were acting and (re-)creating. Whatever one might want to argue about these plays, though, can be grounded in what they do, as linear-yet-repeatable heard experiences. Indeed, as a rendering of various biblical and para-biblical traditions, stories spun across many mediums in the period, the plays show the value of close attention to language and verse-craft: if plot and content were all that mattered, then other renderings of the same familiar stories would have identical resonances and effects—and this is obviously not the case.

That's just a smattering of Middle English drama, the body of Middle English writings in which hearing and audience reception play the most obvious parts. As this chapter underscores at its start, though, all literature was more heard and more dramatic. Just as Middle English poetry tended to be both more local and more supranational than verse today, part of the trick of studying English verse of this period is to think of it as at once both more physical—recall the complexities of manuscripts in Chapter 9—and more heard than we are used to today.

Epilogue
Craft in an Unfixed Time

This book has tried to grasp something of the many crafted styles and pleasures found in Middle English and Older Scots verse. Different aspects of the topic demanded treatment out of historical order, so as to bring in ideas in a logical sequence from small to large, and from familiar to strange. Here at the end, though, the book's parts can rearrange themselves into a sketch history. My sketch will no doubt invite tweaks and corrections. But it can serve as an anchor for readers seeking to place particular forms, and it can sum up the period's interest.

What we have surviving from the twelfth and early thirteenth centuries suggests a time of varied experiment, as poets absorbed Latin and French models alongside bequests from Old English alliterative verse. Experiment does not mean irregularity. If some poems seem transitional when seen from a later point of view, that doesn't mean that people at the time felt the same thing: some of the forms of the twelfth century must have sounded normal to their first audiences. Poems such as 'The Grave' and Layamon's *Brut* display some inheritance from the half-lines of Old English poetry, and mix alliteration and internal rhyme. The *Ormulum* shows us early blank verse—an innovation without surviving successors—and an early instance of regular septenary alternating metre held to strict syllable counts. English's earliest surviving regular rhymed couplets emerge briefly and possibly in the hymns attributed to Godric of Finchale, and securely and at length in the septenary *Poema Morale* and the four-beat *Ure Feder*. A little later, *The Owl and the Nightingale* displays four-beat alternating rhyming couplets with controlled syllable counts, basically the same formal option which would one day be taken by Gower and by the early Chaucer.

The extant material from the thirteenth century includes short poems in a variety of forms with French and Latin models, surviving in increasing numbers over time and exemplified in the trilingual manuscript that is now Oxford, Bodleian Library, MS Digby 86 (Fein ed. 2019a). The earliest extant romances in English also survive from this time. *Havelok the Dane* shows us Middle English romance adopting four-beat stichic couplet verse, probably in imitation of octosyllabic Anglo-Norman narrative poems. *Sir Tristrem* is the earliest known long English narrative in stanzas, and it already displays the use of a bob. Tail rhyme emerges first in shorter poetry, and has not yet become a favoured form for narrative romance.

From the late thirteenth century and through the first half of the fourteenth century, the four-beat couplet dominates long-form poetry. The four-beat couplet underpins some romances, such as *Orfeo* and some of the other works preserved in the Auchinleck Manuscript; other poets writing romances began to use increasingly widespread tail-rhyme forms. The four-beat couplet also serves, in various sub-types, as the standard form of the masterworks of northern Middle English religious instruction: *Cursor Mundi*, the *Northern Homily Cycle*, *Handlyng Synne*, *The Prik of Conscience*, and *Speculum Vitae*. Several of these works will enjoy sustained popularity into and through the fifteenth century, and *The Prik of Conscience* will become the most widespread English poem before print. The four-beat couplet also sustains history-writing in Robert Mannyng's *Chronicle* and in John Barbour's *Bruce*, one of the earliest substantial Scots poems. Subdivided *frons–cauda* stanza forms of around twelve or thirteen lines have emerged by the early fourteenth century, and appear among the poems preserved in the so-called 'Harley Lyrics' of MS Harley 2253.

The middle of the fourteenth century sees the flowering—in the surviving manuscript record—of later Middle English alliterative verse, with its relatively defined a-verse and tightly defined b-verse; it probably descends from Old English alliterative verse. Possibly the earliest works in this group known today are the romance *William of Palerne* and the political poem **Wynnere and Wastour*. Then, in the second half of the fourteenth century, come *St Erkenwald*, *Piers Plowman*, *Patience*, *Cleanness*, *Sir Gawain*, **The Siege of Jerusalem*, alliterative poetry about Alexander the Great, and probably John Clerk's †*Destruction of Troy*, the longest surviving alliterative-verse work across both Old and Middle English. In the later fourteenth century and into the fifteenth century, alliterative-stanzaic verse also crops up, marrying a metre descended from alliterative verse together with the concept of the subdivided *frons–cauda* stanza. *Sir Gawain and the Green Knight* is unique in its shuttling between internally-stichic, orthodox alliterative-metre *frons* and stanzaic, alternating-metre *cauda*.

In the later fourteenth century, Gower and Chaucer write. Both poets use four-beat and five-beat lines, but it is probably Chaucer who introduced the five-beat line, and certainly he who makes extensive use of it. Chaucer also probably invented the rhyme royal stanza, and certainly showed its capacities for meditation and narrative, creating one of the formal mainstays of the next century of English poetry.

English and Scots poets thus started the fifteenth century with a wider range of socially accepted formal options than they had ever had before, or would ever have again. The decades around 1400 form the great pivot-point of the whole history of English verse, from the first millennium to the third and present. Alliterative verse would carry on finding ready audiences and seeing new compositions for some time; Chaucer's innovations, such as the five-beat line, would in due course achieve a privileged, prestigious position—but they hadn't yet. All forms stood in balance.

We shouldn't think too sweepingly about any of these shifts. They took time to spread. The five-beat line first found favour among London and south-eastern poets specifically. Only in the later fifteenth century would it become recognized universally, even making it into drama in the Digby *Conversion of St Paul* (Baker, Murphy, and Hall eds 1982). We also shouldn't think of these shifts as involving forms set in stone. Alliterative verse constitutes a definable grouping, but has both variations and external affiliations. *William of Palerne* and *Piers Plowman* seem somewhat more comfortable than some other alliterative poems with three-lift a-verses, for instance, if those exist; *Sir Gawain* takes a unique approach in its weave of alliterative verse and alternating verse; rhyming alliterative-stanzaic poems clearly differ from true alliterative verse, but they just as clearly relate to it. Similarly, poets innovated in turn on Chaucer's innovations. The five-beat line became in Hoccleve's hands more defined by syllable count, while Lydgate created a different metrical fingerprint with his regular metrical caesura between second and third beats. Many fifteenth-century poets adopted rhyme royal, but most ran syntax across stanza divisions more often than was normal in Chaucer's own stanzaic writing, and some—such as John Metham and the poet of *Asneth*—had their own ideas about metre.

These caveats notwithstanding, the fifteenth century, especially in its later stages, did see much writing influenced to a greater or lesser extent by Chaucer and placing itself in a Chaucerian tradition. This last of the centuries covered in this book also saw much continuing influence from French: where the language had earlier provided models for rhyme and stanza, and raw materials for translated romances, so now it also served up fashionable fixed forms for short lyrics, and source materials for monumental works such as Lydgate's *Fall of Princes*, modelled on a French translation of a Latin prose work by Giovanni Boccaccio. Meanwhile, earlier forms continued in use, and earlier poems continued to be copied and enjoyed. Tail-rhyme stanzas built on a four-beat skeleton, for instance, continued to appear in new romances in the fifteenth century and possibly the sixteenth: examples include *The Turke and Sir Gawain* (Hahn ed. 1995) and *Capystranus*, two poems engaged in different ways with English imaginings of the then-ascendant Ottoman Empire. Consider, also, that one of the three surviving copies of *Orfeo* dates from around 1500, even though the poem itself might have been composed around 1300.

The end-times of Middle English and Older Scots contained the seeds of the new—fourteen-line lyrics like sonnets, rising five-beat lines anticipating Shakespeare and Milton—alongside older tools—in forms such as the septenary and the four-beat couplet—and ancient roots, still living on—alliterative verse, stretching back, in a modified way, to the very earliest English, and before that to its predecessor languages. There was no immediate, conscious purging of forms as the sixteenth century got underway, and of course some linger on and remain with us today in less prestigious yet widespread verse traditions: four-beat lines are a mainstay of present-day pop music. But the formal horizons of 'polite' or 'art' poetry narrowed in the hundred years from 1500 to 1600.

My mention of narrowing shows how the telling-out of facts has brought in argument and judgement, as any telling-out sooner or later must. A story told about early poetry among some non-specialists runs something like this. The poetry is, outside Chaucer, inchoate, chaotic, and often inept; it holds interest primarily as data for language history rather than as a set of objects for literary criticism; and it is neither relevant nor comparable to what came after it. As should be clear by now, I disagree! The poetry discussed here was often well-crafted; it forms a necessary part—the heart, even—of the whole body of English verse; and it offers at least as much excitement as any other grouping of poems. Indeed, in some respects I think it takes the prize as the most exciting grouping of English and Scots poetry. Its excitement come from two overarching qualities: uncentredness and possibility.

Compared to later periods, verse at this time was written, passed around, and read in far more scattered ways. Imagine a map of the public distribution of verse in English in 1650: it would, crudely, be a series of star shapes, with poetry travelling into urban centres housing printers—preeminently, London—entering print, and then emerging again from those centres and travelling outwards. Now imagine the same map for 1400. A certain starry tendency would still appear, for some book-making and certain aspects of literate culture before print already centred on London and other cities and towns, but the map would much more resemble a distributed network, with many individual households being places of literary (re)production in ways small, yet meaningful to their dwellers.

In 1300 or 1400, someone could equal the basic technology of London book artisans if they had ink and writing materials to hand. Someone could copy poems in urban centres such as Bristol, Perth, or Lincoln; they could copy poems in the moving centres of patronage and resources created by the king and the greater nobility as they and their large retinues travelled; they could also copy poems in a single household more or less anywhere. Important examples of such regional readers and transmitters of verse include the scribe of MS Harley 2253, a professional dealer with documents based in or near Ludlow, Shropshire, in the fourteenth century; and Robert Thornton, a gentleman amateur based in the North Riding of Yorkshire in the fifteenth. Both figures created manuscripts preserving unique copies of poems, manuscripts which must stand in for a great many lost books. Much more of the circulation of verse involved personal ties, so that we might think of the coterie circulation seen as special in later periods as the norm for the first reception of many earlier poems. True, books were expensive, only some people could read, and fewer people could write. But literate people were more numerous than is often imagined today, much evidence of book-borrowing survives, and many poems were also read aloud to groups. For many people, verse was a heard phenomenon, its written form only secondary. Moreover, poetry's circulation was not affected, until the late fifteenth century, by printers and publishers, who would inevitably impose their own judgements of taste and marketability on verse as they entered the field.

We might note too that all drama used verse, and drama happened outside and without dedicated private theatres. Audiences didn't wait for drama to spread outward from London. Rather, household enthusiasm, communal initiative, or travelling expertise brought forth plays in various places. The sixteenth century would see the gradual privatization and enclosure of the stage and the coming of the physical, permanent, commercial theatre. The great age of popular plays, unmatched for mass participation by any drama in Great Britain since, falls in the fourteenth and fifteenth centuries.

As with page and stage, so with the tongue: language's decentralized, non-standardized state mirrored and reinforced the uncentred distribution of poetry. Written Older Scots and Middle English undoubtedly differed in some ways from spoken forms, for writing is a different medium, but no standard prestige type of written language exercised a strong centralizing pull on wording and grammar. We can say something similar about verse form. Chaucer and his successors, writing in alternating metre and usually in five-beat lines, might loom large in present-day understandings of this time. But modern tastes and interests caused this, and Chaucer was, in his own lifetime, as regional a poet as any of his contemporaries; his regional distribution simply happened to include the country's greatest power centre. The English language itself lived a more marginal and precarious written life in these centuries than it does today, being by no means the dominant, normative tongue of power and writing even in England. This aspect of the language's history leads us from uncentredness to possibility.

At this time, many options and choices had not yet been closed off. English itself was up for grabs in ways it has not been since, and indeed in ways it had not been during the later parts of the Old English period, when a West Saxon type offered a nascent shared model for writing. Individual scribes had far more say in how Middle English should appear on the page and, similarly, individual poets and small, immediate audiences had far more say in what English and Scots verse should be: what forms it should take and what desires it should serve. At no other time, before or since, have so many different systems of verse-craft coexisted without one dominating, and for Scotland and England this was the greatest age of experiment and ferment in poetry.

Criticism often takes the sixteenth century as an innovative sequel to the Middle English period, hosting such developments as the English sonnet and blank verse. Yet fifteenth-century poets independently wrote both a Shakespearean sonnet, and verse which was blank, free of obligatory alliteration or rhyme. Plus, as we saw in Chapter 4, Orm wrote more than ten thousand lines of blank verse in his *Ormulum* at some point around 1200. The sixteenth century wasn't necessarily more innovative than the arbitrary hundred-year units preceding and following. It merely provided better cultural conditions for forms such as the sonnet and blank verse to take root, flourish, and achieve the kind of dominance which comes to look like innovation in hindsight.

Though Middle English and Older Scots verse does share this next quality with some earlier and later times, readers and writers also took an extraordinarily wide range of types of material into poetry, far wider than the range most readers today think of as being appropriately poetic. Besides imagined narratives and short, emotive first-person poems, poets wrote practical texts such as recipes, guides to behaviour, and what we might anachronistically call self help: material guiding readers in the pursuit of wisdom or holiness. They also wrote philosophy and dietary advice. Many poems emerge from ties of service and obligation which brought people together in ways a little unfamiliar to us now. Some audiences today find most challenging the poems which are charms or (or 'and/or') prayers. But prayers were in their own way practical—what could be more practical than salvation?—and taking them seriously can help us chew over the purposes of literature, and indeed of criticism. The reception of some of Roger Robinson's work hints that criticism today sometimes struggles when contemporary poets write prayers too (Robinson 2019, 71, 80; Sanatan 2020, 163–164).

My chapter exploring textual and manuscript problems hinted at how excitingly varied the different manuscript copies of the same poem can be. This book's period, the final centuries before the gradual success of moveable type, marries all the perils and joys of manuscript transmission in general with, in particular, the highest surviving numbers of pre-print manuscripts containing English, because manuscripts survive in higher proportions when they have to travel through fewer centuries to get to the present. The manuscript situations of poetry make the texts of poems themselves living problems, opening up another fascinating route to take in studying verse. Manuscript contexts also encourage honesty about the messiness of the surviving evidence, in turn helping us to attend to the same issues in modern writing: no literature, from any time, reaches us unmediated.

I haven't pursued cultural history, a different disciplinary focus which already has good introductory guides. Historians tend to claim by forgivable reflex that their particular period ushered in the crucial changes underpinning our present, and I don't want to do that; as a literary critic, I have other vices. It's true, though, that poetry from this time both echoed and shaped a great many modern things which were then beginning to be laid down, or which then existed in interestingly different forms. A list of such things might include childhood, the state, nationalism, literacy, the idea of literature, and conventions in book design. Other ideas and problems have simply stayed consistent. Though they might come to different answers, and involve different personnel, *Wynnere and Wastour* and *Piers Plowman* worry at societal questions about wealth and justice which, sadly but not surprisingly, remain with us. I don't think we can straightforwardly interpret these centuries through their poems, or these poems through their centuries, but early verse is a necessary part of cultural history.

Equally, however, the surviving Middle English and Older Scots poems are also present-day, twenty-first-century works. They travel far faster and further today, and many of them find larger audiences today than they had at their times of writing. If poetry is worthwhile now, then these poems have as much worth as any others. In their differences from younger poetry, and even in their difficulties, they teach us much. The verse is out there, wanting only to be read. I have described its basic workings; I now pass on the task of reading. If you want to read this poetry, then it is all yours: reach out, take it, and make it your own.

Appendix

Scope

This appendix offers help with reading Middle English and Older Scots verse aloud, or hearing it in mind, with better comprehension of its soundscape and its grammar. It is a brief primer, not a systematic account. Space limits nuance and detail, and interested readers should progress to fuller and more knowledgeable treatments: Burrow and Turville-Petre eds 2021, 3–55; Horobin and Smith 2002, 40–68, 89–125; Fulk 2012, 19–133; and, for Scots, Smith 2012.

Abbreviations

This Appendix uses the following abbreviations:

IPA: International Phonetic Alphabet
ME: Middle English
OE: Old English
PDE: present-day English

I write primarily for readers without knowledge of the IPA, but I include IPA pronunciations for those who can read them. For explanations of the IPA see Ferber 2019, 17–27; and Fulk 2012, 21–23.

Sound and spelling

1. Reconstruction. Reading aloud helps criticism: it aids comprehension, brings out structure, breathes life into puns, and, most importantly, makes verse more fun. Of course, language resists exact reconstruction when it dates from before the birth of audio recording. Moreover, ME varied both from place to place and through time. PDE varies in this way, but the variation in ME was more dramatic, because there were neither standard varieties nor prestigious varieties. ME therefore presents a moving and somewhat hazy target for PDE speakers. Nevertheless, scholarship has reconstructed most aspects of the sounds of ME with some confidence using various types of evidence (Horobin and Smith 2002, 42–44), including rhyme and metre: when poets decided that certain words matched each other in rhyme or as metrical patterns, they left hints about consistencies in sound.

2. Lost letters. ME was written using some extra letters. These are 'transliterated' into more familiar letters in this book, but are used in the majority of editions of ME works.
  Thorn—Þ, þ—is equivalent to *th*: *þe* is *the*, *wiþ* is *with*, and so forth.
  Yogh—ȝ, ȝ—is a trickier customer. Within words, it can most often be taken as *gh*: *niȝte* is *nighte* (PDE *night*) and *wroȝte* is *wroghte* (PDE *wrought*). When it appears at the starts of words, it most often fills the role, and indicates the sound, of PDE *y* in the same position: *ȝonge* is the adjective *yonge* (PDE *young*), *ȝesterdai* is *yesterdai* (PDE *yesterday*).

In early ME texts, readers might meet eth—Ð, ð—which, like thorn, was used where we would use *th*, and ash—Æ, æ—which represented something like the *-a-* of PDE *cat*; both letters fell out of use within the ME period, and don't appear in later ME.

I have regularized these letters to *th*, *ae*, and (depending on context) *y* or *gh* throughout quotations in this book, but they will appear in some editions. On the pronunciation of *gh*/ʒ, see the next table.

3. Consonants. Most ME consonants were the same as their PDE equivalents. ME spelling conventions had a closer relationship to sound than PDE spelling, and so readers should usually sound every letter written. This means, for example, that while in many varieties of PDE an egg *yolk* and an animal's *yoke* sound the same, the *l* in ME *yolke* should be sounded, as it should in ME *should*. Similarly, some varieties of PDE make *r* silent in some positions after vowels: neither *r* is audible if I say *further* in my own normal speech, because I speak a variety of PDE in which *r* tends to be silent after vowels, but in ME every *r* should be sounded. The *k* in *knighte* and *knowe* should be sounded before the *n*, unlike in PDE. The *g* should be sounded before the *n* in *gn* where it is silent in PDE, as in *gnat* and *gnaw*. The *h* should be sounded after the *w* in the combination *wh*, as in ME *where* and *what*. Equally, the *w* should be sounded in ME *writen* and *wlonk*.

A few consonants and clusters of consonants deserve further comment:

ME spelling	Sound	IPA
c	Like an *s* before front vowels e.g. before *e* (as in PDE) in *certayne* (PDE *certain*), but also before *i* and vowel *y*, e.g. in *citee* (PDE *city*). The letter is therefore an *s* twice in *cyteceynys* (PDE *citizens*). Hard *k* sound otherwise, as in *calle* (PDE *call*), *cunnyng* (PDE *cunning*) or *socour* (PDE *succour*). The distinction usually maps onto PDE equivalents.	/s/ when soft; /k/ when hard
ch	Has the sound it makes twice in PDE *church* and, indeed, at the start of PDE *Chaucer*.	/tʃ/
h-	*h-* is not pronounced when it appears at the start of words derived from French. PDE retains this in some words, such as *honour* and *hour*—though first-language speakers are often surprised when they notice that they have never been pronouncing the *h-* in these!	
i	At the starts of words, scribes copying ME often wrote (I simplify a complex situation) *i* where PDE spelling would put a *j* for the same sound; the *i* in *iust ioyful ieste* (PDE *just joyful jest*) should be pronounced (roughly) like PDE *j*; readers who have some French can be more precise, and use French *j*. Spellings in this book have been regularized to solve this confusion, but readers should be alert to it in other editions of ME works.	/ʒ/
f	Not normally voiced: pronounced without the vibration it receives in PDE *of*, more like the sound it makes in PDE *off*.	/f/
gh	In PDE *gh* is silent in words such as *light* and *thought*. It should be sounded in ME, for example in *lighte* and *thoghte*. Readers will do well enough if they give it a sound like the *-ch* in present-day Scots *loch*. In some PDE words, such as *enough*, *gh* is not silent but has taken on a different sound; in ME, it indicates a sound like the *-ch* in present-day Scots *loch* in these words too.	/x/ after back vowels; /ç/ after front vowels
sch	Pronounce as PDE *sh*.	/ʃ/
r	Should ideally be trilled, quite like a modern Spanish *r*.	/r/

4. Vowel overview. The letters used to spell vowels in ME were almost identical to those used in PDE spelling, with the exception that *i* and (in its vowel use) *y* were the same. One could display *wit* or *wyt* in ME; it was the same noun and the same sound in both cases.

Some changes have, however, happened since the ME period, most significantly in the sounds of long vowels. Though most first-language speakers rarely think on the difference, PDE distinguishes between short and long vowels. The same distinction, often mapping onto the same words, held in ME. Crudely, short vowels stayed the same as ME became modern English, but long vowels changed. I shall describe the two types separately.

5. Short vowels. The sounds of short vowels in PDE and ME are by and large the same, so *wyt* and *fit* sounded like *wit* and *fit* sound today. ME short vowels can be tabulated roughly as follows:

ME spelling	Sound when short	IPA
a	As in PDE *cat*, *mat*, *ban*	/æ/
e	As in PDE *bet*, *debt*	/ɛ/
i/y	As in PDE *fit*, *wit*	/i/
o	As in PDE *not*, *plot*	/ɒ/
u	As in PDE *put* and the *-oo-* of PDE *soot*	/ʊ/

6. Long vowels. A major historical change in the prounciation of long vowels, today called the Great Vowel Shift, has distanced PDE long vowel sounds from their predecessors in ME. ME long vowels were much closer to the vowels of present-day Spanish, French, or German, and therefore, before the Great Vowel Shift, English was much more audibly similar to its continental relatives. ME long vowels can be tabulated roughly as follows:

ME spelling	Sound when long	IPA
a	The *a* of PDE *hard*, *last*	/a/
e	The vowels of PDE *fête*, *hate*	/e:/
i/y	The vowels of PDE *beam*, *screen*	/i/
o	The vowel of PDE *home* (close) or of PDE *saw* (open)	/o/, /ɔ/
u, sometimes ow or ou	The vowels of PDE *flue*, *crew*	/u/

7. Diphthongs. A diphthong (pronounced *diff-thong*) is a combination within one syllable of two vowels, the sound sliding from the first vowel into the second. Some PDE diphthongs remain close to their ME ancestors: ME *oi* | *oy* indicated a sound much like the vowel sounds in PDE *toys' noise*. Some good ones to know are *aw* | *au*, which indicated the vowel sound of PDE *flout cow*; *eu* | *ew*, which indicated the vowel sound of PDE *feud*; and *ai* | *ay* | *ei* | *ey*, which could represent a range of sounds, but which beginners can give the sound of PDE *slay*.

8. Stress. The basic rule determining the distribution of natural lexical stress in ME was, as in PDE, to stress the first syllable of any word (*knówen*) unless the first syllable was a normally-unstressed prefix (*unknówen*). ME had a similar set of normally-unstressed prefixes as PDE, so examples of this are mostly easy to spot; the extra prefix to look out for in ME is *y-* | *ʒe-* | *i-*, sometimes used to form past participles (see section 12), and this too is always unstressed.

As noted in Chapter 4, linguistic stress could fall multiple ways in some words (*góddesse| goddésse*). Stress fell later in many French-derived words than it does now: the second syllable was often stressed in *natúre, statúre, matére, sesóun*, and *justíce*, for instance.

In ME alternating verse, a metrical beat could fall more easily on word-endings, and as a result *sittýnge:lokýnge* and *sódeynlý:tréwelý:férmelý* were viable rhymes in ME though they are not in PDE (these examples: *Troilus and Criseyde*, II.1014–1015, V.492, V.494–495).

9. **Proper names** were open to a certain amount of crafty variation for rhyme and metre. Chaucer could have *Troilus* be two syllables (*Troi-lus*) or three (*Tro-i-lus*), and was not above very occasionally adding a new sound to a name, so that *Emelye* could become *Emelya* (*Canterbury Tales*, I 1077), and *Criseyde, Criseyda* (*Troilus and Criseyde*, I.169). Similarly, Gower allows the name *Jason* to deliver a metrical beat with either its first or second syllable:

               and seide anon,
x /   x / x /   x/
'Welcome, O worthi kniht Jason'.
                           (**Confessio Amantis*, V.3787–3788)

x   /   x / x / x /
And whan sche mihte Jason se,
Was non so glad of alle as sche.
                           (*CA*, V.3819–3820)

Chaucer does likewise when he tackles the same story (compare *Legend of Good Women* 1580 and 1620).

Grammar

10. **Inflections.** Most of the following comments have to do with inflections, word-endings imparting information about the word's role and its relationship to other words. PDE retains a few inflections, so, for example, the *-s* on the verb *retains* at this sentence's start showed that the subject doing the retaining is a singular rather than a plural noun ('English'), and the *-ed* on the verb *showed* indicated that the showing happened in the past. ME had more inflections than PDE, but fewer than OE.

11. **Present tense verbs and infinitives.** ME infinitives typically end in *-en* or *-e*. The headwords under which the *MED* files verb entries thus usually end in *-en*: to look up the ancestor of modern *speak*, search for *speken*. Verbs in the present tense with plural subjects also typically end in *-en* or *-e*.

This knowledge clarifies the tricksy close to the first stanza of *Troilus and Criseyde*, when the poet begs the muse, 'help me for t'endite [*compose*] / Thise woful vers, that weepen as I write' (I.6–7): *weepen* here cannot be an infinitive, as it is not preceded by 'to' and has an implied subject; if *weepen* is not an infinitive it probably has a plural subject because it ends in *-en*; *vers* is an acceptable plural noun in ME (see section 13); it is therefore probably not the poet, but, in a strange, stimulating metaphor, the lines themselves 'that weepen'.

Present-tense verbs with singular second-person subjects usually end in *-st* or *-est*. Present-tense verbs with singular third-person subjects usually end in *-ith* or *-eth*; in northern ME, they usually end in *-s* or *-es*, and this is the ancestor of the equivalent PDE inflection. In the present participle, by contrast, it is the southern *-ing(e)* | *-yng(e)* ending which survives in standard PDE, not the northern *-and(e)* | *-end(e)*.

12. Past tense verbs. ME verbs normally indicate the past tense through one of the two systems still surviving in PDE: 'strong' verbs change their stem vowel so, for example, *drink* becomes *drank*, while 'weak' verbs acquire a *-d* or *-ed* ending, so *live* becomes *lived*.

Open-class verbs could also be placed in the past by coupling their infinitive with *gan* (that is, *began*) or *did*. With *gan*, the infinitive can be preceded by *to* ('in this wo gan Troilus to dwelle', *Troilus and Criseyde*, V.1566), but need not be ('he gan him dispaire', V.1569); with *did* the infinitive is not preceded by *to* ('many a mannes guttes dide he paine', *Canterbury Tales*, VII 2604). In verse, past tense verbs created using *gan* and *did* had metrical utility.

The past participle sometimes begins with an additional *y-*, *ʒe-*, or *i-*: thus the Wife of Bath's couplet running 'Somme seyde that oure hertes been moost esed / Whan that we been yflatered and yplesed' (III 929–930). Like *gan* and *did*, the *y-* prefix was a useful metrical lubricant. (Readers who know some OE will recognize it as the descendant of earlier *ge-*.)

13. Noun possession and pluralization. Singular nouns indicate possession with *-es* or *-s*. This inflection survives in PDE, and is the ancestor of *-'s* in PDE spelling.

Plural number is normally indicated in ME nouns by *-s*, *-is*, or *-es*, with no distinguishing among plural subjects, plural objects or plural possessives. There are two other types of pluralization in ME, but they are similar to their PDE counterparts, and usually apply to the same words: one *child* but two *children*, one *foot* but two *feet*. Some nouns had lacked a plural ending in Old English and sometimes carried on lacking it in Middle English, so that ME *word* and ME *þing*, for instance, could on occasion occur where PDE would write *words* and *things* (e.g. *Alliterative Morte Arthure, Benson ed. 1994, 8–10). A small number of French-derived nouns that ended in sibilant sounds when singular could stay unchanged when plural. This was true for *cas* (PDE *case*) and for *vers*, as seen in Appendix section 11 and in the mentions of 'two vers' in the Tale of Melibee (*Canterbury Tales* VII 1107, VII 1611).

14. First-person pronouns. *I* is sometimes spelled *Y*; this is simply a spelling difference for the same sound (see section 5). The older form *Ich* sometimes still occurs.

15. Second- person pronouns. The second-person singular pronoun is *thou* (also *thow*, *thu*) when the subject of a verb, *thee* (also *the*) when the object of a verb. Unhelpfully, the opposite vowel contrast operates in the second-person plural personal pronouns, which are *ye* (also *yee*, *yhe*) when the subject of verbs, and *you* (also *yow*) when the object of verbs.

In later ME, *ye* | *you* was also adopted as a formal singular pronoun for courteously addressing social superiors and unfamiliar equals, with *thou* | *thee* sometimes reserved for familiarly addressing social inferiors and well-known equals. This is an analogue to the singular second-person uses of, for example, *Sie* and *du* in German, or *vous* and *tu* in French; ME developed this system in imitation of French. Fulk offers a handy list of ME examples (2012, 95). Note that God was normally addressed intimately as *thou* | *thee* ('Oure fadir that art in heuenes, halewid be *thi* name').

16. Third-person singular pronouns. The OE feminine third-person pronoun—equivalent to PDE *she* | *her*—was *heo* | *hie* | *hire*. In its changes during the ME period *heo* sometimes lost its *-o*, becoming *he*: see, for example, *Orfeo* line 408 (*Laskaya and Salisbury eds 1995), and *'Ichot a burde' in the Harley lyrics, where the male speaker says of his lover that 'He is coral' and 'He is blosme' ('she is coral', 'she is a flower'): it is clear from other pronouns used that the lover is a woman (*NIMEV* 1394 | *DIMEV* 2324; Fein ed. 2014–2015, art. 28, ll. 7, 17). Sometimes, though, *heo* lost its *-e-* rather than its *-o*, producing *ho*. When this pronoun began to start with *sh-* rather than *h-*, the result was sometimes the PDE *she*, but this shift could also produce *sho*.

The OE feminine possessive *hire* eventually became PDE *her*, but scribes can still be found writing *hire* in copies of Chaucer. The OE neuter third-person pronoun, equivalent to PDE *it*, was *hit*, and in later ME this still sometimes survives as *hit* or *hyt*.

Thei (or *they, thai,* and so on) could be a singular third-person pronoun in later ME.

17. Third- person plural pronouns. OE third-person plural pronouns all began with *h-*: where a PDE speaker would say *they, them,* and *their*, OE speakers would use variations on *hi, him | heom,* and *hira*. The Old Norse third-person plural pronoun, which began with *th-*, was adopted into English in the regions of England which experienced extensive Scandinavian settlement, and gradually made its way into the language at large as *thei | thai, them | thaim, their | thair | there*; these are the ancestors of the PDE words *they, them,* and *their*. The usurpation was still in progress for most of the period covered by this book. While northern and/or later ME often offers PDE readers a relatively familiar pattern of *thei, them* and *their*, many southern and/or earlier writers still used *he* for the plural third-person subjects of a verb, *hem* for the objects of a verb, and *hire* (also *here, her*) for the possessive. Readers of Chaucer can meet therefore *hire* where PDE would have *their* (*Troilus and Criseyde*, II.41), as a third-person plural possessive, but also where PDE would have *her* (I.275), as a third-person singular possessive. Some writers who lived in the middle of the transition use *thei* in subject positions, but *hem* and *hire* in other positions.

18. Adjectives. In Chaucer's verse, when an adjective modifies a singular noun, but is itself preceded by the definite article (*the*), by a possessive pronoun, or by a demonstrative, it is, for reasons which need not detain us here despite their interest, what scholarship calls a weak adjective, and typically ended in sounded *-e*.

Strong adjectives—adjectives modifying singular nouns but not preceded by the definite article, a possessive pronoun, or a demonstrative—did not normally end in sounded final *-e*, even when scribes included a written *-e*.

Adjectives modifying plural nouns seem typically to have ended in sounded final *-e*.

Sounded final *-e* was already dwindling away in English by Chaucer's lifetime, and had probably already disappeared in northern English, though it might have kept its significance for some poets in the generations immediately following him, in the early and middle parts of the fifteenth century, as a conscious archaism and metrical event.

19. Negation. Negation in most formal written PDE logically cancels itself out, so that to say 'this is not not the case' means 'this is the case'. In ME, as in some informal and/or spoken types of PDE and in many other present-day languages, negation is cumulative: adding two or any higher number of negative words to a statement simply makes the negation of that statement more emphatic. 'I **ne** can do **no** maner servyse' means 'I really cannot do any kind of service', not 'I can do a kind of service'.

Readers should also note one other feature of negation. Words of negation beginning with *n-* and preceding a verb or preposition sometimes combine with the subsequent word:

n'is	*ne is*	PDE *is not*
n'as	*ne was*	PDE *was not*
n'oot	*ne woot*	PDE *know not	don't know*
n'at... n'at	*nor at... nor at*	PDE *neither at... nor at*

This melding can serve metrical purposes. Some kinder editors will mark such combinations with an apostrophe after the *n-* in their present-day printing of the ME text.

Bibliography

1. Manuscripts

Cambridge, Trinity College
  MS R.3.19 (<https://mss-cat.trin.cam.ac.uk/Manuscript/R.3.19/UV>)
Cambridge, University Library
  MS Ff.i.6 (<https://cudl.lib.cam.ac.uk/view/MS-FF-00001-00006/1>)
Edinburgh, National Library of Scotland
  MS Advocates' 19.2.1 (<https://auchinleck.nls.uk/index.html>)
London, British Library
  MS Additional 37049 (<http://www.bl.uk/manuscripts/Viewer.aspx?ref=add_ms_37049>)
  MS Cotton Nero A.X/2 (<http://www.bl.uk/manuscripts/Viewer.aspx?ref=cotton_ms_nero_a_x!2>)
  MS Harley 682
  MS Harley 978 (http://www.bl.uk/manuscripts/Viewer.aspx?ref=harley_ms_978)
  MS Harley 2253 (<http://www.bl.uk/manuscripts/Viewer.aspx?ref=harley_ms_2253>)
  MS Harley 2255 (<http://www.bl.uk/manuscripts/Viewer.aspx?ref=harley_ms_2255>)
  MS Harley 3810
  Loan MS 70/8
Manchester, John Rylands Library
  MS Eng. 1 (<https://www.digitalcollections.manchester.ac.uk/view/MS-ENGLISH-00001/1>)
Oxford, Bodleian Library
  MS Ashmole 33
  MS Ashmole 61 (<https://digital.bodleian.ox.ac.uk/objects/69462c25-b481-4643-9942-34f7243ea921>)
  MS Digby 86 (<https://digital.bodleian.ox.ac.uk/objects/2d6dfc9f-2ab9-46bf-9b32-e52f0e6eabb3>)
  MS Douce 104 (<https://digital.bodleian.ox.ac.uk/objects/a241fe3e-e78e-498a-8c6d-7eae61464e54/>)
  MS Junius 1 (<https://digital.bodleian.ox.ac.uk/objects/90a06f70-880a-4b5b-bd30-798710afff11>)
  MS Rawlinson poet. 163
Oxford, Jesus College
  MS 29 (<https://digital.bodleian.ox.ac.uk/objects/432a9599-3dc1-40d8-b997-83dbb5ff8df6/>)
San Marino, Henry E. Huntington Library
  MS HM 114

2. Editions and translations

Agbabi, Patience, 2008. *Bloodshot Monochrome* (Edinburgh)
Agbabi, Patience, 2014. *Telling Tales* (Edinburgh)
Andrew, Malcolm, and Ronald Waldron, eds, 2007. *The Poems of the 'Pearl' Manuscript: 'Pearl', 'Cleanness', 'Patience', 'Sir Gawain and the Green Knight'*, 5th edn (Liverpool)
Armitage, Simon, 2012. *The Death of King Arthur* (London)

Ashe, Laura, ed., 2015. *Early Fiction in England from Geoffrey of Monmouth to Chaucer* (London)
*Audelay, John the Blind, 2009. *Poems and Carols (Oxford, Bodleian Library MS Douce 302)*, ed. Susanna Greer Fein (Kalamazoo)
Auden, W. H., 2007. *Collected Poems*, ed. Edward Mendelson, rev. edn (London)
Baker, Donald C., John L. Murphy and Louis B. Hall, eds, 1982. *The Digby Plays*, EETS o.s. 283 (Oxford)
Barbour, John, 1997. *The Bruce*, ed. A. A. M. Duncan (Edinburgh)
Barratt, Alexandra, ed., 2010. *Women's Writing in Middle English*, 2nd edn (London)
*Benson, Larry D., ed., and Edward E. Foster, rev., 1994. *King Arthur's Death: The Middle English Stanzaic 'Morte Arthur' and Alliterative 'Morte Arthure'* (Kalamazoo)
Bergvall, Caroline, 2011. *Meddle English* (New York)
Bergvall, Caroline, 2019. *Alisoun Sings* (New York)
Bishop, Elizabeth, 2004. *Complete Poems* (London)
Bjork, Robert E., ed. and trans., 2014. *Old English Shorter Poems. Volume II: Wisdom and Lyric* (Cambridge, MA)
Bliss, A. J., ed., 1966. *Sir Orfeo*, 2nd edn (Oxford)
Bokenham, Osbern, 1938. *Legendys of Hooly Wummen*, ed. Mary S. Serjeantson (London)
Bokenham, Osbern, 2020–2022. *Bokenham's 'Lives of Saints'*, ed. Simon Horobin, 2 vols, EETS o.s. 356, 359 (Oxford)
*Braswell, Mary Flowers, ed., 1995. *'Sir Perceval of Galles' and 'Ywain and Gawain'* (Kalamazoo)
'Brother Hans', 1963. *Bruder Hansens Marienlieder*, ed. Michael S. Batts (Tübingen)
Capildeo, Vahni, 2013. *Utter* (Leeds)
Cartlidge, Neil, ed. and trans. 2003. *The Owl and the Nightingale: Text and Translation*, corrected repr. (Exeter)
†Caxton, William, 1490. *Eneydos* ([London])
*Chance, Jane, ed., 1999. *The Assembly of Gods* (Kalamazoo)
Charles d'Orléans, 1923–1927. *Poésies*, ed. Pierre Champion (Paris)
Charles d'Orléans, 1994. *'Fortunes Stabilnes': Charles of Orleans's English Book of Love*, ed. Mary-Jo Arn (Binghamton)
Chaucer, Geoffrey, 1995. *The Legend of Good Women*, ed. Janet Cowen and George Kane (East Lansing)
Chaucer, Geoffrey, 2019. *The Norton Chaucer*, gen. ed. David Lawton (New York)
†[Clerk, John], 1869–1874. *The 'Gest Hystoriale' of the Destruction of Troy*, ed. G. A. Panton, 2 vols, EETS o.s. 39 and 56 (London)
Conlee, John W., ed. and trans., 1991. *Middle English Debate Poetry: A Critical Anthology* (East Lansing)
*Cook, Megan L., and Elizaveta Strakhov, eds, 2019. *John Lydgate's 'Dance of Death' and Related Works* (Kalamazoo)
Cowen, Janet, ed., 2015. *On Famous Women: The Middle English Translation of Boccaccio's 'De mulieribus claris'* (Heidelberg)
*Davidson, Clifford ed., 2011. *The York Corpus Christi Plays* (Kalamazoo)
*Dean, James M., ed., 1996. *Medieval English Political Writings* (Kalamazoo)
Dickinson, Emily, 1999. *The Poems of Emily Dickinson*, ed. R. W. Franklin (Cambridge, MA)
Duggan, Hoyt N., and Thorlac Turville-Petre, eds, 1989. *The Wars of Alexander*, EETS s.s. 10 (Oxford)
*Dunbar, William, 2004. *The Complete Works*, ed. John Conlee (Kalamazoo)
Duncan, Thomas G., ed., 2013. *Medieval English Lyrics and Carols* (Cambridge)
*Epp, Garrett P. J., ed., 2017. *The Towneley Plays* (Kalamazoo)

*Fein, Susanna, ed., 1998. *Moral Love Songs and Laments* (Kalamazoo)
*Fein, Susanna, ed., with David Raybin and Jan Ziolkowski, 2014–2015. *The Complete Harley 2253 Manuscript*, 3 vols (Kalamazoo)
*Fein, Susanna, ed. and trans., 2022. *'The Owl and the Nightingale' and the English Poems of Oxford, Jesus College, MS 29 (II)* (Kalamazoo)
Flügel, Ewald, ed., 1905. 'Eine Mittelenglische Claudian Übersetzung (1445)', *Anglia* 28: 255–299, 421–438
*Forni, Kathleen, ed., 2005. *The Chaucerian Apocrypha: A Selection* (Kalamazoo)
*Foster, Edward E., ed., 2007. *'Amis and Amiloun', 'Robert of Cisyle', and 'Sir Amadace'* (Kalamazoo)
Garlick, Raymond, and Roland Mathias, eds, 1984. *Anglo-Welsh Poetry 1480–1980* (Bridgend)
Gates, Robert J., ed., 1969. *The Awntyrs off Arthure at the Terne Wathelyne* (Philadelphia)
*Ginsberg, Warren, ed., 1992. *'Wynnere and Wastoure' and 'The Parlement of the Thre Ages'* (Kalamazoo)
*Gower, John, 2000–2004. *Confessio Amantis*, ed. Russell A. Peck with Andrew Galloway, 3 vols (Kalamazoo)
*Gower, John, 2006–2013. *Confessio Amantis*, ed. Russell A. Peck with Andrew Galloway, 2nd edn, 2 vols (Kalamazoo)
*Gower, John, 2011. *The French Balades*, ed. R. F. Yeager (Kalamazoo)
Greenlaw, Lavinia, 2014. *A Double Sorrow: Troilus and Criseyde* (London)
Gunn, Thom, 1993. *Collected Poems* (London)
Gunn, Thom, 2017. *Selected Poems*, ed. Clive Wilmer (London)
*Hahn, Thomas, ed., 1995. *Sir Gawain: Eleven Romances and Tales* (Kalamazoo)
Hanna, Ralph, ed., 2008. *Speculum Vitae: A Reading Edition*, 2 vols, EETS o.s. 331, 332 (Oxford)
Hayes, Terrance, 2010. *Lighthead* (London)
Hayes, Terrance, 2018. *American Sonnets for My Past and Future Assassin* (London)
*Henryson, Robert, 2010. *The Complete Works*, ed. David Parkinson (Kalamazoo)
†Herrtage, Sidney J., ed., 1879. *The English Charlemagne Romances, Part 1: 'Sir Ferumbras'*, EETS e.s. 34 (London)
*Herzman, Ronald B., Graham Drake, and Eve Salisbury, eds, 1997. *Four Romances of England: 'King Horn', 'Havelok the Dane', 'Bevis of Hampton', 'Athelson'* (Kalamazoo)
*Hoccleve, Thomas, 1999. *The Regiment of Princes*, ed. Charles R. Blyth (Kalamazoo)
Holland, Richard, 2014. *The Buke of the Howlat*, ed. Ralph Hanna (Woodbridge)
*Hudson, Harriet, ed., 2006. *Four Middle English Romances: 'Sir Isumbras', 'Octavian', 'Sir Eglamour of Artois', 'Sir Tryamour'*, 2nd edn (Kalamazoo)
Johnston, Dafydd, ed. and trans., 1998. *Canu Maswedd yr Oesoedd Canol/Medieval Welsh Erotic Poetry*, 2nd edn (Bridgend)
Jones, Christopher A., ed. and trans., 2012. *Old English Shorter Poems. Volume I: Religious and Didactic* (Cambridge, MA)
*Klausner, David N., ed., 2008. *Two Moral Interludes: 'The Pride of Life' and 'Wisdom'* (Kalamazoo)
*Klausner, David N., ed., 2010. *The Castle of Perseverance* (Kalamazoo)
*Knight, Stephen, and Thomas H. Ohlgren, eds, 1997. *Robin Hood and Other Outlaw Tales* (Kalamazoo)
*Kooper, Erik, ed., 2005. *Sentimental and Humorous Romances* (Kalamazoo)
Langland, William, 1995. *The Vision of Piers Plowman: A Critical Edition of the B-Text Based on Trinity College Cambridge MS B.15.17*, ed. A. V. C. Schmidt, 2nd edn (London)
Langland, William, 2014. *Piers Plowman: A New Annotated Edition of the C-Text*, ed. Derek Pearsall (Liverpool)

*Laskaya, Anne, and Eve Salisbury, eds, 1995. *The Middle English Breton Lays* (Kalamazoo)
Layamon, 1963–1978. *Brut*, ed. G. L. Brook and R. F. Leslie, 2 vols, EETS o.s. 250, 277 (London)
Layamon, 2001. *Layamon's Arthur: The Arthurian Section of Laymon's 'Brut' (Lines 9229–14297)*, ed. and trans. W. R. J. Barron and S. C. Weinberg, rev. edn (Exeter)
*Lupack, Alan, ed., 1990. *Three Middle English Charlemagne Romances* (Kalamazoo)
*Lupack, Alan, ed., 1994. *'Lancelot of the Laik' and 'Sir Tristrem'* (Kalamazoo)
Lydgate, John, 1911–1934. *The Minor Poems of John Lydgate*, ed. H. N. MacCracken, 2 vols, EETS e.s. 107 and o.s. 192 (London)
Lydgate, John, 1924–1927. *Lydgate's 'Fall of Princes'*, ed. Henry Bergen, 4 vols, EETS e.s. 121–4 (London)
*Lydgate, John, 2001. *The Siege of Thebes*, ed. Robert R. Edwards (Kalamazoo)
*Lydgate, John, 2007. *The Temple of Glas*, ed. J. Allan Mitchell (Kalamazoo)
†Mannyng, Robert, 1862. *Robert of Brunne's 'Handlyng Synne'*, ed. Frederick J. Furnivall (London)
Marsden, Richard, ed., 2015. *The Cambridge Old English Reader*, 2nd edn (Cambridge)
*Metham, John, 1999. *Amoryus and Cleopes*, ed. Stephen F. Page (Kalamazoo)
*Minot, Laurence, 1996. *The Poems of Laurence Minot 1333–1352*, ed. Richard H. Osberg (Kalamazoo)
Moffat, Douglas, ed., 1987. *The Soul's Address to the Body: The Worcester Fragments* (East Lansing)
*Mooney, Linne R., and Mary-Jo Arn, eds, 2005. *'The Kingis Quair' and Other Prison Poems* (Kalamazoo)
*Morey, James H., ed., 2012. *Prik of Conscience* (Kalamazoo)
†Morris, Richard, ed., 1871. *Legends of the Holy Rood, Symbols of the Passion and Cross-Poems*, EETS o.s. 46 (London)
†Morris, Richard, ed., 1872. *An Old English Miscellany Containing a Bestiary, Kentish Sermons, Proverbs of Alfred, Religious Poems of the Thirteenth Century*, EETS o.s. 49 (London)
†Morris, Richard, ed., 1874–1893. *'Cursor Mundi' ('The cursur o the world'): A Northumbrian Poem of the XIVth Century in Four Versions, Two of Them Midland*, 7 vols, EETS o.s. 57, 59, 62, 66, 68, 99, 101 (London)
Morris, Richard, ed., 1898. *Old English Homilies and Homiletic Treatises*, 2 vols, EETS o.s. 29, 34 (1867–68), repr. in one volume (Woodbridge)
Oliver, Douglas, 1990. *Three Variations on the Theme of Harm: Selected Poetry and Prose* (London)
Oliver, Lisi, ed., 2004. 'The Laws of Æthelberht: A Student Edition', *Old English Newsletter* 38: 51–72
Orm, 2023. *Ormulum*, ed. Nils-Lennart Johannesson and Andrew Cooper, 2 vols, EETS o.s. 360, 361 (Oxford)
*Pearsall, Derek, ed., 1990. *'The Floure and the Leafe', 'The Assembly of Ladies', 'The Isle of Ladies'* (Kalamazoo)
*Peck, Russell A., ed., 1991. *Heroic Women from the Old Testament in Middle English Verse* (Kalamazoo)
Putter, Ad, and Myra Stokes, eds, 2014. *The Works of the 'Gawain' Poet: 'Sir Gawain and the Green Knight', 'Pearl', 'Cleanness', 'Patience'* (London)
†Raine, James, ed., 1836. *The Towneley Mysteries*, Surtees Society 3 (London)
*Reames, Shelley L., ed., 2003. *Middle English Legends of Women Saints* (Kalamazoo)
Robbins, Rosell Hope, ed., 1955. *Secular Lyrics of the XIVth and XVth Centuries*, 2nd edn (Oxford)
Robinson, Roger, 2019. *A Portable Paradise* (Leeds)

Roth, Pinchas, 2020. 'A Hebrew Debate Poem from Medieval England', *Early Middle English* 2: 83–89
*Salisbury, Eve, ed., 2002. *The Trials and Joys of Marriage* (Kalamazoo)
*Saupe, Karen, ed., 1997. *Middle English Marian Lyrics* (Kalamazoo)
Shakespeare, William, 1604–1605. *The Tragicall Historie of Hamlet, Prince of Denmarke* (London); London, British Library, C.34.k.2
Shakespeare, William, 1623. *Mr. William Shakespeares Comedies, Histories, & Tragedies* (London); Oxford, Bodleian Library, Arch. G c.7
Shakespeare, William, 2021. *The Arden Shakespeare, Third Series: Complete Works*, ed. Richard Proudfoot and others (London)
Shelley, Mary, and Shelley, Percy Bysshe, 1817. *History of a Six Weeks' Tour through a Part of France, Switzerland, Germany, and Holland; with Letters Descriptive of a Sail Round the Lake of Geneva and of the Glaciers of Chamouni* (London)
Shockley, Evie, 2017. *semiautomatic* (Middletown)
*Shuffelton, George, ed., 2008. *Codex Ashmole 61: A Compilation of Popular Middle English Verse* (Kalamazoo)
Skelton, John, 2015. *The Complete English Poems of John Skelton*, ed. John Scattergood, rev. edn (Liverpool)
*Stanbury, Sarah, 2001. *Pearl* (Kalamazoo)
Stevens, Martin, and A. C. Cawley, eds, 1994. *The Towneley Plays*, 2 vols, EETS s.s. 13, 14 (Oxford)
*Sugano, Douglas, ed., 2007. *The N-Town Plays* (Kalamazoo)
*Symons, Dana M., ed., 2004. *Chaucerian Dream Visions and Complaints* (Kalamazoo)
Treharne, Elaine, ed., 2010. *Old and Middle English, c.890–c.1450: An Anthology*, 3rd edn (Chichester)
Turville-Petre, Thorlac, ed., 1989. *Alliterative Poetry of the Later Middle Ages* (London)
Turville-Petre, Thorlac, ed., 2015. *Poems from BL MS Harley 913, The Kildare Manuscript*, EETS o.s. 345 (Oxford)
Wace, 1999. *Wace's 'Roman de Brut', A History of the British: Text and Translation*, ed. and trans. Judith Weiss (Exeter)
Wilde, Oscar, 1909. *A Woman of No Importance*, 3rd edn (London)
*Wimsatt, James I., ed., 2009. *Chaucer and the Poems of 'Ch'*, rev. edn (Kalamazoo)

3. Secondary works

Akbari, Suzanne Conklin, 2019. 'Read It Out Loud', in *How We Read: Tales, Fury, Nothing, Sound*, ed. Kaitlin Heller and Suzanne Conklin Akbari ([Santa Barbara]), 24–32
Allen, Rosamund, Jane Roberts, and Carole Weinberg, eds, 2013. *Reading Laʒamon's 'Brut': Approaches and Explorations* (Amsterdam), doi:10.1163/9789401209526
Ashe, Laura, 2017. *The Oxford English Literary History, Volume I, 1000–1350: Conquest and Transformation* (Oxford)
Atherton, Mark, 2022. 'Rhyme and Reason in *The Battle of Maldon*', in *Tradition and Innovation in Old English Metre*, ed. Rachel A. Burns and Rafael J. Pascual (Leeds), 103–119, doi:10.2307/j.ctv310vqj8.13
Attridge, Derek, 1995. *Poetic Rhythm: An Introduction* (Cambridge)
Attridge, Derek, 2013. *Moving Words: Forms of English Poetry* (Oxford)
Baechle, Sarah, Carissa M. Harris, and Elizaveta Strakhov, eds, 2022. *Rape Culture and Female Resistance in Late Medieval Literature; with an Edition of Middle English and Middle Scots Pastourelles* (University Park)

Barney, Stephen A., 1993. *Studies in 'Troilus': Chaucer's Text, Meter, and Diction* (East Lansing)

Beadle, Richard, 1994. 'English Autograph Writings of the Later Middle Ages: Some Preliminaries', in *Gli Autografi medievali: Problemi paleografici e filologici*, ed. Paolo Chiesa and Lucia Pinelli (Spoleto), 249–268

Beadle, Richard, 2008. 'The York Corpus Christi Play', in *The Cambridge Companion to Medieval English Theatre*, ed. Richard Beadle, 2nd edn (Cambridge), 99–124, doi:10.1017/ccol9780521864008.005

Bellis, Joanna, 2016. *The Hundred Years War in Literature, 1337–1600* (Cambridge)

Bennett, J. A. W., 1990. *Middle English Literature, 1100–1400*, ed. and completed by Douglas Gray (Oxford)

Bliss, A. J., 1953. '*Sir Orfeo*, Lines 1–46', *English and Germanic Studies* 5: 7–14

Boffey, Julia, 1993. 'Women Authors and Women's Literacy in Fourteenth- and Fifteenth-Century England', in *Women and Literature in Britain, 1150–1500*, ed. Carol M. Meale (Cambridge), 159–182

Boffey, Julia, and A. S. G. Edwards, 2005. *A New Index of Middle English Verse* (London)

Brantley, Jessica, 2022. *Medieval English Manuscripts and Literary Forms* (Philadelphia), doi:10.2307/j.ctv2cw0s41

Brown, Carleton, and Rossell Hope Robbins, 1943. *The Index of Middle English Verse* (New York)

Burrow, J. A., 2008. *Medieval Writers and Their Work: Middle English Literature, 1100–1500*, 2nd edn (Oxford)

Burrow, J. A., and Thorlac Turville-Petre, 2021. *A Book of Middle English*, 4th edn (Oxford)

Busby, Keith, 2023. 'The Poetic Field, III: Anglo-French', in *Medieval Poetry, 1100–1400*, ed. Helen Cooper and Robert R. Edwards, Oxford History of Poetry in English 2 (2023), 104–117

Butterfield, Ardis, 1991. 'Lyric and Elegy in *The Book of the Duchess*', *Medium Ævum* 60: 33–60, doi:10.2307/43629381

Butterfield, Ardis, 2009. *The Familiar Enemy: Chaucer, Language, and Nation in the Hundred Years War* (Oxford)

Butterfield, Ardis, 2016. 'Poems without Form? *Maiden in the mor lay* Revisited', in *Readings in Medieval Textuality: Essays in Honour of A. C. Spearing*, ed. Cristina Maria Cervone and D. Vance Smith (Cambridge), 169–194

Butterfield, Ardis, 2022. 'Lyric Editing', in *What Kind of a Thing is a Middle English Lyric?*, ed. Cristina Maria Cervone and Nicholas Watson (Philadelphia), 30–60

Byrne, Aisling, 2016. *Otherworlds: Fantasy and History in Medieval Literature* (Oxford)

Byrne, Aisling, 2020. 'From Hólar to Lisbon: Middle English Literature in Medieval Translation, c.1286–c.1550', *Review of English Studies* 71.300: 433–456, doi:10.1093/res/hgz085

Cable, Thomas, 2009. 'Progress in Middle English Alliterative Metrics', *Yearbook of Langland Studies* 23: 243–264, doi:10.1484/J.YLS.1.100478

Calabrese, Michael, 2016. *An Introduction to 'Piers Plowman'* (Gainesville)

Cannon, Christopher, 2008. *Middle English Literature: A Cultural History* (Cambridge)

Cannon, Christopher, 2016. *From Literacy to Literature: England, 1300–1400* (Oxford)

Carlson, David, 1991. '*Pearl*'s Imperfections', *Studia Neophilologica* 63: 57–67, doi:10.1080/00393279108588061

Casling, Dennis, and V. J. Scattergood, 1974. 'One Aspect of Stanza-Linking', *Neuphilologische Mitteilungen* 75: 79–91

Chaganti, Seeta, 2018. *Strange Footing: Poetic Form and Dance in the Late Middle Ages* (Chicago)

Chickering, Howell, 1997. 'Stanzaic Closure and Linkage in *Sir Gawain and the Green Knight*', *Chaucer Review* 32: 1–31

Clanchy, Michael, 2013. *From Memory to Written Record: England 1066–1307*, 3rd edn (Chichester)
Clanchy, Michael, 2018. *Looking Back from the Invention of Printing: Mothers and the Teaching of Reading in the Middle Ages* (Turnhout)
Cohen, Helen Louise, 1915. *The Ballade* (New York)
Coleman, Joyce, 1996. *Public Reading and the Reading Public in Late Medieval England and France* (Cambridge)
Cooper, Helen, 2023. 'The Naming of Will in *Piers Plowman*', *Chaucer Review* 58: 456–467, doi:10.5325/chaucerrev.58.3-4.0456
Corèdon, Christopher, with Ann Williams, 2004. *A Dictionary of Medieval Terms and Phrases* (Cambridge)
Cornelius, Ian, 2017. *Reconstructing Alliterative Verse: The Pursuit of a Medieval Metre* (Cambridge)
Cornelius, Ian, 2022. 'Language and Meter', in *What Kind of a Thing is a Middle English Lyric?*, ed. Cristina Maria Cervone and Nicholas Watson (Philadelphia), 106–134
Cuddon, J. A., 1998. *The Penguin Dictionary of Literary Terms and Literary Theory*, 4th edn, rev. C. E. Preston (London)
Dance, Richard, 2019. *Words Derived from Old Norse in 'Sir Gawain and the Green Knight': An Etymological Survey* (Chichester)
Drimmer, Sonja, 2019. *The Art of Allusion: Illuminators and the Making of English Literature, 1403–1476* (Philadelphia)
Duffell, Martin J., 2008. *A New History of English Metre* (London)
Duffell, Martin J., 2018. *Chaucer's Verse Art in its European Context* (Tempe)
Duncan, Thomas G., 2005. 'Middle English Lyrics: Metre and Editorial Practice', in *A Companion to the Middle English Lyric*, ed. Thomas G. Duncan (Cambridge), 19–38
Eagleton, Terry, 2007. *How to Read a Poem* (London)
Edwards, A. S. G., 2001. 'The Middle English Translation of Claudian's De consolatu Stilichonis', in *Middle English Poetry: Texts and Traditions; Essays in Honour of Derek Pearsall*, ed. A. J. Minnis (York), 267–278
Engler, Bernd, 1990. 'Literary Form as Aesthetic Program: The Envoy in English and American Literature', *REAL: Yearbook of Research in English and American Literature* 7: 61–97
Evans, Ruth, 2018. 'Chaucerian Rhyme-Breaking', in *Contemporary Chaucer across the Centuries: Essays for Stephanie Trigg*, ed. Helen M. Hickey, Anne McKendry, and Melissa Raine (Manchester), 56–73, doi: 10.7228/manchester/9781526129154.001.0001
Fallows, David, 1992. 'Polyphonic Song', in *Companion to Medieval and Renaissance Music*, ed. Tess Knighton and David Fallows (London), 123–126
Faulkner, Mark, 2022. *A New Literary History of the Long Twelfth Century: Language and Literature between Old and Middle English* (Cambridge)
Fein, Susanna, 1997. 'Twelve-Line Stanza Forms in Middle English and the Date of *Pearl*', *Speculum* 72: 367–398, doi:10.2307/3040975
Fein, Susanna, ed., 2019a. *Interpreting MS Digby 86: A Trilingual Book from Thirteenth-Century Worcestershire* (Woodbridge)
Fein, Susanna, 2019b. 'Designing English: Early Middle English Verse on the Page in Oxford, Jesus College MS 29 (II)', *Journal of the Early Book Society*, 22: 43–71
Ferber, Michael, 2019. *Poetry and Language: The Linguistics of Verse* (Cambridge)
Flannery, Mary C., 2020. *Practising Shame: Female Honour in Late Medieval England* (Manchester)
Fulk, R. D., 2002. 'Early Middle English Evidence for Old English Meter: Resolution in *Poema morale*', *Journal of Germanic Linguistics* 14: 331–355

Fulk, R. D., 2012. *An Introduction to Middle English: Grammar, Texts* (Peterborough, ON)
Galloway, Andrew, 2006. *Medieval Literature and Culture* (London)
Gardner, Helen, 1949. *The Art of T. S. Eliot* (London)
Gasparov, M. L., 1996. *A History of European Versification*, trans. G. S. Smith and Marina Tarlinskaja, ed. G. S. Smith and Leofranc Holford-Strevens (Oxford)
Ghosh, Amitav, 2016. *The Great Derangement: Climate Change and the Unthinkable* (Chicago)
Gillespie, Vincent, 2005. 'Moral and Penitential Lyrics', in *A Companion to the Middle English Lyric*, ed. Thomas G. Duncan (Cambridge), 68–95
Gillespie, Vincent, 2008. 'Religious Writing', in *The Oxford History of Literary Translation in English, Volume One: To 1500*, ed. Roger Ellis (Oxford), 234–283
Gillespie, Vincent, and Anne Hudson, eds, 2013. *Probable Truth: Editing Medieval Texts from Britain in the Twenty-First Century* (Turnhout), doi:10.1484/m.tt-eb.6.09070802050003050306080305
Görlach, Manfred, 1974. *The Textual Tradition of the South English Legendary* (Leeds)
Gray, Douglas, 2008. *Later Medieval English Literature* (Oxford)
Greenham, David, 2019. *Close Reading: The Basics* (Abingdon)
Griffith, David, 2011. 'A Newly Identified Verse Item by John Lydgate at Holy Trinity Church, Long Melford, Suffolk', *Notes and Queries* 58: 364–367
Guy-Bray, Stephen, 2022. 'Notes on the Couplet in the Sonnet', *Shakespeare* 18: 322–331, doi: 10.1080/17450918.2022.2091651
Hanna, Ralph, 1995. *Pursuing History: Middle English Manuscripts and Their Texts* (Stanford)
Hanna, Ralph, 2013. *Introducing English Medieval Book History: Manuscripts, their Producers and their Readers* (Liverpool)
Hanna, Ralph, 2015. *Editing Medieval Texts: An Introduction, Using Exemplary Materials Derived from Richard Rolle, 'Super Canticum' 4* (Liverpool)
Hanna, Ralph, 2019. 'Latin and English: Unnoticeable Middle English Verses', *Notes and Queries* 66: 36–47, doi:10.1093/notesj/gjy179
Hardman, Phillipa, 2006. 'Lydgate's Uneasy Syntax', in *John Lydgate: Poetry, Culture, and Lancastrian England*, ed. Larry Scanlon and James Simpson (Notre Dame), 12–35
Henry, Avril, 1997. 'The Dramatic Function of Rhyme and Stanza Patterns in *The Castle of Perseverance*', in *Individuality and Achievement in Middle English Poetry*, ed. O. S. Pickering (Cambridge), 147–183
Hilmo, Maidie, 2017. 'Did the Scribe Draw the Miniatures in British Library, MS Cotton Nero A.x (The *Pearl-Gawain* Manuscript)?', *Journal of the Early Book Society* 20: 111–136
Hilmo, Maidie, 2018. 'Re-Conceptualizing the Poems of the *Pearl-Gawain* Manuscript in Line and Color', *Manuscript Studies* 3: 383–40, doi:10.1353/mns.2018.0020
Hodgson, Andrew, 2021. *The Cambridge Guide to Reading Poetry* (Cambridge)
Hopwood, Llewelyn, 2021. 'Creative Bilingualism in Late-Medieval Welsh Poetry', *Studia Celtica* 55: 97–120, doi:10.16922/SC.55.5
Horobin, Simon, 2013. *Chaucer's Language*, 2nd edn (Basingstoke)
Horobin, Simon, and Jeremy Smith, 2002. *An Introduction to Middle English* (New York)
Hsy, Jonathan, 2013. *Trading Tongues: Merchants, Multilingualism, and Medieval Literature* (Columbus)
Inoue, Noriko, 2023. 'The "Extra-Long" Dip in the Poems of the *Gawain* Poet', *Chaucer Review* 58: 232–258, doi:10.5325/chaucerrev.58.2.0232
Jefferson, Judith A., Donka Minkova and Ad Putter, 2014. 'Perfect and Imperfect Rhyme: Romances in the *abab* Tradition', *Studies in Philology* 111: 631–651, doi:10.1353/sip.2014.0026

Johnson, David, and Elaine Treharne, eds, 2005. *Readings in Medieval Texts: Interpreting Old and Middle English Literature* (Oxford)
Kelemen, Erick, 2009. *Textual Editing and Criticism: An Introduction* (New York)
Kerby-Fulton, Kathryn, 2020. 'Making the Early Middle Hiberno-English Lyric: Mysteries, Experiments, and Survivals before 1330', *Early Middle English* 2: 1–26
Kerby-Fulton, Kathryn, Maidie Hilmo, and Linda Olson, 2012. *Opening up Middle English Manuscripts: Literary and Visual Approaches* (Ithaca, NY)
Lawton, D. A., 1980. 'Larger Patterns of Syntax in Middle English Unrhymed Alliterative Verse', *Neuphilologus* 64: 604–618
Leahy, Connor, 2019. 'Middle English in Early Auden', *Review of English Studies* 70.295: 527–549, doi:10.1093/res/hgy112
Lennard, John, 2005. *The Poetry Handbook: A Guide to Reading Poetry for Pleasure and Practical Criticism*, 2nd edn (Oxford)
Lerer, Seth, 1985. 'Artifice and Artistry in *Sir Orfeo*', *Speculum* 60: 92–109, doi:10.2307/2852135
Lerer, Seth, 2003. 'The Endurance of Formalism in Middle English Studies', *Literature Compass* 1: ME 1–15, doi:10.1111/j.1741-4113.2004.00006.x
Lester, G. A., 1996. *The Language of Old and Middle English Poetry* (Basingstoke)
Lumiansky, R. M., 1951. 'Chaucer's "For the nones"', *Neophilologus* 35: 29–36, doi:10.1007/bf01513152
Lundeen, Stephanie Thompson, 2009. 'The Earliest Middle English Interludes', *Comparative Drama* 43: 379–400, doi:10.1353/cdr.0.0069
Lynch, Deidre Shauna, 2015. *Loving Literature: A Cultural History* (Chicago)
Machan, Tim William, 1994. *Textual Criticism and Middle English Texts* (Charlottesville)
Matthews, David, 2016. 'Enlisting the Poet: The List and the Late Medieval Dream Vision', *Style* 50: 281–295, doi:10.5325/style.50.3.0280
Meyer-Lee, Robert J., 2010. 'The Emergence of the Literary in John Lydgate's *Life of Our Lady*', *Journal of English and Germanic Philology* 109: 322–348, doi:10.5406/jenglgermphil.109.3.0322
Mikics, David, 2013. *Slow Reading in a Hurried Age* (Cambridge, MA)
Minkova, Donka, 2007. 'The Forms of Verse', in *A Companion to Medieval English Literature and Culture, c.1350–c.1500*, ed. Peter Brown (Oxford), 176–195
Murton, Megan, 2020. *Chaucer's Prayers: Writing Christian and Pagan Devotion* (Cambridge), doi:10.2307/j.ctvxhrk7b
Myklebust, Nicholas, 2022. 'Historicising Hoccleve's Metre', in *Thomas Hoccleve: New Approaches*, ed. Jenni Nuttall and David Watt (Cambridge), 25–46, doi: 10.1017/9781800106420.002
Nolan, Maura, 2007. 'Beauty', in *Middle English*, ed. Paul Strohm (Oxford), 207–221, doi:10.1093/oxfordhb/9780199287666.013.0014
Nolan, Maura, 2013. 'Performing Lydgate's Broken-Backed Meter', in *Interpretation and Performance: Essays for Alan Gaylord*, ed. Susan F. Yager and Elise E. Morse-Gagné (Provo), 141–159
Nuttall, Jenni, 2016. 'The Vanishing English Virelai: French *Complainte* in English in the Fifteenth Century', *Medium Ævum* 85: 59–79, doi:10.2307/26396470
Nuttall, Jenni, 2018. 'Lydgate and the Lenvoy', *Exemplaria* 30: 35–48
Nuttall, Jenni, 2020. 'The English Roundel, Charles's Jubilee, and Mimetic Form', in *Charles d'Orléans' English Aesthetic: The Form, Poetics, and Style of 'Fortunes Stabilnes'*, ed. R. D. Perry and Mary-Jo Arn (Cambridge), 82–101, doi:10.2307/j.ctvxhrm5t.10
Orme, Nicholas, 2006. *Medieval Schools: From Roman Britain to Renaissance England* (New Haven)
Perry, R. D., and Mary-Jo Arn, eds, 2020. *Charles d'Orléans's English Aesthetic: The Form, Poetics, and Style of 'Fortunes Stabilnes'* (Cambridge), doi:10.2307/j.ctvxhrm5t

Phelpstead, Carl, 2004. 'Auden and the Inklings: An Alliterative Revival', *Journal of English and Germanic Philology* 103: 433–457

Pickering, O. S., 1992. 'Newly Discovered Secular Lyrics from Later Thirteenth-Century Cheshire', *Review of English Studies* 43.170: 157–180; doi:10.1093/res/xliii.170.157

Prendergast, Thomas, and Jessica Rosenfeld, eds, 2018. *Chaucer and the Subversion of Form* (Cambridge), doi:10.1017/9781108147682

Purdie, Rhiannon, 2008. *Anglicising Romance: Tail-Rhyme and Genre in Medieval English Literature* (Cambridge), doi:10.1515/angl.2010.061

Purdie, Rhiannon, 2018. '*King Orphius* and *Sir Orfeo*, Scotland and England, Memory and Manuscript', in *The Transmission of Medieval Romance: Metres, Manuscripts and Early Prints*, ed. Ad Putter and Judith A. Jefferson (Cambridge)

Putter, Ad, 2004. 'The Language and Metre of *Pater Noster* and *Three Dead Kings*', *Review of English Studies*, n.s. 55.221: 498–526, doi:10.1093/res/55.221.498

Putter, Ad, 2012. 'A Prototype Theory of Metrical Stress: Lexical Categories and Ictus in Langland, the *Gawain*-Poet and Other Alliterative Poets', in *The Use and Development of Middle English: Proceedings of the Sixth International Conference on Middle English, Cambridge 2008*, ed. Richard Dance and Laura Wright (Frankfurt am Main), 281–298

Putter, Ad, 2015. 'Adventures in the Bob-and-Wheel Tradition: Narratives and Manuscripts', in *Medieval Romance and Material Culture*, ed. Nicholas Perkins (Cambridge, 2015), 147–163

Putter, Ad, 2017. 'In Appreciation of Metrical Abnormality: Headless Lines and Initial Inversion in Chaucer', *Critical Survey* 29: 65–85, doi:10.3167/cs.2017.290306

Putter, Ad, 2018. 'The Singing of Middle English Romance: Stanza Forms and *Contrafacta*', in *The Transmission of Medieval Romance: Metres, Manuscripts and Early Prints*, ed. Ad Putter and Judith A. Jefferson (Cambridge), 69–90

Putter, Ad, Judith Jefferson, and Myra Stokes, 2007. *Studies in the Metre of Alliterative Verse* (Oxford)

Rajabzadeh, Shokoofeh, 2019. 'The Depoliticized Saracen and Muslim Erasure', *Literature Compass* 16: e12548, doi:10.1111/lic3.12548

Renevey, Denis, 2018. '"Short song is good in ale": Charles d'Orléans and Authorial Intentions in the Middle English *Ballade 84*', in *Middle English Lyrics: New Readings of Short Poems*, ed. Julia Boffey and Christiana Whitehead (Cambridge), 201–210, doi:10.1017/9781787442993.015

Revard, Carter, 2003. 'Crossing Cultures: An Online Interview with Carter Revard', *Studies in American Indian Literatures*, s. 2, 15: 139–141

Roscow, G. H., 1981. *Syntax and Style in Chaucer's Poetry* (Cambridge)

Russom, Geoffrey, 2017. *The Evolution of Verse Structure in Old and Middle English Poetry: From the Earliest Alliterative Poems to Iambic Pentameter* (Cambridge)

Rust, Martha D., 2016. '"Qui bien aime a tarde oblie": Lemmata and Lists in the *Parliament of Fowls*', in *Chaucer: Visual Approaches*, ed. Susanna Fein and David Raybin (University Park, PA), 195–217

Sanatan, Amílcar Peter, 2020. Review of Roger Robinson, *A Portable Paradise* (2019), in *Journal of West Indian Literature* 28: 162–164

Saunders, Corrine, 2010. 'Epilogue: Afterlives of Medieval English Poetry', in *A Companion to Medieval Poetry*, ed. Corrine Saunders (Oxford), 647–660, doi:10.1002/9781444319095.epil

Sawyer, Daniel, 2020. *Reading English Verse in Manuscript c.1350–c.1500* (Oxford), doi:10.1093/oso/9780198857778.001.0001

Sawyer, Daniel, 2021a. 'Form, Time, and the "First English Sonnet"', *Chaucer Review* 56: 193–224, doi:10.5325/chaucerrev.56.3.0193

Sawyer, Daniel, 2021b. 'The Influence of *Pearl* on Thom Gunn's "Lament"', *Notes and Queries* 68: 363–366, doi:10.1093/notesj/gjab133

Scase, Wendy, 2022. *Visible English: Graphic Culture, Scribal Practice, and Identity, c.700–c.1550* (Turnhout)
Schmidt, A. V. C., 1987. *The Clerkly Maker: Langland's Poetic Art* (Cambridge)
Shepherd, Stephen H. A., and Courtney Harshbarger, 2020. 'Text-Image Alignment in MS Douce 104 (*Piers Plowman*): "Articulation", Pre-Drawing, and Proximal Allusion', *Medium Ævum* 89: 267–300, doi:10.2307/27089791
Shillingsburg, Peter, 2017. *Textuality and Knowledge: Essays* (University Park, PA), doi:10.5325/j.ctv14gpfnz
Simpson, James, 2002. *The Oxford English Literary History, Volume II, 1350–1547: Reform and Cultural Revolution* (Oxford)
Smith, Jeremy, 2012. *Older Scots: A Linguistic Reader*, Scottish Text Society, 5th series, 9 (Woodbridge)
Solopova, Elizabeth, 1994. 'Studies in Middle English Syllabic Verse before Chaucer', unpublished DPhil thesis, University of Oxford
Solopova, Elizabeth, ed., 2017. *The Wycliffite Bible: Origin, History, and Interpretation* (Leiden), doi:10.1163/9789004328921
Spearing, A. C., 1964. *Criticism and Medieval Poetry* (London)
Spearing, A. C., 2005. *Textual Subjectivity: The Encoding of Subjectivity in Medieval Narratives and Lyrics* (Oxford), doi:10.1093/acprof:oso/9780198187240.001.0001
Stagg, Robert, 2022. *Shakespeare's Blank Verse: An Alternative History* (Oxford), doi:10.1093/oso/9780192863270.001.0001
Stanley, E. G., 1972. 'The Use of Bob-Lines in *Sir Thopas*', *Neuphilologische Mitteilungen* 73: 417–426
Stanley, E. G., 1988, 'Rhymes in English Medieval Verse: From Old English to Middle English', in *Medieval English Studies Presented to George Kane*, ed. Edward Donald Kennedy, Ronald Waldron, and Joseph S. Wittig (Woodbridge), 19–54
Strakhov, Elizaveta, 2020. 'Charles d'Orléans' Cross-Channel Poetics: The Choice of Ballade Form in *Fortunes Stabilnes*', in *Charles d'Orléans' English Aesthetic: The Form, Poetics, and Style of 'Fortunes Stabilnes'*, ed. R. D. Perry and Mary-Jo Arn (Cambridge), 34–81, doi:10.2307/j.ctvxhrm5t.9
Strakhov, Elizaveta, 2022. *Continental England: Form, Translation, and Chaucer in the Hundred Years' War* (Columbus)
Strohm, Paul, 2000. *Theory and the Premodern Text* (Minneapolis)
Strohm, Paul, ed., 2007. *Middle English* (Oxford), doi:10.1093/oxfordhb/9780199287666.001.0001
Terasawa, Jun, 2011. *Old English Metre: An Introduction* (Toronto)
Tolmie, Jane, 2002. 'Mrs Noah and Didactic Abuses', *Early Theatre* 5: 11–35, doi: 10.12745/et.5.1.623
Turner, Marion, ed., 2013. *A Handbook of Middle English Studies* (Chichester), doi:10.1002/9781118328736
Turner, Marion, 2019. *Chaucer: A European Life* (Princeton), doi:10.2307/j.ctv941rbz
Turner, Marion, 2023. *The Wife of Bath: A Biography* (Princeton)
Turville-Petre, Thorlac, 1974. '"Summer Sunday", "De Tribus Regibus Mortuis", and "The Awntyrs off Arthure": Three Poems in the Thirteen-Line Stanza', *Review of English Studies* 25.97: 1–14, doi:10.1093/res/XXV.97.1
Turville-Petre, Thorlac, 1988. 'The Author of *The Destruction of Troy*', *Medium Ævum* 57: 264–269, doi:10.2307/43629212
Turville-Petre, Thorlac, 2007. *Reading Middle English Literature* (Malden, MA)
Turville-Petre, Thorlac, 2018. *Description and Narrative in Middle English Alliterative Poetry* (Liverpool), doi:10.2307/j.ctv62hg7x

Twycross, Meg, 2008. 'The Theatricality of Medieval English Plays', in *The Cambridge Companion to Medieval English Theatre*, ed. Richard Beadle, 2nd edn (Cambridge), 26–74, doi:10.1017/ccol0521366704.002

Vendler, Helen, 2010. *Poems, Poets, Poetry: An Introduction and Anthology*, 3rd edn (Boston)

Wakelin, Daniel, 2018. *Designing English: Early Literature on the Page* (Oxford)

Weber, Ben, 2011. '"Smothe and plain and al grene": *Sir Orfeo*'s Flat Fairyland', *Notes and Queries*, 58: 24–28, doi:10.1093/notes/gjq252

Weiskott, Eric, 2016. *English Alliterative Verse: Poetic Tradition and Literary History* (Cambridge), doi:10.1017/9781316718674

Weiskott, Eric, 2021a. *Meter and Modernity in English Verse, 1350–1650* (Philadelphia), doi:10.2307/j.ctv16qjz9w

Weiskott, Eric, 2021b. 'Stanza-Linking in *Sir Gawain and the Green Knight*: The Phenomenology of Narrative', *Neophilologus* 105: 457–461, doi:10.1007/s11061-021-09677-7

Weiskott, Eric, 2023. 'Verse Forms and Prosody', in *Medieval Poetry, 1400–1500*, ed. Julia Boffey and A. S. G. Edwards, Oxford History of Poetry in English 3 (Oxford), 76–90

Wenzel, Siegfried, 1986. *Preachers, Poets, and the Early English Lyric* (Princeton)

Whiting, Bartlett Jere, and Helen Wescott Whiting, 1968. *Proverbs, Sentences, and Proverbial Phrases from English Writings Mainly before 1500* (Cambridge, MA)

Williams, Raymond, 1983. *Keywords: A Vocabulary of Culture and Society*, rev. edn (London)

Wogan-Browne, Jocelyn, ed., 2009. *Language and Culture in Medieval Britain: The French of England, c.1100–c.1500* (Woodbridge)

Wolfson, Susan, and Marshall Brown, eds, 2006. *Reading for Form* (Seattle)

Zaerr, Linda Marie, 2005. '*The Weddynge of Sir Gawen and Dame Ragnell*: Performance and Intertextuality in Middle English Popular Romance', in *Performing Medieval Narrative*, ed. Evelyn Birge Vitz, Nancy Freeman Regalado and Marilyn Lawrence (Cambridge), 193–208

4. Electronic resources

Dance, Richard, Sara Pons-Sanz, and Brittany Schorn, 2019. *The Gersum Project: The Scandinavian Influence on English Vocabulary* (Cambridge, Cardiff and Sheffield), <https://www.gersum.org>

Dictionaries of the Scots Language/Dictionars o the Scots Leid <https://dsl.ac.uk>

Greene, Roland, and others, eds, 2017. *The Princeton Encyclopedia of Poetry and Poetics*, 4th edn, doi:10.1093/acref/9780190681173.001.0001

Kurath, Hans, and others, eds. *Middle English Dictionary* <https://quod.lib.umich.edu/m/middle-english-dictionary/dictionary>

Mooney, Linne R., and others, eds. *The 'DIMEV': An Open-Access, Digital Edition of the 'Index of Middle English Verse'* <https://www.dimev.net>

Nuttall, Jenni. *Stylisticienne*, <http://stylisticienne.com>

Oxford English Dictionary, <https://www.oed.com>

Indexed Glossary of Technical Terms

This glossary lists all technical words and phrases that are printed in **bold type** at their first appearance in the main text, and provides page numbers for discussion. I have my preferred terms but, to help in further reading, I cross-reference from some words and phrases sometimes used in other scholarship discussing Middle English and early Scots verse. These are underlined.

The glossary doesn't cover the full range of analytical vocabulary for English verse in general: I have kept in the main to words specifically useful for the study of Middle English verse. For more general vocabulary, see resources such as Lennard's *Poetry Handbook* (2005, 360–89), *The Penguin Dictionary of Literary Terms and Literary Theory* (Cuddon 1998), and the online *Princeton Encyclopedia of Poetry and Poetics* (Greene and others eds 2017).

a-verse: the first of the two half-lines in a line of **alliterative verse**, preceding the **b-verse**. Typically contains two **lifts** and avoids b-verse patterns, so that full lines are asymmetric. The a-verse is often longer than the b-verse, and often contains more grammatically- and semantically-central material. (72, 74–75, 106)

accentual-syllabic metre: see **alternating metre**.

alliterative lexis: words found in Middle English **alliterative verse**, but never or almost never in any other context; many are used almost exclusively to provide **lifts**. Many examples gave poets useful synonyms for repeated concepts, such as 'man' or 'warrior'. Examples include *freke*, *gome*, *hathel*, *renk*, *segg*, *tulke*, and *wyghe*. (71, 80–82, 87)

alliterative metre: metre in which each line is divided by a regular **metrical caesura** into two **half-lines**, the **a-verse** and the **b-verse**, which contain patterns of **lifts**, **long dips**, and **short dips**. Contrasted with **alternating metre**. Descended from, but not identical to, the metre of Old English verse. (70–8)

alliterative-stanzaic verse: a tradition of verse featuring obligatory, regular alliteration *and* obligatory, regular end-rhyme, organized into stanzas. No single stanza-form defines alliterative-stanzaic verse. Alliterative-stanzaic poems often have stanzas subdivided into *frons* and *cauda*, but not all poems in such **subdivided stanzas** are alliterative-stanzaic, and the earliest surviving English *frons-cauda* poems are in **alternating metres**. The role of obligatory rhyme at the ends of lines in alliterative-stanzaic poetry might have gradually pulled the tradition's metrical norms away from typical **alliterative metre**. Alliterative-stanzaic verse emerges in the written record in the fourteenth century. (86–88, 106, 178)

alliterative verse: verse written in **alliterative metre**; since this is a metrical distinction, not all verse with **regular alliteration** qualifies as alliterative verse. Middle English alliterative verse has a historical relationship to Old English alliterative verse, but emerges in its orthodox form in the written record only in the middle of the fourteenth century. Some early Middle English poems, most notably Layamon's *Brut*, also show signs of descent from Old English alliterative verse, but their relationship to later Middle English alliterative verse from c. 1350 on is a matter of scholarly debate. (34–35, 70–78, 178, 179)

202 Indexed Glossary of Technical Terms

alternating metre: metre created by the predictable alternation of perceived **beats** and **offbeats**. The majority of Middle English and early Scots poetry was written in various types of alternating metre, and it is the ancestor of the standard metrical systems of the sixteenth to the nineteenth centuries. Contrasted with **alliterative metre**. (46–69, 70–88)

anacrusis: the omission of a normally-expected offbeat at the start of a line of verse in **alternating metre**. Creates a **headless line**.

anisometric: adjective describing verse forms in which the metrical lengths of the lines change; the word means 'not equally measured'. Verse in **septenary** lines is anisometric. Most **tail rhyme** stanzas and **subdivided stanzas** split between metrically-distinguished *frons* and *cauda* are anisometric. Contrasted with isometric forms.

aureation / aureate diction: the use of rare, polysyllabic French- or (especially) Latin-derived words to 'gild' poetry and display a poet's learning and creativity. A feature of some fifteenth-century poetry. (28–30)

autograph: a **manuscript** copy of a work in the handwriting of the work's author. Rare for early English and Scots poetry. (47, 61, 68, 148)

autorhyme: rhyming a word with itself, in exactly the same sense and as the same part of speech. Used cunningly in some early Middle English poems. Generally avoided in later Middle English verse. Compare **punning rhyme**. (94–95)

b-verse: the second half-line of a full line of **alliterative verse**, following the **a-verse**. Typically contains two **lifts** and one **long dip**; the long dip occurs either *before* both lifts or *between* the lifts; the b-verse ends in a **short dip**. The b-verse is often shorter than the a-verse, and often contains syntactically subordinated material. (72, 75–6, 106, 144)

ballade: most commonly used in modern scholarship to mean a short poem of multiple (most often three) **through-rhymed** stanzas, and the only one of the French fixed forms to find widespread use among poets writing in English in this period. A *ballade* sometimes ends with an **envoy**. In Middle English itself, the word was sometimes used generically to mean 'a stanza' or 'a short poem'. (116–17)

beat: in **alternating verse**, a perceived strong point in a metrical pattern. (48–50)

blank: metrical verse is blank when it has neither regular rhyme nor regular alliteration. In the sixteenth and seventeenth centuries, poets codified blank verse as unrhymed poetry in five-beat lines with a dominant rising pattern of **offbeat** and **beat** (x/x/x/x/x/). But at least two poets writing in Middle English had independently invented it, using other metres, in the twelfth and fifteenth centuries. (100–1, 177, 181)

bob: one single-beat line in a stanza. Usually linked by syntax to preceding lines and by rhyme to following lines. Though poets frequently used bobs to separate a *frons* from a formally-distinct *cauda* within a **subdivided stanza**, and though the bob is most well-known from its use in *Sir Gawain*, not all subdivided stanza models used a bob. (104, 106–7, 110, 134)

bob and wheel: combination of a **bob** and a *cauda* ('wheel'). These were distinct features which could be combined, as they are in *Sir Gawain*, but did not have to appear together.

broken-backed line: Lydgatean line in which John Lydgate's consistent **metrical caesura** between the second and third **beats** allows him to put two beats next to each other without an intervening **offbeat** for a x/x/|/x/x/(x) metrical pattern. (66–8)

burden: the repeated portion of a **carol**. Burdens vary in length. Editions normally print the burden at the carol's head, and then indicate that it should be repeated after each main stanza. (114–16, 157)

caesura: a pause within a line, caused either by predictable rules about metre (**metrical caesura**) or simply by local syntax (**rhetorical caesura**). For clarity's sake, it is best to specify whether a rhetorical or a metrical caesura is meant. Both *caesurae* and *caesuras* are acceptable plural forms. (65)

carol: a stanzaic poem beginning with a **burden**, which then recurs after each stanza. Many carols either originate in song or were written to be sung, and some survive with music. Middle English carols tackle all kinds of topics, sacred and secular, and the form has no automatic link to Christmas or to religion. (114–16)

cauda: a formally distinguished set of two or more lines at the end of a **subdivided stanza** form. The plural form is *caudae*. Although in many poems the *cauda* is separated out from the stanza's initial *frons* by a **bob**, *caudae* could appear without bobs, usually distinguished by metrically shorter lines. In **alliterative-stanzaic** poems, the *cauda* is typically three **a-verses** followed by one **b-verse**. (104–8)

closed-class word: a word in one of the classes which do not readily accept new members: prepositions, conjunctions, pronouns, determiners, auxiliary verbs, interjections, and numerals. Compare **open-class word**. (24, 72–3)

closed couplet: a couplet which is one self-contained syntactic unit, the syntactic unit matching the extent of the two-line rhyme unit. Compare **open couplet**. (35–6)

concatenatio: see **concatenation**.

concatenation: the 'chaining' of one verse unit to the next by the repetition of one or more open-class words from the last line of one unit in the first line of the next unit. Units can be subdivisions within stanzas ('intrastanzaic concatenation'), or whole stanzas ('interstanzaic concatenation'). The repeated words may be in different parts of speech, and may arrive in a different order. (105, 120–3)

content word: see **open-class word**.

diction: see **lexis**.

dip: name for the two types of metrically weak position in **alliterative verse**, normally occupied by one or more unstressed syllables. Dips can be divided into **long dips** and **short dips**. (73–4)

double offbeat: in **alternating verse**, an **offbeat** consisting of two syllables. (48–9)

elision: the absorption of an unstressed vowel at one word's end into the following vowel, producing a single sound. A normal linguistic event in everyday speech, adopted by poets and used to their metrical advantage. (51)

end-stopping: when syntax ends at the end of a metrical line, so that a natural pause and the metrical line-division coincide. Compare **enjambment**. (33–4, 124)

enjambment: when syntax continues on over the end of a metrical line and into the next line. Compare **end-stopping**. (33–34, 91, 112, 174)

envoi: see **envoy**.

envoy: a passage at the end of a poem, wrapping the poem up, often by telling the poem itself how to behave and/or by commending it to readers. Often in a different stanza-form to that used for the rest of the poem. The envoy to a shorter poem is often a single stanza, while the envoy to a longer poem can run for several stanzas. (117)

etymology: a word's origins; also used for the study of those origins. Best explored using the *OED*, *MED*, and (for Scots) the *DOST*. Often—but not always—indicates a word's associations. (22–4)

feature rhyme: a sub-type of **imperfect rhyme** in which consonants after the rhyming vowels are close rather than identical, e.g. *time:thine* or *on:long*. (94)

feminine rhyme: rhyme in which the first rhyming syllable is followed by one or more additional unstressed syllables, which for perfect rhyme must also match in both rhyme sounds. Modern English examples include *forbidden:ridden, slighted:united, motion:ocean*, and (a comically wrenching example from Byron's *Don Juan*) *this did:assisted*. Middle English examples include *steven:heven, assailid: faillid, comprehended:amended*. Compare **masculine rhyme**. (27, 57, 66, 92–3, 109)

filler rhyme: a rhyme phrase probably added primarily to complete a rhyme, rather than to advance the verse's other purposes. (98–9)

fixed form: one of a number of relatively 'set' verse forms originating in French verse-craft. The most notable are the *virelai, rondeau*, and **ballade**. Of these, only the *ballade* achieved much purchase in Middle English verse-craft. The *rondeau* had a Middle English descendant, the **roundel**, which appears in the works of a few poets but never became widespread. (116–20)

folio: one physical leaf in a book. Therefore two pages. (140)

forme fixe: see **fixed form**.

fourteener: later term for **septenary**, as a line of this sort most commonly has fourteen syllables.

frons: a set of lines at the start of a **subdivided stanza**, formally distinguished (usually by metre) from a following **cauda**. Sometimes a **bob** sits at the transition between *frons* and *cauda*. The plural form of the word is *frontes*. (104–8)

full rhyme: see **perfect rhyme**.

function word: see **closed-class word**.

half-line: half of a line of **alliterative verse**. The first half-line is the **a-verse** and the second half-line is the **b-verse**. A **metrical caesura** separates the two half-lines. (72, 83)

half-rhyme: see **imperfect rhyme**.

headless line: a line in an **alternating metre** missing a normally-expected initial **offbeat**, and therefore beginning with a **beat**. Compare lines with **initial inversion**, which also begin with a beat but achieve this by repositioning the initial offbeat rather than by losing it. (54, 58–9, 64)

hypotaxis: subordination. Hypotactic writing uses syntactically-subordinate clauses, e.g. 'The scholar, who was tired, finished her book' rather than 'The scholar was tired. She finished her book.' Compare **parataxis**. (43–5)

imperfect rhyme: rhyme with a looser correspondence between the sounds involved. Sub-types relevant in Middle English include **feature rhyme** and **subsequence rhyme**. (94)

initial inversion: reversal of the expected order of the *first* **offbeat** and **beat** in a line of alternating metre. Since most early English and Scots alternating metres default to an offbeat–beat (x/) order, initial inversion normally results in a line beginning with a beat followed by a **double offbeat** before the next beat (/xx/), without changing the number of syllables in the line. Compare **headless lines**, which also begin with a beat but do so by losing their initial offbeat. (64–5)

inset lyric: a short poem, usually formally distinguished in some way, embedded within a longer poem. (128–9, 147)

isometric: adjective for verse forms in which all lines have the same metrical length. Means 'equally measured'. Compare anisometric.

laisse: a section of lines sharing the same end-rhyme (**monorhymed**), with no rule that all *laisses* in a poem should have the same number of lines. Verse composed in *laisses* sits somewhere between **stichic** and stanzaic. Each *laisse* is internally stichic; although the *laisses* are distinct units, they do not mutually echo form as stanzas do. The term comes from the study of early French epic, in which the *laisses* were often tied by assonance at line-endings rather than rhyme. (102)

lenvoy: see **envoy**.

lexis: in criticism, used to mean a writer's wording. (20–30)

lift: one of the three components of **alliterative metre**, and the only type of metrically strong component. One stressed syllable. In the most conventional alliterative lines, each half-line has two lifts, and the first three of the four lifts in the whole line alliterate with each other, while the fourth does not alliterate. Very crudely, lifts are normally supplied by the lexically-stressed syllables of **open-class words**. (73–4)

long dip: one of the two types of weak position in **alliterative metre**. Two *or more* unstressed syllables; the exact number does not matter but the plurality does. Compare **short dip** and **lift**. (73–4)

macaronic: adjective for verse which integrates multiple languages together. Sometimes, more rarely, used as a noun ('a macaronic') for a poem which displays such integration. (157–63)

manuscript: a written object created by hand writing. Until the coming of moveable-type printing in the late fifteenth century, English was only preserved in manuscripts. (7, 131–48)

masculine rhyme: rhyme in which the rhyme syllable bearing the line's final **beat** is also the last syllable of both rhyme sounds. Present-day English examples: *await:mate, pie:dry, gong:belong*. Middle English examples: *bond:lond, yhent:torment, regioun:toun*. Note that, although two rhyming monosyllabic words will always produce masculine rhyme, many polysyllabic words also produce masculine rhyme. Compare **feminine rhyme**. (92–3, 109)

metrical caesura: a pause within a line required by metrical rules which the poet consistently observes. A metrical caesura separates the two **half-lines** in each line of **alliterative verse**. Four-beat alternating-verse lines have an inherent tendency to develop a metrical caesura between the second and third beats. John Lydgate used a metrical caesura between the second and third beats in his five-beat **alternating-verse** lines. Distinct from a caesura present not because of a consistent metrical rule but because of a local syntactic pause, for which see **rhetorical caesura**. (65–8)

mnemonic: as an adjective, this word means 'having to do with memory' or 'helpful in remembering something'. Sometimes used as a noun to describe poems designed to be learned as aids to the memory of useful information. Mnemonics in use today include '*i* before *e* except after *c*' and 'Thirty days has September'. (40)

Monk's tale stanza: stanzas of eight lines rhyming *ababbcbc*, possibly invented by Chaucer, and named for its use in his Monk's Tale. (111–12, 114, 116, 126)

monorhyme: the persistence of the same rhyme sound throughout a stanza or *laisse*. (102, 128)

near rhyme: see **imperfect rhyme**.

off-verse: see **b-verse**.

offbeat: a weak position in an alternating metrical pattern, normally occupied by either one unstressed syllable (**single offbeat**) or two unstressed syllables (**double offbeat**). (48–50)

on-verse: see **a-verse**.

open-class word: a word in one of the classes which readily absorb new vocabulary: nouns, verbs, adjectives, and adverbs. Compare **closed-class words**. (24, 72–3)

open couplet: a couplet which joins syntactically to its neighbours at either its beginning, its end, or both its beginning and its end. Compare **closed couplet**. (35–6)

parataxis: the lack of syntactic subordination. Paratactic writing proceeds via independent, free-standing clauses only. e.g. 'The scholar was tired. She finished her book' rather than 'The scholar, who was tired, finished her book.' Compare **hypotaxis**. (43–5)

perfect rhyme: complete, conventional rhyme, in which the vowels of the rhyming syllables and all following sounds match; contrasted with **imperfect rhyme**. (94)

punning rhyme: the rhyme of words which sound identical but differ in meaning. To achieve identical sounds, the rhymed sylllables must match not only in their vowels and any following sounds, but also in the consonants preceding the vowels. Prized in much French poetry, and in some Middle English works. Compare **autorhyme**. (95–8, 122–3, 159)

refrain: a line or later part of a line which repeats across different stanzas, most typically at each stanza's end. (114, 116, 117, 121, 129)

regular: in the study of poetry, often used to mean 'rule-bound'; when experts call a form 'regular', they mean that it obeys observable rules, not necessarily that it involves things happening at evenly-spaced intervals. In Middle English the word was used, in a pleasingly analogous way, to describe people bound by religious or monastic rules: see *reguler* in the *MED*. (47)

rhetorical caesura: a pause within a metrical line caused only by local syntax, and not replicated in other lines, not being a **regular** feature of the metre; a caesura of choice. Compare **metrical caesura**. (65, 174)

rhyme-breaking: placing syntactic divisions in counterpoint to divisions between units of rhyme. For example, when syntactic units in a work written in couplets break at the ends of the *first* lines of couplets. (36–9, 56, 142)

rhyme royal: stanza of seven lines rhyming *ababbcc*. Probably invented by Chaucer, and used by him in a number of major poems, including *Troilus and Criseyde*. Later used by other poets in the fifteenth century. Tension between an interlaced quatrain (*abab*) and a pair of couplets (*bbcc*) overlapping in the fifth line and third *b*-rhyme is central to the stanza's effect. (93, 101, 110–11, 116, 126, 127, 129, 178)

rhyming-alliterative: see **alliterative-stanzaic**.

rhyming tag: see **filler rhyme**.

rime couée: see **tail rhyme**.

rime equivo(c)que: see **punning rhyme**.

rime riche: see **punning rhyme**. Some critics use this to describe punning rhyme, but since in French versification *rime riche* and 'enriched rhymes' mean something slightly different, 'punning rhyme' is safer and avoids confusion.

rime royal: alternate spelling of **rhyme royal**.

roundel: a **through-rhymed** four-stanza **fixed form** built on a 'I+II, 1+I, 1+2, I+II' structure, in which Roman numerals represent the repetition of both words and rhyme, and Arabic numerals represent the repetition of the same rhyme with different words; both parts of the first stanza therefore become refrains. The name 'roundel' would be revived for English verse by Algernon Charles Swinburne in the late nineteenth century, but the form he used derived from the French ancestors of the Middle English roundel, not from the Middle English roundel itself; present-day English roundels are cousins, not descendants, of early English roundels. (117–20)

septenary: an **alternating-verse** metre of longer, seven-**beat** lines, split between a four-beat first unit and a three-beat second unit separated by a regular **metrical caesura**. Septenary lines could have end-rhyme. They could also feature internal rhyme on the fourth beat. With internal rhyme, septenary couplets resemble $a_4b_3a_4b_3$ quatrains; in this form, Middle English septenaries are the ancestors of many song, ballad, and hymn forms common in modern English. (59–62, 101, 133, 177, 179)

short dip: one of the three components of alliterative metre, and one of the two types of weak position in alliterative metre. One unstressed syllable. Compare **long dip** and **lift**. (73–4)

single offbeat: in **alternating verse**, an offbeat consisting of just one syllable. 48–50

stanza-linking: see **concatenation**.

stanzaic: adjective for verse in regular stanzas; opposite of **stichic**. Some examples of stanzaic poems are *Sir Tristrem*, *Sir Perceval of Galles*, *The Awntyrs off Arthure*, the Man of Law's Tale, *The Fall of Princes*, and *The Bowge of Court*. (102–12)

stave: see **lift**.

stichic: adjective for verse which is written continuously rather than in regular stanza units; the opposite of **stanzaic**. In this period, stichic verse is normally written in either rhymed **alternating-verse** couplets or in lines of **alliterative metre**. Some examples of stichic poems are the *Ormulum*, Layamon's *Brut*, *The Owl and the Nightingale*, *The Prik of Conscience*, *Piers Plowman*, and the Knight's Tale. 102

stress-syllabic metre: see **alternating metre**.

strong dip: see **long dip**.

strophe: a word requiring caution, as different writers use it in different senses. Used by some critics interchangeably with 'stanza', and by other writers for looser types of large-scale division. In a perceptive article (1997), Howell Chickering uses 'strophe' for the first part of the *Sir Gawain* stanza, what I would call the *frons*. The word is also sometimes used specifically for the twenty-four-line units into which the **alliterative-verse** *Wars of Alexander* appears to be syntactically divided.

subdivided stanza: a stanza split between *frons* and *cauda* by means of a **bob** and/or by a metrical shift in the *cauda*, typically towards shorter lines. Some poems in subdivided stanzas use **alternating metre** and others are **alliterative-stanzaic**; uniquely in the surviving evidence, the poet of *Gawain* joined an internally **stichic** orthodox **alliterative verse** *frons* to an alternating-meter *cauda*. Subdivided stanzas often come in thirteen or twelve lines; see Turville-Petre 1974 and Fein 1997. (103–8, 121, 134, 173–4, 178)

subsequence rhyme: a sub-type of **imperfect rhyme** in which some of the words rhymed together have unstressed word-endings and others do not, e.g. *fyght: knyghtes*. 94

syllabic metre: see **alternating metre**

syncope: when an unstressed vowel is dropped within a word. A normal linguistic event in everyday speech, adopted by poets and used to their metrical advantage. (51)

synizesis: when the vowel sound of $y|i$, itself followed by a vowel, becomes the consonant sound represented in present-day English by word-initial *y-*. A normal linguistic event in everyday speech, adopted by poets and used to their metrical advantage. (51–2)

tail rhyme: a group of stanza forms subdivided by repeated 'tail' lines, such as *aabccb, aaabcccb, aabccbddb*, and so on. The *b*-rhymed 'tail' lines are usually metrically shorter than the other lines. Tail-rhyme is an approach to stanza design, not one fixed stanza form. (62, 93, 108–10, 126, 128, 158, 179)

through-rhyme: in a **stanzaic** poem, through-rhyme occurs when one or more of the rhyming sounds is sustained across multiple stanzas. If a **refrain** is present in a poem, then that usually guarantees at least one through-rhymed sound, but not all through-rhyme is caused by refrains. Strict **ballades** and **roundels** have full through-rhyme with all rhyme sounds repeating across all stanzas. In a **stichic** poem, through-rhyme occurs when multiple abutting rhyme-units hammer on the same sound, e.g. in a poem in stichic couplets (*aabbccddee*...) when multiple abutting couplets share a rhyme (*aabbccccdd*...). (27, 91, 116, 117, 142)

total consonance: the matching of syllables through identical initial and closing consonants (technically, identical syllable 'onset' and 'coda') despite different vowel sounds, e.g. *syght: saght, bere: bare, row: rew*. Occasionally used as a **regular** ornament (Putter 2004, 512–13). (17, 105)

trochaic inversion: see **initial inversion**.

verse: usually used to mean **regular** poetry in general. In alliterative metrics, sometimes used to refer to one **half-line**: the **a-verse** is the first half-line in a line, and the **b-verse** is the second half-line in a line. In studies of present-day popular music, 'verse' is sometimes used to distinguish stanzas from a repeating **refrain** or **burden**; we normally avoid this use in discussing historical poetry, because it confuses more than it clarifies.

virelai: a French **fixed form**. Middle English works sometimes mention *virelais*, but the form does not in practice seem to have found a home in English: Nuttall 2016.

weak dip: see **short dip**.

wheel: see *cauda*.

General Index

Works with known authors are indexed under the author's name. Anonymous works with agreed modern titles are indexed by title. Works lacking agreed titles are indexed by *NIMEV* number under 'untitled works'. Tenuously titled works are indexed by title but cross-referenced under 'untitled works'.

Adam 173–5
Agbabi, Patience 15, 123, 130
Agincourt, battle of 116–17
Alexander the Great 178
Alliterative *Morte Arthure*
   alliteration 79, 113
   lists in 40
   metre 70, 75, 76
   in translation 10–11
'Amazing Grace' 62
Antigone 42
antisemitism 18, 35
architecture 16
Armitage, Simon 10–11
Arthur 10–11, 82–3, 122
Ashby, George
   Complaint of a Prisoner in the Fleet 33, 94, 111, 112, 125
aside (dramatic technique) 168
Assembly of Gods, The 68
Assembly of Ladies, The 68, 94, 125, 161
astronomy 36
Athena (goddess) 127
Auchinleck Manuscript, the *see* manuscripts
Audelay, John the Blind 109, 115, 158
   Three Dead Kings 17–18, 87, 106, 107, 121
Auden, W. H. 15, 71
   Letter to Lord Byron 111
aurality 8–9, 32, 47
author-function 43, 135
Awntyrs off Arthur, The 87–8, 106, 107, 122–3

Barbour, John
   Bruce 56–7, 178
Barlaam and Josaphat tradition 149
bathos 91
Battle of Maldon, The 89
battle poetry 56–7, 84–5
Bergvall, Caroline 15
Bible
   English versifications of 34, 60–1, 111, 134, 157, 172–6

Latin Vulgate 82, 151, 159
   quotations from 157, 158, 159
   Wycliffite Bible 150
Bird with Four Feathers, The 125–6
Bishop, Elizabeth
   'Burglar of Babylon, The' 94
Boccaccio, Giovanni 57, 146, 153, 179
Boethius
   Consolation of Philosophy 42, 129
Bokenham, Osbern 68, 100–11, 127, 148
Bradstreet, Anne 63
Brews (later Paston), Margery 151
Brittany 42
Brother Hans 158
Bruce, Edward 56–7
Bruce, Robert the 56
Buddha, the 149

Calais, siege of 122
canonicity 7, 10
Canterbury 36, 51
Capgrave, John 68, 111
Capildeo, Vahni 15
Capystranus 179
Carthusians 164
Castle of Perseverance, The 128
Caxton, William 14, 144
characterization 16–17
Charles d'Orleans 68, 112, 162
   Fortunes Stabilnes 114, 116–17, 118–19
Charter of Christ tradition 136–7
Chaucer, Geoffrey
   Anelida and Arcite 169–70
   Boece 42
   Book of the Duchess 58–9, 130
   Canterbury Tales
      absorption of *Gamelyn* 147
      dramatic qualities 170
      formal play in 126, 146
      influence 15, 36
      in early print 144

210 General Index

Chaucer, Geoffrey(*Continued*)
   Clerk's Tale 93, 147
   Cook's Tale 147
   Friar's Tale 21, 48
   General Prologue 32–3, 49, 51
   Knight's Tale 15, 37, 64, 79–80, 96
   Man of Law's Tale 123, 147, 156, 161
   Manciple's Tale 98
   Miller's Tale 119
   Monk's Tale 111–12
   Nun's Priest's Tale 64–5, 160, 165
   Pardoner's Tale 98
   Parson's Tale 71, 126
   Prioress's Tale 18
   Second Nun's Tale 147
   Shipman's Tale 36
   Squire's Tale 98
   Summoner's Tale 96
   Tale of Melibee, The 126
   Tale of Sir Thopas, The 110, 170
   Wife of Bath's Prologue 138
   'Complaint of Chaucer to His Purse' 117
   Complaint of Venus 90, 117
   early metre 53, 58–9
   'Envoy to Bukton' 117
   'Envoy to Scogan' 117
   final -*e* 52
   'Fortune' 116, 117
   House of Fame 58, 80, 82
   'Lack of Steadfastness' 117
   Legend of Good Women, The 57, 80, 156
   'Merciles Beauté' 118
   metrical fastidiousness 55, 177
   metrical inventions 63–5, 178
   model for tradition 5–6, 28, 59, 66–9, 94, 127, 179
   Parliament of Fowls, The 39–40, 110, 147, 165
   rhyming practice 94, 99
   'To Rosemounde' 116
   stanzaic inventions 110–12
   Troilus and Criseyde
      editing of 133
      French in 161
      influence of 15
      listing in 39
      love in 119
      manuscript transmission of 47, 131–2
      metre in 50, 64
      middle of 126
      prayer in 166
      rhyme in 93, 97, 98
      social reading in 152
      stanzas in 111, 124–5
      translation in 130
   'Truth' 117
   vocabulary 28

Christine de Pizan 153
church buildings 16, 80, 136
circularity 123
Clanvowe, John
   Boke of Cupide, The 165
Classical Chinese 89
Claudian
   De consulatu Stilichonis 100–1
Clerk, John
   Destruction of Troy, The 57, 81, 126, 178
climate change 18–19
close reading 1–3, 9, 46, 77, 82, 132–3, 142, 147
codicology *see* manuscripts
complaint 109, 129, 130, 169
concrete poetry 90, 132
cookery 40
Cornish 154
craft
   and freedom 46, 177–82
   of intricacy 17–18, 43, 142–3
   nature of 2–3
   persistence of 16
   in rote phrases 99
   variety in 55, 115
criticism
   early poetry's value to 15, 46, 133, 148, 161, 165, 179–82
   practice of 3, 5, 6, 9, 19, 130, 133, 143, 168, 182
Crucifixion *see* Jesus
Cursor Mundi 128–9, 178
Cynewulf 89

Dame Sirith 171–2
dance 3, 115, 117, 164
Dante 82, 102
   Comedy 94–5
death 121, 159
debasement of coinage 119
debate poetry 55–6, 65, 165
Denmark 40
Denston, Katherine Clopton 127
Deor 102
devil, the *see* Satan
Dickinson, Emily 6, 62
dictionaries 9–10
   Middle English 9–10, 29, 153, 161, 173
   of the Older Scottish Tongue 10, 20
   Oxford English 10
Digby *Conversion of St Paul*, the 178
Dispute between Mary and the Cross, The 106, 126
drama 128, 155, 171–6, 180
dream visions 40
Dryden, John 63
Dunbar, William 68, 112
   'Ballad of Our Lady' 29

Flyting of Dunbar and Kennedy, The 165–6
'Lament for the Makars' 144–5
Tretis of the Twa Mariit Wemen and the Wedo, The 165
Dutch 154

editions
　accessibility of 5, 6–8, 47, 140–1
　craft in 147
　foreign words in 161
　layout in 134–5
　metre improved in 47, 78, 93
　necessity of 134–5, 140–1, 147
　punctuation added in 8, 33, 174
　spelling changed in 7, 133, 147
　text emended in 144
education 43, 151–2
Edward III of England 112
Edward IV of England 120
Egerton, Sarah Fyge 63
Eliot, T. S.
　'Love Song of J. Alfred Prufrock, The' 63
　Waste Land, The 164
Elizabeth of York 120
embodiment 3, 46, 175
England 119
　multilingual culture in 149
　peripherality of 14, 23, 152
English
　changing prestige of 4–5, 149–50
　changes within 24, 71, 181
　as experimental language 5, 7–8, 14, 154
　as peripheral language 14, 154, 161
　ties to Scots 4
　as world language 5, 13–14
Eteocles 42–43
etymology 22–24, 29, 153
Eve 173–5
exophonic writers 117

Fachliteratur 181
fairy land 138, 141
Fall, the 173–5
Festivals of the Church, The 106
Flemish 154
Fletcher, John 15
Flood, the 175
Floure and the Leafe, The 68, 125, 167
flytings 165–166
Fortune 37, 116, 151
Four Leaves of the Truelove, The 106
France 61, 119, 152–3
Franciscans 150
free verse 46
French
　in macaronic verse 158
　source of form 55, 66, 89, 107, 108, 116–20, 129, 177, 179
　source for translation 67–8, 84–85, 118–20, 126, 153
　source of words 23, 26, 48–9, 55, 63, 67–8, 81, 149, 161
　status in England 4–5, 150, 152–3
Frideswide (saint) 146, 168–9

Gaelic 4, 154
Gamelyn *see Tale of Gamelyn, The*
Gardner, Helen 8
Gawain Poet *see Pearl* Poet
Generydes 68
Geoffrey of Monmouth 82
Germany 40
Godric of Finchale 89, 102–3, 177
Gower, John
　Cinkante Ballades 117, 149
　Confessio Amantis 49, 51, 52, 57, 65, 92, 95–6, 155
　In Praise of Peace 65
　literary moment 178
　metre 53, 55, 57
　Mirour de l'Omme 149
　reception of 15–16, 127
　rhyme 94, 95–6, 98
　Vox Clamantis 149
graffiti 164
'Grave, The' 21–2, 85–6, 177
Greece 40
Greenlaw, Lavinia 15
Guinevere 122
Gunn, Thom 15
　'Gas Poker, The' 114
　'Lament' 92
　'Merlin in the Cave' 111

hagiography *see* saints' lives
Harley lyrics 59–60, 70, 80, 93, 105, 109, 121
Havelok the Dane 54, 161, 177
Hayes, Terrance 20
Hebrew 154
Henry V of England 151
Henry VI of England 151
Henry VII of England 120
Henryson, Robert 68, 80, 111, 112
　Orpheus and Eurydice 129–30
Herbert, George
　'Easter Wings' 126
Herod (biblical king) 134
Hiberno-English 154–5
Hoccleve, Thomas 28, 52, 92, 94, 112, 118
　metrical innovations 68–9, 179
　Regiment of Princes, The 31–2, 45, 90–1, 117
Holland, Richard
　Buke of the Howlat, The 87, 106

212 General Index

Holofernes 111–12
Hundred Years' War 152–3
Hutchinson, Lucy 63
hymns 62

Ieuan ap Hywel Swrdwal 163
images 135–138
inscription 80, 136, 164
insults 55–6, 165–6
interludes 171–2
Interludium de clerico et puella 171
intertextuality 17, 159–60
invention 86, 100–1, 117, 130, 177, 179–81
Ireland 154–5
Irish 154–5
  as source of form 102
Italian vernaculars 63, 150

James I of Scotland 68
  Kingis Quair, The 111, 125
Jason (legendary hero) 57
Jesus
  birth 60–61, 134
  crucifixion 35, 93, 128, 136–7
  resurrection 35
John II of France 153
Judith (biblical hero) 111–12

Kennedy, Walter
  Flyting of Dunbar and Kennedy, The 165–6

Lalibela, churches of 16
Langland, William 88, 145–6
  Piers Plowman
    alliteration 79
    circulation 71
    dramatic qualities 170
    editorial challenge 145–6
    literary moment 178
    as macaronic verse 159
    manuscript decoration 135
    metre 73
    rhyme 100
    social concerns of 182
Latin
  gloss in 155
  in macaronic verse 157, 158, 159
  as normative language 4–5, 150–1
  source of form 60, 89, 102, 107, 108
  source for translation 100–1, 155–6
  source of words 22, 26, 29, 32, 55, 60, 61, 81
Laud *Troy Book* 81
Laurence de Premierfait 153, 179
Layamon (Lawman) 70
  Brut 82–5, 177
Leapor, Mary 63
Leir (Lear, legendary king) 83–4

letter-poems 28
lexicography *see* dictionaries
lists 39–40
literacy 151–2, 156, 180
literary history
  omissions in 61, 86, 100–11, 117, 120, 130
  Whiggishness in 16
literature (concept) 14
London 4, 71, 164, 178, 180
Lydgate, John
  alliteration by 80
  aureation by 28
  Complaint of the Black Knight 24
  Dance of Death 67–8, 164
  Debate of the Horse, Goose, and Sheep, The 165
  early career 151
  Fall of Princes, The 117, 153, 179
  final -*e* 52
  Floure of Courtesye, The 116
  metrical invention 66–8, 179
  roundels 118
  Siege of Thebes, The 36–7, 38, 42–3, 67
  Temple of Glas, The 66
  Testament of Dan John Lydgate, The 126
  in tradition 94, 111, 112, 127
  as translator 67–8, 81, 153
  Troy Book 15, 81
lyric cycle 117

Magnificat, the 157
Malory, Thomas
  Morte Darthur 39, 110
Mannyng, Robert, of Brunne 145
  Chronicle 178
  Handlyng Synne 21, 178
manuscripts 7–8, 181–2
  abbreviations in 132
  circulation of 144, 146
  challenges of 33, 97, 118
  cost of 151
  facsimiles of 133, 141
  images in 135–8
  layout in 15, 101, 126, 132, 134–5
  loss of 6, 53, 89, 103, 115, 144, 182
  rhyme in 111
  textual variation in 131–2, 138–8
  Cambridge
    Trinity College, MS R.3.19 33
    University Library, MS Ff.i.6 ('Findern Manuscript') 109–10
  Edinburgh
    National Library of Scotland, MS Advocates' 19.2.1 ('Auchinleck Manuscript') 138–43, 177
  London
    British Library, MS Additional 5465 136
    British Library, MS Additional 37049 136–7

British Library, MS Cotton Caligula
    A.ix 143-4
British Library, MS Cotton Nero A.X/2
    ('*Pearl* Manuscript') 135
British Library, MS Harley 978 170
British Library, MS Harley 2253 ('Harley
    Manuscript') 93, 154, 178, 180
British Library, MS Harley 3810 138-43
British Library, Loan MS 70/8 148
Manchester
    John Rylands Library, MS Eng. 1 cover, 3
Oxford
    Bodleian Library, MS Ashmole 33 61
    Bodleian Library, MS Ashmole 61 138-43
    Bodleian Library, MS Digby 86 103, 177
    Bodleian Library, MS Douce 104 135
    Bodleian Library, MS Junius 1 61
    Bodleian Library, MS Rawlinson poet.
        163 131-2
    Jesus College, MS 29 143
San Marino
    Henry E. Huntington Library, MS
        HM 114 145
Manx 154
Mary (mother of Jesus) 29, 62, 80, 93, 102-3, 115,
    156, 158
Medea 28, 57
medievalism 15-16, 71, 92, 110, 111, 123, 130,
    147
merchants *see* trade
Merlin 82-83
metatheatre 172
Metham, John 179
    Amoryus and Cleopes 111, 112, 126-7, 130
midrash 111
Milton, John 5, 63, 179
    Paradise Lost 32, 89, 100, 173, 174
Minot, Laurence 109, 122, 152
miracles 168
Montagu, John 153
moralization 130
music 179
    and carols 115
    creating stanzas 103
    in manuscripts 93, 136
    in *Orfeo* 44, 138, 141
    pop 47, 94, 164, 179
    religious 164
    and roundels 117
    in *Troilus and Criseyde* 170

N-Town plays 157
narration 129-30, 168
nationalism 149, 154
Norman Conquest 4, 152
Northern Homily Cycle, The 178

Northern Passion, The 3, 143
Norway 40
numerology 126
nursery rhymes 40

Octavian 166
Oedipus 38, 42
Old English 4, 23, 46, 70-1, 81, 88, 89, 102, 178,
    181
Old Norse 22-3, 81
Oliver, Douglas
    Infant and the Pearl, The 123
onomatopoeia 78-9
Orleans, Charles Duke of *see* Charles d'Orleans
Orm
    Ormulum 60-1, 86, 100-1, 177, 181
Orpheus and Eurydice legend 20, 42, 129
Ottoman Empire 179
Ovid
    Metamorphoses 42, 129
Owl and the Nightingale, The 55-6, 96, 143-4,
    165, 177
Oxford 146

Paris 67
parchment 136, 165
pastourelles 162-3
Paternoster (prayer) 53, 89, 173
Pearl Poet 34-5, 82, 126
    Cleanness 75, 112-13, 130, 178
    Patience 34, 112-13, 178
    Pearl 70, 123, 126, 161
    Sir Gawain and the Green Knight
        alliteration in 79
        editing of 144
        local concatenation in 123
        literary moment 178
        metre 72-3, 75, 76-7
        numbers in 126
        mentions drama 171
        stanza of 71, 103-4, 108
        syntax 34-5
        use of delay 167
Penllyn, Tudur 162-3
performance
    and filler rhyme 98
    and tail rhyme 109
    bob in 107
    carols in 114, 115
    drama in 171-6
    depicted 170
    importance 164
    ties to metre 47, 55, 59
periodization 3-4, 6, 179-80
Petrarch 106, 130
Pistil of Swete Susan, The 87, 106, 107

pleasure
  in constraint 17–18, 116, 120, 127
  in editing 133
  in familiarity 99
  in metrics 46
  in rhyme 90, 92, 112
  in selection 6
  as theme 3
  in variation 39, 40
Poe, Edgar Allen
  'Raven, The' 114
Poema Morale 60, 62, 89, 177
Poitiers, battle of 153
Polynices 42–3
Pope, Alexander 63
  Essay on Criticism 36
prayer 53, 166
present, the 12, 18–19, 46, 163, 182
Pride of Life, The 155
Prik of Conscience, The 36, 39, 98, 99, 155–6, 178
printing 4, 7, 144–5, 148, 180
prose 6, 32, 126
Proverbs of Alfred, The 85

Ralph the Collier (Rauf Coilyear) 87
rape culture 162
reading
  aloud 8–9, 32, 47, 114, 127, 129, 152, 180
  alone 164
  and cognition 30, 99, 107
  discontinuously 40, 167
  socially 152, 164–7
regionalism 146, 149, 178, 181
register 23–4, 26–9, 91
Revard, Carter 15, 71
'Rhyming Poem, The' 89
Robinson, Roger 181
romances 53–4, 61–2, 94, 99, 109, 126, 164, 177
Romans of Parthenay, The 68
Roos, Richard 68
Ruin, The 70

Saint Eustace 108
saints' lives 127, 146–7, 168–9
Satan 173–5
satire 100, 109, 115
schools 151
Scotland 4, 56, 87, 119, 152
Scots 4, 87, 88, 150, 152, 153–4
Scottish Troy Book 81
scribes
  and layout 113, 118, 126, 133–5
  and rhyme 90
  and textual variation 123, 131–2, 138, 144
  distant from poets 47
  multilingual 154

power of 181
  as readers 113
  local 180
Second World War 12
sermons 128–9, 150, 164, 171
Shakespeare, William 5, 8, 63, 68, 100, 126, 179
  A Midsummer Night's Dream 15
  As You Like It 15, 114, 147
  editorial spelling in 7
  Hamlet 7
  King Lear 84
  Pericles 15–16
  Rape of Lucrece, The 111
  Troilus and Cressida 15
  Two Noble Kinsmen, The 15
Shelley, Percy Bysshe 132
  Mont Blanc 148
Shockley, Evie
  'the way we live now ::' 111
'Short Charter of Christ, The' 136, 143
Siege of Jerusalem, The 112, 178
Sir Amadace 109
Sir Bevis of Hampton 126
Sir Cleges 166
Sir Ferumbras 61–2
Sir Golagros and Gawain 87
Sir Orfeo 20–1, 38, 41–2, 44–5, 91, 138–43, 177, 179
Sir Perceval of Galles 109, 121
Sir Tristrem 103, 106–107, 177
Skelton, John 94, 111
  Bowge of Court, The 125
  Phyllyp Sparowe 158–9
Somer Soneday 106, 107
sonnet 106, 116, 123, 130, 179, 181
Soul's Address to the Body, The 85
South English Legendary, The 146–7, 168
Speculum Vitae 40, 99, 178
spelling 7–8, 61
Sphinx (creature) 42
Squire of Low Degree, The 144
St Erkenwald 71, 112, 178
Stilicho 101
stock phrases 20–1, 26–7, 65, 98–9, 143
Storie of Asneth, The 111, 179
Strode, Ralph (philosophical) 150
subordination 40–5
Sultan of Babylon, The 94
'Sumer is icumen in' 170
Swinburne, Algernon Charles
  Tale of Balen, The 110

Tale of Gamelyn, The 15, 147
tangibility 3
Temple of Heaven, the 16
theory 1–2

Thomas of Hales
  Love Rune 150
Thornton, Robert 180
time travel 46
Towneley plays 128, 134–5
trade 13, 152, 154
translation
  from early to modern 10–11
  from English or Scots 154
  into Scots or English 29, 32, 118–20, 126, 153, 155
Tristan and Iseult legend 106
Trojan War 52, 81–2
Turke and Sir Gawain, The 179

universities 43, 151, 152
untitled works
  NIMEV 16 158
  NIMEV 39 150
  NIMEV 72 115
  NIMEV 99 80
  NIMEV 205 112
  NIMEV 378 157
  NIMEV 433 85
  NIMEV 585 122
  NIMEV 709 109
  NIMEV 780 128
  NIMEV 1330 59
  NIMEV 1449 162
  NIMEV 1460 157
  NIMEV 1526 100–1
  NIMEV 1650 156–7
  NIMEV 1885 128
  NIMEV 2179 120
  NIMEV 2182 25–8
  NIMEV 2468 109
  NIMEV 2684.5 85
  NIMEV 2709 see Ure Feder
  NIMEV 2988 89, 102–3
  NIMEV 3031 89
  NIMEV 3208 128
  NIMEV 3211 93
  NIMEV 3415 106
  NIMEV 3497 see 'Grave, The'
  NIMEV 3838 see Somer Soneday
  NIMEV 3932 157
  NIMEV 4085 103
  NIMEV 4162 103
  NIMEV 4184 see 'Short Charter of Christ'
Ure Feder 53, 89, 95, 96–7

Valentine's Day 151
variants see editions
Venus (goddess) 50
vernacularization 152
verse indexes 11–12
Visitation, the 157
Virgil
  Georgics 42, 129

Wace
  Roman de Brut 84–5
Wakefield Master 106
Wales 163
Wars of Alexander, The 75, 76, 113
Welsh 150, 154, 162
  as source of form 102, 163
Wilbur, Richard 71
Wilde, Oscar
  A Woman of No Importance 81
William of Palerne 178
Winchester 44–5
Woodville, Elizabeth 120
Woolf, Virginia
  To the Lighthouse 148
Wulf and Eadwacer, excellence of 102
Wynnere and Wastoure 72, 75, 76, 78, 165, 178, 182

York 172–3
York plays 128, 172–6

The manufacturer's authorised representative in the EU for product safety is Oxford
University Press España S.A. of El Parque Empresarial San Fernando de Henares,
Avenida de Castilla, 2 – 28830 Madrid (www.oup.es/en or product.safety@oup.com).
OUP España S.A. also acts as importer into Spain of products made by the manufacturer.

Printed in the USA/Agawam, MA
July 31, 2025

891340.015